Reasons from Within

Reasons from Within

Desires and Values

Alan H. Goldman

OXFORD
UNIVERSITY PRESS

OXFORD

UNIVERSITY PRESS

Great Clarendon Street, Oxford OX2 6DP

Oxford University Press is a department of the University of Oxford.
It furthers the University's objective of excellence in research, scholarship,
and education by publishing worldwide in

Oxford New York

Auckland Cape Town Dar es Salaam Hong Kong Karachi
Kuala Lumpur Madrid Melbourne Mexico City Nairobi
New Delhi Shanghai Taipei Toronto

With offices in

Argentina Austria Brazil Chile Czech Republic France Greece
Guatemala Hungary Italy Japan Poland Portugal Singapore
South Korea Switzerland Thailand Turkey Ukraine Vietnam

Oxford is a registered trade mark of Oxford University Press
in the UK and in certain other countries

Published in the United States
by Oxford University Press Inc., New York

© Alan H. Goldman 2009

The moral rights of the author have been asserted
Database right Oxford University Press (maker)

First published 2009

British Library Cataloguing in Publication Data

Data available

Library of Congress Cataloging in Publication Data

Goldman, Alan H., 1945-
Reasons from within : desires and values / Alan H. Goldman.
p. cm.
Includes index.
ISBN 978−0−19−957690−6 (hardback : alk. paper) 1. Values. 2. Desire. I. Title.
BJ324.V35G65 2009
128'.4—dc22   2009027510

Typeset by Laserwords Private Limited, Chennai, India
Printed in Great Britain
on acid-free paper by
MPG Books Group, Bodmin and King's Lynn

ISBN 978−0−19−957690−6

10 9 8 7 6 5 4 3 2 1

For those who provide my deepest reasons (but only because I care about them): Joan, Michael, David, Carolyn, Bridget, Merritt, Florence, and Shelly

Acknowledgments

This book was written with the support of year-long fellowships from the American Council of Learned Societies and the National Endowment for the Humanities, as well as summer research grants from the College of William and Mary. It could not have been written without that support and release time from teaching, for which I am most grateful. I am also grateful for the continued support of the William R. Kenan Charitable Trust. Articles that were modified and expanded into material for the book appeared in *Philosophical Psychology*, *Philosophy and Phenomenological Research*, *Ethical Theory and Moral Practice*, *American Philosophical Quarterly*, and the *Southern Journal of Philosophy*. Additional material derived from papers read at the tenth anniversary conference of *Ethical Theory and Moral Practice*, at colloquia at the University of Miami, and at the Virginia Philosophical Association. I received helpful comments from referees for those journals and from attendees at those conferences. Anthony Price and John Robertson provided astute criticisms of the entire manuscript, which led to substantial revisions. Other helpful comments on portions of the book came from Noah Lemos, Toni Ronnow-Rasmussen, Stephen Darwall, Andrea Scarantino, Patricia Marino, my students at William and Mary seminars on practical reason, my wife Joan, and my cousin Sherry Suib Cohen, a successful writer who urged me to lighten up on the usual grim philosophical style. Given all this input from readers, any remaining errors must be due to their having overlooked them.

All epigraphs at the beginnings of sections are from Yogi Berra.

Contents

1

Introduction: The Debate

I. Deliberation

"It was a once-in-a-lifetime opportunity, and I've had a couple of those."

Days, weeks, months go by in which I engage in no real deliberation about what to do. I do not think I am unusual in this regard. On an average day in which I am not teaching, I read or write for an hour or two, drive to my office, check correspondence, go to lunch with colleagues, work for another hour or two, then return home for some exercise, and so on. I might briefly ask myself what to work on next, whether to play tennis or bike, whether to eat in or out, but noting the alternatives, I simply opt for one or another (with permission from my wife). It is similar if I more rarely pause to ask myself whether I should be doing what I initially planned, whether, for example, the laundry would be done on time for me to keep my lunch appointment. Here I simply make sure that my action does not prevent the satisfaction of some concern more important to me.

In none of these ordinary situations is there deliberation in anything like the way philosophers typically describe: listing and weighing of reasons on each side of a contemplated action, assigning rough numerical values to reflect the weights, summing and reflectively forming the intention to perform the action with the greatest weight of reasons behind it. In my case something remotely like this happens maybe a few times a year, if that much. In all their writing about practical reasoning and weighing reasons in a detached and reflective frame of mind, philosophers have ignored the fact that the process they attempt to describe almost never occurs. But this fact is significant. I will attempt a more accurate description of the process below in preparation for a proper interpretation of it in later chapters. But before considering the process as it actually occurs, it is worthwhile to reflect on why it is so rare. Are we irrational in so rarely considering the reasons for our actions? I assume not.

Practical deliberation is the exception and not the rule, but that does not mean that agents ordinarily act without reasons for what they do. In ordinary contexts of action we are rational in doing what we are immediately motivated to do. Simply doing what we feel like doing ordinarily reflects our coherent motivational states at the time. Our inclinations line up with our implicit judgments about what it would be good to do, and action automatically follows.[1] Because unreflective action is typically rational, we normally do not need to consciously consider our reasons, stand back from our desires, and deliberately choose to do what is most rational, what we have most reason to do. We need not do this because acting without deliberation nearly always reflects the reasons we have or the values of the actions and their likely outcomes at the time for us. And this is already significant for the main argument of this book.

Either we are somehow (automatically, magically, evolutionarily?) in tune with the objective values our actions can embody or produce and motivated to maximize such value in the world, or our reasons reflect the motivations we have, what we are concerned to do at various times, what we care about, what has value for us at any given time simply because we value doing that at that time. The second explanation sounds less mysterious and initially more plausible. We can trust our actions in general to be rational neither because of some magical connection to objective values that generate our reasons, nor because we must view agents as rational in order to interpret or explain their actions (many people act irrationally at least some of the time, and we have no problem understanding and explaining their actions—we see, for example, that they were overwhelmed by emotion or temptation). We can trust our unreflective decisions because they reflect our motivations and hence the reasons that derive from our motivations. We need not deliberate because our actions automatically flow from our desires or concerns, and

---

[1] If we typically act for reasons without deliberation, when, if ever, do we act for no reason or without reason? We do so when we act on a pure whim, just because we feel like it, when this feeling is unconnected to any more stable concerns, or when we falsely believe we have a reason. Such action is irrational, as opposed to arational, only if it blocks the satisfaction of those other deeper concerns.

our reasons too derive from these motivations, reflecting shifting priorities among immediate desires, which in turn derive from and specify our longer standing, deeper, and more general concerns.

States of affairs that present themselves as opportunities or threats, as reasons for or against certain actions, themselves already reflect our motivations, what we care about. If we care about enough, have a variety of major concerns, we will have a couple of once-in-a-lifetime opportunities. But even on those occasions the same situation may present itself as both opportunity and threat, an opportunity to fulfil certain important desires and a threat to the fulfilment of others. This is when deliberation typically occurs. Serious deliberation occurs when one is pulled in opposite directions by conflicting reasons affecting important concerns and relating to the same prospect.

Consider an example of such deliberation in which something important hangs on a decision and conflicting considerations present themselves. Not too long ago I had to decide whether to accept a position at another university or remain where I was and had been for many years. Then I certainly did have to consider carefully the pros and cons, the reasons for and against the move. On the pro side, it seemed that I would be joining a lively and productive department and leaving a meddlesome administrator (little did I anticipate a change for the worse in administration at the new university), would be gaining on average brighter and more serious undergraduate students, would be living in a more pleasant environment with more trees, changing climates, and fewer rude people and traffic jams, would be closer to my sons, and would be near a city with cultural attractions second only to New York. On the con side, I would be leaving close friends and colleagues, would be giving up graduate students, stone crabs, and late night restaurants, would have to find new tennis opponents on my level, would have to sell and buy a house and arrange a move. To these I had to add my wife's concerns (of course counted above mine if she is reading this).

Did I assign rough numerical weights to these reasons and attempt to sum so as to maximize net benefit? No. What I did was try to make sure my list of important considerations was complete (did I need to find out if the new location has good Thai food or level surfaces for rollerblading?) and to picture as vividly as I could what each outcome would be like. I also considered whether I might integrate other actions that might compensate for the negatives or add to the positives. Might I move to a nicer neighborhood in my current city instead of moving to a new town? Might I move to a golf as well as tennis community in the new location? (For long-range planning, integration is crucial—making plans that will allow for the satisfaction of my sports, aesthetic, family, and gustatory interests, as well as my academic interests, whatever the secret priorities among these concerns might be.) Finally, I attempted to gather some further information. How much would the move cost? What was the housing market like in both locations? One point to emphasize about this process is that at no point did I call any of my desires or concerns into question: I took for granted that the pros were pros and cons were cons. I was not standing back and reflecting on my desires (as some philosophers describe deliberation). I did not focus on my desires at all, but on these possible future states of affairs that immediately struck me as positive or negative, reflecting my motivations without foregrounding them. And then I simply made a decision.

Before considering yet a third sort of case, we can note the similarities and differences in the two contexts briefly described. In the first and most common, we simply act without deliberating. Here action, like belief, is more or less automatic. Here we can assume that there are no major conflicts in motivations, that inclination lines up with implicit evaluative judgment about what it would be good to do, leading to action without conscious forming of intention or choice. In the second less common but not altogether rare context there are conflicting reasons that must be brought vividly to mind, informed, prioritized, and integrated in deliberation. The prioritizing is again more or less automatic, however, once the other steps are complete. When the priorities are clearly felt, decision again follows without meditative choice, much as belief follows from full consideration of the evidence for and against a proposition when there is evidence on both sides. And just as evidence for belief is typically clearly for or against, indicative of truth or falsity, so reasons for action are rarely ambiguous, but instead clearly in line with one's concerns or opposed to them.

The only ambiguity in the list of reasons for and against the move was the status of changing college administrators: was it a reason for the move, as it appeared to be at the time, or a reason against, as it turned out? The question arises not because of any lack of clarity in my preferences or in the relations of the possible states of affairs to them, but simply because of a lack of relevant information—I had no clue about the impending change in administrators where I might go. It seems that I was subjectively rational to count the new administration as a reason in favor of the move, given the information available to me at the time, but in the next chapter I will argue that in such a case I only appeared to have a reason in favor of the move; in fact, I had a reason against it of which I was not aware.

I have been emphasizing the automaticity of action in the absence of deliberation and of decision after deliberation once the relevant factors are brought to mind, and I have suggested a comparison of the context of action to that of belief. Belief probably would not be as reliable as it is, would not be true as often, if we had to choose what to believe after considering evidence. We are better off for being programmed to automatically believe what strikes us as true. Similarly, action would probably not be as successful, would not as often satisfy our desires and concerns, if we had to constantly stand back and assess our motivations and reasons and choose what to do. It may be more common in the case of action for neither of the opposing decisions to be clearly indicated by the opposing reasons, and then decision itself will determine the priorities for the future. But in both cases it is normally clear what counts for and against belief or action, clear whether reasons once brought to mind are pro or con, and equally clear what to believe or how to act once the evidence or reasons are in.

In the case of action as opposed to belief, some of these pros and cons seem clearly relative to personal preferences. I prefer teaching more motivated and brighter students; better teachers than I might welcome the challenge of teaching less independently motivated students. For them the prospect of "better" students would be a reason against a move; for me it was a reason in favor of one. Good tennis facilities are important to me; they count for nothing for others. Thus many of the considerations or possible states of affairs that count as reasons for me seem to do so only by reflecting my personal concerns.

By contrast, there may seem to be other reasons that are not so person-ally relative. It might be thought that moral reasons should not have been absent from my list of reasons for and against the move. Should not I have considered the hardship caused by abandoning graduate students whose half finished dissertations I was advising, or the demand for loyalty to an institu-tion that had treated me well for much of my long tenure there? In point of fact, I did arrange not to abandon the dissertations, but loyalty to institution counted for nothing for me. Being unconcerned about it, I did not consider it a reason against the move. But did that lack of concern imply that I had no such reason? Many would argue that there is no such implication, that the moral reasons I have are independent of whether I recognize or care about them. I cannot escape my moral obligations by not caring about them, and therefore I have these reasons whether I recognize them or not.

The same point of view might be supported by a third type of case, much rarer still, in which one does question one's desires or concerns, in which they are brought to the fore instead of being automatically reflected in what strikes one as pro and con reasons. Somehow I seemed to have missed my midlife crisis (was it hiding behind the move?), but those who do not miss that landmark ask themselves such questions as, "Do I really want to continue in this career (or this marriage)?" "Is what I spend my life pursuing really worthwhile; is there real value in what I am doing, or am I wasting my life chasing insignificant goals?" Such questions are raised in periods of crisis (or after a particularly bad day in the classroom). When we are reasonably content, our deliberations leave structuring deep concerns in the background, or our actions flow smoothly from more superficial desires. But these periods of discontent do occur, and they indicate that deep concerns and projects too can be called into question. The worries expressed seem to call into question whether our subjective values, even those most fundamental to the course of our lives, measure up to what is truly or objectively valuable, what we ought to be pursuing as opposed to what we are pursuing. As in our attitude toward moral demands, we seem to be presupposing here objective values or reasons independent of our current motivations, reasons that we ought to care about and take into account whether we are doing so or not. We seem to be holding up our subjective values to such objective standards.

But again such questions can be given a different interpretation. Even when I call the ongoing course of my life into question, even when I ask whether what I am doing is really worth my concern, I may not be asking for a comparison between my values as so far expressed in my actions and objective values as what I or anyone else ought to be pursuing, but instead asking whether what I am doing, what I continue to do perhaps out of force of habit, inertia, or lack of energy, is what I really care about most deeply, what will continue to satisfy me in the long run by answering to these genuine concerns. When I ask whether continuing my current life plan will really satisfy me, I am not asking whether it would satisfy anyone independently of their dispositions and concerns. I am not interested in whether it would satisfy an investment banker or whether it is valuable from the point of view of the universe as a whole, but whether it is really what I want out of my life. Do I really deeply care about what I am doing any more, or are there other things that I care about more, or things that I would be disposed to care about if I took the time to think about them?

Those who favor the former interpretation would insist that our actions need and can be given a deeper justification. Whatever our deepest concerns, they argue, we can always ask whether satisfying them is objectively worthwhile, whether objective values and reasons ultimately justify our concerns and pursuits. For reasons must not only explain our actions, and must not only justify them in our own eyes, but must justify them *tout court*. Genuine reasons are normative: they determine what we ought to do if we are rational. What we really ought to do cannot simply be a function of what we want to do. Typically the point of asking what we ought to do is to call into question what we want or feel like doing. I feel like going back to sleep in the morning when the alarm rings, but I know that I ought not to. I have many reasons not to go back to sleep and no reason to do so. Hence, according to these philosophers, if reasons are to be genuinely normative, they must be independent of our motivations and reflect objective values.

Reasons are what we deliberate about on those relatively rare occasions in which we do deliberate. They are what motivate us if we are rational. They indicate how our actions can satisfy our concerns. If my moving to a new job would satisfy my desire for more income, the higher salary is a reason for me to apply. We do not deliberate about our desires, but about such things as living in a better climate versus losing friends and colleagues. Desires are not what motivate us: they are states of being motivated.[2] And particular desires in themselves do not seem to create reasons. As suggested in the alarm clock example, just feeling like doing something is not in itself a reason for doing it. If you wake up on a morning when you have a busy schedule before you, and you feel like going back to sleep, that does not give you a reason to do so. The fact that you have appointments is a reason

---

[2] As pointed out by Jonathan Dancy, *Practical Reality* (Oxford: Oxford University Press, 2000), pp. 85–94.

for you not to go back to sleep, and it would be a reason for anyone in similar circumstances, a seemingly objective reason independent of what you feel like doing.

But again on the other side, how would the claim that there is a reason to do something motivate me to do it if it did not connect to any of my concerns? If someone reminds me that there is a religious reason not to work on a Saturday or Sunday, that would not strike me as a reason for me, precisely because I do not care about the demands of religions. Reasons must be capable of motivating us. They explain the actions of rational agents as well as justifying them. We are rational agents most of the time, so we must be motivated by reasons. But how could they motivate us if they do not reflect or connect with what we care about?[3]

From the second person point of view too, when we try to convince another person that she ought not to act in the way she seems to intend, we try to appeal to what we know she cares about. If she is about to act irrationally by taking some unnecessary or pointless risk, we do not argue that aversion to this risk is included in some list of objective rational requirements, but instead point out that the likely outcome will threaten the continued satisfaction of her other concerns, that it will endanger completion of cherished projects, or will likely harm her or those she cares about in some way she finds unacceptable. An agent will be convinced of irrationality only when incoherence with her concerns or deepest motivations is demonstrated to her, not when she is presented with some purported objective requirement that might not appear to her to be a requirement for her.

First person deliberation, as described above, does not typically directly address desires of the agent, but focuses instead on states of affairs that present themselves as good or bad, as opportunities or threats. But their so presenting themselves may be relative to an agent's concerns, including personal and idiosyncratic concerns. When these concerns themselves are called into question, they seem to be held up to a more objective standard. Is what we are doing really worthwhile? But this question too may be addressed to the relation between day-to-day routine or superficial desires and deeper concerns. If deepest concerns—for oneself or one's family, or

---

[3] This argument resembles one given by Bernard Williams, "Internal and External Reasons," in E. Millgram (ed.), *Varieties of Practical Reasoning* (Cambridge, MA: MIT Press, 2001).

for those projects that have structured and given meaning to so many of one's other pursuits—themselves come into question, this again seems to call for an objective validation in terms of reasons or values independent of these concerns. But it may reflect instead a despair of there being any such ultimate reasons, or of there being any point to doing anything at all. Fortunately, few of us ever do call these fundamental concerns into serious question. We do not seem to need a reason to care for our children or ourselves.

Negotiations with others, as opposed to first person deliberation, generally also take the concerns of others as fixed, once known. And we appeal to those concerns or to states of affairs that we know to relate to them when trying to convince others of alternative courses of action. We aim to find shared values and base our negotiations on them. Does such sharing point to a deeper objective basis, or does it end there? Is appeal to what we value the ultimate appeal, or is there an independent truth about what we ought to value?

II. Internalism versus Externalism

"Nobody goes there any more because it's too crowded."

The debate to which the last question points is that between internalists and externalists regarding reasons, or between subjectivists and objectivists regarding value. Internalists hold that the reasons we have for acting are limited by our pre-existing motivational states, by our desires and concerns. A reason is not a reason intrinsically: in itself it cannot demand on pain of irrationality that agents be motivated by it. It is because agents have certain concerns or desires that they have reasons; their motivational states limit what reasons they can have. Externalists deny such limitation, holding that reasons determine what we ought to do whether we care to do so, indeed whether we have any cares that require us to care to do so, or not. They hold that we are rationally motivated because we recognize the independent force of reasons, while internalists believe that reasons are such because they motivate us or relate to previously existing motivations. The question, in short, is whether, ultimately, motivations generate reasons or reasons generate motivations. Do I have a reason to exercise because I care about my health, or simply because it is good for me, independently of my concerns? Are reasons internal or external?

Internalists do not claim that reasons always result in actions in rational agents. They need not be overriding reasons. Motivation can consist in a disposition that is not actualized most of the time. I am concerned about music and therefore motivated to go to concerts, but I do not go constantly even when opportunities arise, because other motivations are often stronger. Indeed, internalists can allow that agents can have reasons even though they are not motivated by them at all at particular times. They may be in irrational frames of mind at those times, too depressed, for example, to care about any of their usual concerns. Or, again irrationally, they may not realize that they need to specify their deeper and broader concerns into specific desires and intentions if they are not to go unsatisfied.

If I am concerned about my health, I need to be motivated to do some kind of exercise and to translate that motivation into an intention to jog or play tennis or . . . Many people are concerned about their health but irrationally never become motivated to exercise. For the internalist there must be such concerns in relation to which reasons are reasons, before a lack of motivation can count as irrational. But agents may not be motivated by the reasons they have. Again, perhaps faultlessly this time, they may not be motivated because they are not aware of certain reasons or opportunities for satisfying their desires, unaware of and so once more unmotivated by reasons they have. Rational agents are motivated by the reasons they have of which they are aware, but agents can fail to be motivated by reasons they have because of ignorance or irrationality.

On the other side, externalists can posit desires whenever we are motivated to act on reasons, but they will see many of these desires as themselves motivated by the reasons, as are the actions that result. If I exercise voluntarily, then in some sense I must have desired to do so, but that desire can spring from the recognition that exercising is good for me. On this account, we come to desire things because we recognize the independent values in them, and those independent values provide the reasons for the desires. Desires themselves can be justified or not, and their justification derives from those reasons that give rise to the desires. Desires that lack reasons should not be acted on and provide no reasons themselves. Again, desiring to go back to sleep does not in itself give me a reason to do so.

The question regarding external reasons is equivalent to the question whether there are objective values. Since reasons are considerations that count for or against actions, they are indicative or constitutive of positive or negative values to be pursued or avoided. Reasons exist independently of persons' motivations or concerns if and only if values or normative facts exist independently of persons' evaluations or valuings, as what they ought to value whether or not they do so. Reasons imply values. But values also imply reasons. If values are to be relevant to our lives, they must have practical import. They must be normatively significant: they must give us reasons to act. They must be what we ought to pursue and protect. This is so whether or not they are independent of our current motivations.

The subjectivist, of course, has an obvious explanation for why recognition of value, expressed by certain evaluative judgments about what it would be good to do, should be motivating. Such judgments on that account already express our motivations. The values we recognize according to this view reflect what we care about: there is no question why we should be motivated to achieve or protect what we care about. Caring *is* just being motivated. Conversely, what seems valuable to us when we have coherent motivations and are relevantly informed is valuable for us. For the subjectivist, values exist only for and because of valuing beings, beings motivated to seek or avoid certain states of affairs. Value subjectivists will be reason internalists. Because values are relations between objects or states of affairs and subjects who value them, and because reasons reflect values, reasons are also relative to subjective values or concerns. The demand to value various objects or objectives follows only from the demand for coherence with deeper existing concerns and motivations. If I ought to exercise, it is because I am concerned about my health, and coherence demands sometimes acting in ways that satisfy that concern.

Likewise, for the current objectivist, objective values reduce to external reasons, reasons to desire certain objects or outcomes.[4] This reduction depends on positing an impersonal perspective from which such reasons are grasped. From this perspective, which corrects for our partial valuings, value requires or merits motivation. Rational agents viewing the states of affairs in question properly, will recognize and respect these values. The impersonal perspective must still be one that we can adopt, from which

---

[4] See, for example, Thomas Nagel, *The View from Nowhere* (Oxford: Oxford University Press, 1986), p. 139.

we can still recognize reasons for us. But once we recognize objective value, we recognize that it provides reasons for our desires and actions. This claim may not be quite as transparent as the counterpart claim of the subjectivist. If values exist independently of our motivations, they might connect to none of our concerns. But if they connect to none of our concerns, possibly demanding instead that our concerns be other than they are, how and why should these purported values motivate us? The question admits of no obvious answer.

Internalism these days, however, is much like Yogi Berra's restaurant that no one goes to any more because it is too crowded. Philosophers call it the dominant position, but then they all attack it. Among the most prominent philosophers, only Bernard Williams has argued for the position in one or two articles, and Harry Frankfurt has eloquently defined and endorsed it, but without addressing many of the arguments for and against.[5] On the

---

[5] Bernard Williams, "Internal and External Reasons"; Harry Frankfurt, *The Reasons of Love* (Princeton: Princeton University Press, 2004). After publishing the articles on which this book is based and writing most of its first draft, I discovered a just published book by Mark Schroeder, *Slaves of the Passions* (Oxford: Oxford University Press, 2007) that also defends the internalist position. We share the basic thesis that reasons derive from desires, but his arguments for the position, his analyses of desires and reasons, and his corollary theses are very different from mine. In his initial argument for the position, for example, he assumes that all philosophers agree that some reasons derive from desires and that we should therefore seek a unified account according to which all reasons share this source. But the premise is false: most objectivists will claim that when one person has a reason to go to a party, desiring to dance there, and another person who does not like to dance does not have that reason (Schroeder's example), this difference in reasons derives not simply from a difference in desires, but from the fact that the first person will derive pleasure from the party and the second will not, pleasure being an objective value that we all have reason to pursue. Objectivists hold that we need reasons to satisfy our desires, and these reasons derive from objective values. And the inference that if some reasons depend on desires, we should seek an account in which all do simply seems to assume that there is one source of all reasons. I too will argue for a unified account, but the unity in my theory derives from an analysis of rationality that encompasses both epistemic and practical rationality. Our different analyses of reasons leads me to explain away what Schroeder accepts and to accept what he attempts to explain away. Specifically, he accepts that every desire in itself can generate reasons that explain why certain actions tend to satisfy the desire. By contrast, I agree with objectivists that desires to go back to sleep or to count blades of grass in themselves generate no reasons, but I provide an internalist explanation for this. Schroeder attempts to provide an internalist explanation for the central claim of objectivists that we all have moral reasons of equal weight. But his explanation fails, as I will argue later, and I reject the claim. Finally, Schroeder attempts to reduce the normative concept of reasons directly by an analysis is non-normative terms. Once more his analysis implies that every desire can generate reasons, which I reject. I share the goal of naturalizing the normative, but proceed to do so indirectly by analyzing reasons in terms of rationality and then providing a naturalistic account of rationality. I provide further argument in the text for why this order of analysis is preferable. All these major differences in our approaches will become clearer in my subsequent chapters. I recommend the reader to compare our defenses of the central internalist thesis that reasons derive from desires, and especially recommend reading his excellent discussion of the nature of metaphysical reduction, a meta-theoretical discussion of the sort that I do not attempt to provide here.

other side are a slew of the most famous names in philosophical circles, all arguing for objective values and external reasons.[6]

Bernard Williams opened the current debate for the internalists by arguing that there is no rational route to an agent's future motivation except through reasoning from her present motivational set. Reasoning can motivate us only by proceeding from prior motivation, and reasons must be capable of motivating us. If we do not begin from something we care about, we will not end by caring about something. If I do not care about playing golf, for example, then the only way I can be argued into being motivated to play is by appeal to something I do care about—my health, my desire for relaxation, exercise, competition, or business deals, my aesthetic appreciation of the outdoors. No objective features of the game will motivate me unless connected to such concerns or dispositions to enjoyments.

Externalists have replied to Williams that an agent can come to be motivated by coming to see the true values and disvalues in things,[7] much as we can come to have new beliefs and even new concepts by perceiving things we had not seen before. In dramatic cases a person can undergo a character conversion, acquiring entirely new sets of motivations and losing old ones, by vividly experiencing others' needs to which she was formerly insensitive, or by coming to see that what she was formerly pursuing, for example wealth or fame, was not really worth the effort. Once again for externalists the sources of reasons that will motivate rational agents are such facts about what is or is not worth doing or promoting. My reason to play golf is not that I desire to or have other desires, but simply that I would enjoy it, and enjoyment is objectively good.[8] On the other side, suffering ought to be relieved, and a person unmotivated to do so can come to be so motivated by coming into close contact with another's suffering. We need no prior motivations in order to be able to discover true value or disvalue.

---

[6] e.g. Thomas Scanlon, *What We Owe to Each Other* (Cambridge, MA: Harvard University Press, 1998), pt. I; John Searle, *Rationality in Action* (Cambridge, MA: MIT Press, 2001); Joseph Raz, *Engaging Reason* (Oxford: Oxford University Press, 1999); Derek Parfit, *Climbing the Mountain*, unpublished but widely circulated manuscript; Warren Quinn, *Morality and Action* (Cambridge: Cambridge University Press, 1993); Nagel, *The View from Nowhere*; Dancy, *Practical Reality*.

[7] See e.g. Brad Hooker, "Williams' Argument against External Reasons," in Millgram (ed.), *Varieties of Practical Reasoning*.

[8] The internalist replies that I have reason to pursue only those enjoyments I care about, if I do not care about pursuing every possible enjoyment.

Both sides to this debate can agree that we can care about what is not truly valuable for us, that which we have no reason to care about. Both can agree also that we can fail to care about that which is good for us, what we have reason to pursue. Finally both can agree that reasons are not necessarily what motivate us, but what ought to motivate, what motivates if considered correctly or rationally. Here the externalist's interpretation of these claims may strike us as simpler and more straightforward, since he sees value as independent of all our actual motivations. If value exists independently of people's concerns, it is clear why it can come apart from those concerns.

The internalist, by contrast, views irrational desire in terms of incoherence within motivational sets. We may be motivated to pursue what is bad for us when an urge to do so opposes a more stable evaluative judgment reflecting a deeper concern. I may desire my next cigarette, but this urge opposes my deeper concern for avoiding terminal illness. Conversely, we may be unmotivated to pursue what is good for us because we lack information or awareness or because we suffer from depression or other irrational frames of mind. I may fail to work on an article or book despite caring deeply about a successful career because I am unaware that I could succeed in publishing it or because I am too lazy or depressed to make the effort. Correct consideration that reveals the true value for a person of various objects or objectives is that which derives from coherent and informed sets of motivational states. Ultimately, values reflect our deepest concerns.

The crucial point regarding the argument of Williams and the externalist's reply to it is that the internalist can always argue that whatever motivations we come to have through encounters with new situations, we must have been disposed to become so motivated. Whenever externalists employ the perceptual model, holding that we can come to see normative facts as they are, come to see the true values in objects and thereby become motivated to pursue them, the internalist can reply that we could not have become motivated had we not been so disposed, had we not already had related concerns or perhaps hidden character traits. A rational action may seem to be out of character to an observer who does not know the details of an agent's dispositions or motivational sets, but it remains true that we do only what we are disposed to do. Trivially, when we act for reasons, we must be the sorts of persons who are motivated to act for those kinds of reasons.

If I see people suffering and become motivated to help them when I took no interest in them before, the internalist will believe that I was nevertheless of such a character as to be sensitive to that kind of suffering—after all, some others would remain insensitive in the presence of such pain. The externalist will believe that I acquired a new disposition from the novel experience—after all, people undergo character conversions prompted by new life-changing experiences. And even if we respond only in ways in which we were disposed to respond, this does not refute externalism about reasons, since we could be disposed to respond to objective reasons or values.

But if the internalist can claim that we are always disposed to do what we do and to value what we come to value, and if these dispositions count as part of the motivations to which reasons are relative, does this not trivialize his central thesis that reasons depend on prior motivations? Does it not trivialize the entire debate, since there will no longer be any difference between his position and the externalist's, for whom it can also be said that we desire to do what we voluntarily do (at least desire the likely outcome more than the available alternatives)? No. While it is true that in some sense we must have been disposed to react positively to anything to which we do react positively, this does not trivialize the internalist's thesis or her debate with the externalist. It implies only that we cannot have an empirical test to differentiate these theories, either from the agent's or the observer's point of view. (An agent may learn of her own character only by noting how she reacts in various circumstances.) But the question remains whether rationality can demand of us that we be motivated by what does not in fact motivate us or connect to our current concerns. This again is equivalent to the question whether value is objective, whether it ought to motivate us however we happen to be disposed. Can objective states of affairs in themselves require motivation from a rational agent?

The answer may be not only of philosophical interest and importance, but may have practical import as well, not only in terms of our broad attitudes toward ourselves and the world, but from the point of view of a moral educator or of someone trying to convince another to change his behavior. Can such advice succeed by getting the other person to see the normative facts or rational requirements as they are? Or must one aim at a gradual change of attitudes and feelings through appeal to present concerns for self and others? Ethics teachers who hope to affect their students' behavior and not just their beliefs may well favor the second approach.

If there is no empirical evidence clearly supporting one side or the other to this debate, then it must be adjudicated in terms of broader theoretical considerations. Some might want to include pragmatic or practical effects of belief among the criteria for choice as well, such as the possible positive effect of belief in internalism noted in the previous paragraph. On the other side, and perhaps more significantly, objective reasons and values play the role of God for contemporary philosophers. Their pursuit gives our lives meaning and purpose without our having to create them. Their presence validates the ways we value things. They provide a standard for our subjective values and pursuits to meet and provide reasons for our having the motivations we have. Such considerations, however, aside from providing a contentious explanation for the inclination to belief in objective values in terms of a quasi-religious yearning, are epistemically irrelevant. They provide no evidence for the existence of objective values, no reasons to believe in them. Aside from removing one bad argument in favor of externalism (namely, why should so many philosophers believe in objective values if they do not exist?), these considerations do not provide evidence against belief in objective values either (Just 'cause you're paranoid doesn't mean they're not out to get you; just 'cause you believe for bad reasons doesn't mean your beliefs aren't true.)

But there is a related argument that is epistemically relevant, if not sound. A philosopher might compare belief in objective values to belief in real physical objects. Realism about physical objects provides a deeper explanation of our perceptual experiences than does phenomenalism, the theory that countenances only perceptual experiences and views objects as regular patterns or collections of experiences. Similarly, it can be claimed, realism about values, appeal to values independent of our desires, provides a deeper justification for our desires and subjective values. Appeal to physical objects explains not only when, but why our perceptual experiences occur. Phenomenalists cannot provide that explanation. Likewise, appeal to objective values justifies even our deepest concerns. Subjectivists cannot provide that justification. Motivations, the source of values for the subjectivist, can themselves be supported by reasons, and, lacking such support, can be irrational. Objective values provide the reasons for those deep concerns that otherwise would lack them.

There is, however, an important disanalogy between these arguments and a closer analogy from the epistemology of belief to the debate over values that supports internalism. The disanalogy is the difference between appeal to explanation in the one argument and the appeal to justification in the other. The analogy relates to justification itself in the two domains. If we stick to explanation in both domains, the analogy disappears. While appeal to physical objects explains our perceptual experiences (my desk causes me to have visual experiences by reflecting light, and so on), and natural selection perhaps explains how we have all come to perceive physical objects as we do, the explanation of motivations in terms of objective values remains mysterious. Natural selection might explain the common instinctual desires with which we begin life, but what we come to value differs among individuals and often has little to do with survival or reproduction. And while the physical causal chains involved in perceiving objects can be specified in detail, the causal chains presumed to connect objective values to desires remain unspecified.

An objectivist can reply that, since objective values are instantiated or realized in ordinary physical objects or states of affairs, the causal chains linking such values to our motivations and actions are the usual physical causal chains. If it is then asked how the values themselves enter into the causal explanations, how they, and not simply the physical states of affairs in which they are realized, are causally efficacious, the objectivist replies that the explanation in terms of value is better because we react in the same ways to the same values however they are realized physically. The same values will have multiple physical realizations. Broader explanations of our motivations in terms of the values themselves instead of their particular physical instantiations are preferable if we would react in the same way to any instantiations of the same values. If a baseball batter cannot hit any curve ball, then his striking out is normally best causally explained by the pitch having been a curve ball, and not by the particular physical path it took. Broader explanations are often better than narrower when the narrower or more specific explanations are part of a common class of causes any of which would have worked in the circumstances.[9]

In this way the objectivist can claim that values enter best causal explanations for motivations and actions, even though the particular causes of these desires and actions are the physical causes we all believe in. But the answer is not entirely satisfactory. The question remains why our motivations track these particular sets of physical states of affairs that are said to realize the same values. It still seems that we must be magically tuned in to these values if we do not reverse the explanation and say that we see them as values because we care about them or are motivated by them. And the latter explanation also explains why people disagree over what is objectively valuable. If I admit that I cannot hit a curve ball, we understand why I cannot hit all pitches of that type (perhaps I am always swinging over them). But if I say that I like baseball and other competitive sports because they are good, it remains mysterious why goodness attaches to all of them. And when I specify what for me are their good-making properties, the question remains why all these properties are good, and why other people do not react in the same positive way to them.

Turning to justification in both domains, a different analogy appears but ultimately points in different directions in the two domains. The analogy is best brought out by extending a point made by Harry Frankfurt. Bernard Williams, we noted, had argued that we cannot reason to new motivation except from other current motivations. Frankfurt argues in similar fashion that we cannot assess claims of value except in terms of what we find valuable, in terms of what we value or care about.[10] Just as we cannot look beyond our set of beliefs to compare them to the world as it is in itself, so we cannot stand back from all our concerns at once in order to compare them to our impersonal grasp of objective values.

Traditional foundationalists in epistemology deny the former claim. They hold that we can check our perceptual beliefs against "the given," unconceptualized raw perceptions. Such non-conceptual content might exist as a source of empirical concepts. One cannot acquire the full concept "red" except by first perceiving red things. But once conceptualized, once

---

[9] For expansion on this point, see Alan Goldman, *Empirical Knowledge* (Berkeley: University of California Press, 1988), p. 34; for its application to values, see Ralph Wedgwood, *The Nature of Normativity* (Oxford: Oxford University Press, 2007), p. 195.

[10] Compare Frankfurt, *The Reasons of Love*, p. 26.

perceived objects appear to be some way or to have certain properties, perceptions immediately give rise to beliefs. It is then doubtful that we can bracket these beliefs, strip away the concepts, and return to the raw experience to verify the truth of the beliefs. Once I have the concept "red," in certain conditions I cannot help believing that I am seeing something red. Justification here, as in the case of values, must be a matter of coherence within the belief system.

But if depth of explanation adds to the coherence of a set of empirical beliefs, if beliefs about the physical world are more coherent if they receive an explanation by appeal to physical objects as the causes of our perceptual beliefs, then the criterion of coherence in itself justifies a realist stance toward the physical world.[11] If physical objects and their properties are to explain the ways we perceive, then these objects must really exist. In the case of values, by contrast, we add only mystery and not deeper understanding by appealing to objective values as the cause of our subjective values. As noted, the full account of the causal connections remains unspecified, as opposed to the detailed and complete causal explanations we have in the case of perceiving physical objects.

Realism in both domains posits a set of objects or objective states of affairs existing independently of our subjective states. It implies that those subjective states that represent those objective states of affairs as being some way or having certain properties could misrepresent them. If objects and values are independent of our beliefs and concerns, then our beliefs about them can be mistaken and our values misguided. Realism implies a wholesale possibility of error. But while the logical possibility of wholesale error in our beliefs about the physical world is intelligible (although probably we would not have survived such universal misrepresentation), there seems to be no sense to the claim that we all ought to care about things completely unrelated to any of our present concerns and ought to give up all of those concerns. Could the true nature of the world and of the values objectively in it demand that we not care for ourselves or our children? Would you respond to or care about such a demand? If not, what practical relevance could objective values have?

---

[11] This is not an epistemology book, and so not the place to defend these claims made by way of comparison. But for a defense and an alternative kind of foundationalism, see Alan Goldman, *Empirical Knowledge* (Berkeley: University of California Press, 1988), chs. 4, 7, 9.

III. Advantages of Internalism: A Modified Humeanism

"If you can't imitate him, don't copy him."

This book, you may have by now surmised, will defend reason internalism, the view that all practical reasons derive ultimately from our concerns. There are no objective values or external reasons. This position is favored by its transparent intelligibility as well as its metaphysical and epistemological economy. While your judgment of its intelligibility will have to await its full presentation in subsequent chapters, it certainly enjoys an initial advantage in this regard. Reasons on this view are states of affairs that motivate rational agents, and values are states of affairs that are rationally evaluated positively. Rationality consists in being relevantly informed and coherent, in which case one acts on the reasons one has. We have at least an initial grasp of what it is to desire, to evaluate, and to be informed and coherent, although all these concepts will be analyzed fully in what follows. We come to see certain facts as reasons when they indicate how to satisfy our desires. And indeed they normally are then reasons for us. Here it is not mysterious how reasons motivate us and how we know they are reasons.

The full analysis of desire to be presented in a later chapter will be controversial—somewhat more so than a parallel analysis of emotion—but both analyses are rooted in our intuitive grasp of what it is to have a desire or to be in the grip of an emotion. And this intuitive grasp is in turn grounded in our common experiences of desiring things, having emotions, and ascribing these states to others. We understand what subjects' desires and evaluations are and how they perceive reasons to act in terms of them. It is not mysterious that if I desire to play tennis and think that playing is good for me, and if this desire coheres with my other concerns for health, competition, and so on, then I see that I have a reason to play. We understand the claim that reasons are states of affairs that motivate rational agents, and we see why they should motivate if they reflect already existing motivations or concerns.

By contrast, I have pointed out that appeal to objective values as the causes of our desires remains mysterious. Objective values or brute, irreducible normative facts involve non-natural properties, properties not countenanced by any scientific theories. Furthermore, these properties demand motivation from us, demand to be pursued and protected. The mysterious nature (or "queerness," as J. L. Mackie put it)[12] of such properties is perhaps reduced somewhat by holding first that they need not necessarily or intrinsically motivate us, but only determine what we ought to value or desire, only provide external reasons. Second, it is widely claimed by believers in them that objective values supervene on natural properties. This means that there can be no differences in value without some differences in ordinary natural properties. If two objects share all their other properties, they must have the same value. The ordinary natural properties provide our reasons, not the additional fact that they are valuable. If golf provides exercise, and exercise is objectively good, then you have a reason (perhaps easily defeasible) to play golf. The fact that it provides exercise and promotes health, a natural fact, is your reason to play, not the additional non-natural fact that health and exercise are good. Their being good just *is* their providing such (external) reasons; it is not an additional source of the reasons.

But, as in the case of causal explanations discussed earlier, while this "buck-passing" account of objective value[13] perhaps reduces the mystery somewhat, it does not eliminate it. The question remains why these properties provide value or constitute reasons, and the natural answer that they do so by connecting to our concerns or motivations is unavailable to the objectivist. For her it remains a brute inexplicable fact that values as non-natural properties attach to certain physical objects and states of affairs. By contrast, the subjectivist or internalist need not ask how motivations create values, if to desire an object is in part just to judge or see it as valuable for oneself (part of the analysis of desire to be defended below). What we desire and judge to be valuable is so if we are coherent and informed of the nature of the object. When fulfilment of desire fails to create value for a subject, it is because the subject was not informed of what its satisfaction would be like, or because the satisfaction blocks that of more central concerns; that is, is inconsistent with them.

Furthermore, as others have pointed out, the concept of supervenience itself is mysterious if values do not reduce to natural properties. Why

[12] J. L. Mackie, *Inventing Right and Wrong* (New York: Penguin, 1977), pp. 38–42. I use the term "mysterious" because I take it to be no longer politically correct to call properties queer.

[13] The account is found in Scanlon, *What We Owe to Each Other*, pp. 95–100.

should there be no difference in values or reasons without a difference in natural states of affairs if the former do not somehow consist in the latter? The answer might be offered that values supervene on ordinary natural properties because they are always realized or instantiated in those other properties. Value is realized in the form of an artwork, in the courage of an heroic act, in the pleasure of a relaxing day at the beach. But it remains mysterious why objective values attach to just these properties from which they are distinct and why they should demand motivation from us.

Thus the intelligibility of the subjectivist account is tied to its metaphysical economy, since the excess metaphysical baggage of the appeal to objective values and brute, non-natural normative facts as causally efficacious renders the objectivist account mysterious. Epistemological clarity and economy are also connected. If there are non-natural normative facts, and if we are to know of them, then our ordinary perceptual, affective, and cognitive abilities would seemingly need to be augmented by a special faculty of value intuition. Once more, even if values reduce to other natural properties in their instantiations, we would have to intuit that these properties are valuable. It can be claimed that intuition is not a special faculty, but simply a matter of certain propositions that are not inferred from others seeming true to us when we think about them.[14] Certain value judgments, such as "pain is bad," seem true to us in that way. But the subjectivist can explain why this proposition seems true, namely, because those who judge it to be true are motivated to avoid pain: they desire its absence. The objectivist or intuitionist cannot provide any such explanation, and so her intuition remains mysterious.

Objectivists can reply that we need a faculty of intuition anyway to apprehend logical or mathematical truths. We do not literally perceive that two plus two is four, but must intuit the truth of this proposition. And we do not know how we do that; certainly it has nothing to do with desires. But even if that is correct for mathematics, mathematical truths seem quite different from values. It cannot be the same faculty that apprehends both, although it often goes by the same name. It seems instead that intuition is just a name for some way of knowing things that we cannot understand or locate. There must be mathematical truths that we know whether or not we can understand how we know them, but the same is not true of objective

---

[14] Michael Huemer, *Ethical Intuitionism* (New York: Palgrave, 2005), p. 101.

values. Being more controversial, it is a strike against belief in them that we cannot understand how we could know or be motivated by them.

By contrast, we generally know our own desires and concerns. For the subjectivist, to know whether something is valuable or good for me, I only need reflect on what I find valuable or am motivated to pursue when relevantly informed and coherent. If reasons are relative to desires, and if desiring something is in part to be disposed to bring it about (again part of my analysis), then we understand both why states of affairs that reflect our desires are perceived as reasons and why apprehension of reasons results in action. Once again reasons simply indicate ways to satisfy our rational desires or concerns.

In addition to being more intelligible and economical, the internalist account to be defended presents a unified view of the entire domain of reason. As indicated, both theoretical and practical rationality, rationality in belief as well as desire and action, consist mainly in coherence. Coherence will be analyzed as the avoidance of self-defeat. Believing what is unlikely to be true based on other beliefs and evidence is self-defeating, since the aim of belief is truth. Similarly, failing to act on the strongest reasons one has, those which reflect one's deepest concerns and evaluative judgments at the time, is also self-defeating, since the aim of action is to satisfy those desires or concerns. Thus rationality in belief and rationality in desire and action will be given similar analyses.

While there are both reasons for beliefs and reasons for action, there can be one account of what reasons are. They are states of affairs that motivate rational subjects, either to believe or to act. If we are rational, we are all motivated to believe what strikes us as true, and so we will base our beliefs on evidence or indications of truth. Epistemic reasons are the same for all since we all aim at truth, and truth is not relative to our beliefs or desires. And if we are rational, we will form intentions to act on what will satisfy our coherent and informed concerns and desires: we will act on the strongest reasons we have at the time of which we are aware. In fact, as pointed out at the beginning, since most of us are rational most of the time and tend to act on our desires, we will tend to act on reasons automatically. But since we do not all have the same desires or concerns, practical reasons will not be the same for all.

Nevertheless, although practical reasons are not all shared, the nature of reasons, both practical and epistemic, admits of a single analysis. Reasons motivate rational agents, and agents are rational if coherent and relevantly informed. While my account will assimilate theoretical to practical reason with the aim of avoiding self-defeat as central in both domains, the objectivist will tend to go in the other direction, assimilating practical to theoretical reason. Practical rationality for her will consist first in forming true beliefs about what is valuable. But there are two problems here. First, she will have to explain how we come to have mostly true beliefs in this domain: how we come to track independent values through their disparate instantiations. Then there will be the additional and different step of explaining why we should be motivated to act so as to achieve what is objectively valuable, if it connects to none of our current concerns. At best the theory will be less simple and unified.

Given all these theoretical advantages of the internalist account of reasons and subjectivist account of values, why do so many philosophers these days, not all of whom are not as smart as I am, argue for the opposing position?[15] First, despite its simplicity, unity, and intelligibility—all criteria for theory choice—they believe that it fails to satisfy the one prior criterion: they believe that it cannot account for all the data. According to them, it cannot account for reasons that seem to exist independently of our motivations. These include reasons for desires or basic concerns themselves, reasons that seem to give rise to new motivations instead of deriving from existing desires, moral reasons that we seem to have whether we care to have them or not, and certain seemingly rationally required prudential reasons, concern for our own welfare. In regard to the latter classes of reasons, a person who is banging his head against a wall or ignoring his own child's acute suffering appears irrational no matter how much he desires to do the one or is unconcerned about the other.

Given the theoretical advantages of internalism, the burden of proof is on the externalist to show that there are reasons for which the internalist cannot account. But once the externalist produces these purported examples, that burden shifts to the internalist to show that he can indeed explain or reasonably dismiss these cases. That is a burden I cheerfully accept for the fourth chapter. I will argue that there is no universal rational requirement to accept moral or prudential reasons as one's own, and that the internalist can explain both reasons for desires that have reasons and the acquisition of

---

[15] I am discounting Yogi Berra's explanation, that they simply made too many wrong mistakes.

new motivations in the course of experience. Basic concerns, by contrast, need no reasons to explain or justify them. I need no reason to care for myself or my loved ones.

A second reason for favoring objectivism and externalism is the phenomenology of seeming to encounter values or reasons in the world and the experience of deliberating. As noted earlier, we do not normally focus on our desires in deciding what to do, but instead focus on states of affairs or possible outcomes that immediately strike us as good or bad. We evaluate objects and not our own motivations. And these objects seem in themselves to be of positive or negative value. Whether a book should be recommended for a prize is determined by the value of the book, not by how many people desire to read it. Reasons, as what we deliberate about, are themselves good and bad states of affairs—that the book contains new ideas or is written in a dull style. Often we discover our own motivations and the priorities among them only by seeing what strikes us as more important or valuable in the world, by how we react to various objects or opportunities.

We know, however, from science and philosophical reflection in other domains that phenomenology can be misleading as a guide to metaphysics. Colors seem in experience to be not only real, but objective—out there on the surfaces of objects independent of our visual systems. But we know that colors are relational properties, analyzed only by appeal to the ways they appear to us, to subjects with our visual systems. Similarly, reasons are states of affairs out in the world, but their status as reasons may still be relative to subjects' motivational sets. That a tennis racquet is on sale is a reason for me to go to the sporting goods store, but only because of my interest in playing tennis. Although such concerns remain in the background as various states of affairs present themselves as opportunities or threats, it still seems that every evaluative judgment is made from the perspective of a person with a set of concerns more or less widely shared. We need not think about our desires or their connection to reasons in order correctly to see certain facts as reasons, or in order for the connection to determine their status as reasons.

The most philosophically astute reader might already question my claim of transparent intelligibility for the position I defend, in that she might already have noted some apparent contradiction or at least tension in my earlier claims. For one, it was claimed that "just feeling like it," a single desire in itself, provides no reason to do anything, although it is desires or concerns that give rise to reasons. My claim will be that only some desires give rise to reasons, and the third chapter will clarify which ones do so. I will claim that only coherent and informed sets of desires anchored by deeper concerns give rise to reasons. Furthermore, the plausibility of the claim that any desires give rise to reasons depends on a proper analysis of desire. If desires were simply felt urges or purely affective states, they would not generate reasons. But desires include implicit evaluative judgments as components that reflect deeper concerns with which they cohere. Such desires do create reasons that indicate how to satisfy them.

The student desires to party, and seemingly does not desire to study, but she has every reason to study and no reason to party. This is because she is concerned not to fail and has other concerns that cannot be satisfied if she does fail, although none of these concerns may be felt as urges; none may involve any yearning sensations or purely affective states. These concerns may be reflected only in her sober judgment that she had better not fail. But such evaluative judgments can be themselves parts of desires or motivational states. Usually they reflect deeper concerns and more stable or standing desires that do not always generate the sensations that attach to urges. These cognitive components of desires are normally better indications of reasons than are the purely affective components. But again, only some evaluative judgments count as motivational, and the third chapter will once more clarify which ones do.

Thus desires, like emotions, will be seen to be complex states involving different affective, dispositional, cognitive, and functional components none of which is necessary or sufficient in itself for ascribing the states. The concepts of desires, emotions, and attitudes are all what philosophers call cluster concepts, different clusters of components in each case, some of which may be absent in particular instantiations. My desire for a piece of cheesecake involves a yearning sensation, but not an evaluative judgment that eating one would be good, while my desire to finish this chapter involves the judgment that finishing it would be good, but not a felt urge. Motivational states that generate reasons include not only such occurrent or superficial desires, but deeper concerns that organize and explain the more specific and superficial desires. These concerns almost always include evaluative judgmental components. My concern for my own welfare includes the implicit judgment that it would be good for me to promote it, and this concern generates more specific desires related to my health and comfort.

The position I will defend, the thesis that all value and practical reasons derive from desires or "passions," derives from Hume. But I advocate a very much modified Humeanism. Transforming the quotation at the start of this section, we should imitate Hume's position but not copy him. Hume himself believed that practical rationality reduces to rationality in belief and instrumental rationality. It demands only that we act on true beliefs and adopt efficient means to our ends. Ends themselves are beyond criticism. I will argue that this requirement to adopt effective means to our ends is itself part of the demand for coherence as the avoidance of self-defeat. This demand generates broader concepts of practical rationality and irrationality than Hume recognized.

Most contemporary Humeans view reasons as complexes of desires and beliefs. According to this view, my reason to go to the sporting goods store is my desire for a new racquet and my belief that I can buy one there. I reject that analysis. Desires are not reasons even when combined with beliefs, and single desires in themselves do not provide reasons. Reasons are what we deliberate about, and they justify and explain our actions. While desires and beliefs are parts of the explanatory causes of our actions, they are not typically objects of deliberation and do not singly in themselves justify our actions. If I want to find out whether I have a reason to go to the sporting goods store, I inquire whether there is a racquet on sale there. That there is one on sale is my reason, and if there were not, I would have no reason to go there, whatever my desires and beliefs about racquets may be. But that there is one on sale there is a reason for me because it indicates how to satisfy my desire for a racquet, which connects to my concern to play better tennis, to exercise and compete successfully, and so on.

The claim that motivational states include cognitive components in the form of implicit evaluative judgments, and that these are generally more reflective of our reasons than are the purely affective components of desires, may seem to be anti-Humean. The complex analysis of desire so as to include judgment is indeed opposed to much of what Hume says about passions. In regard to judgment itself, however, he held only that beliefs about or judgments of objective facts lack motivational force unless connected to desires. For him, evaluative judgments, specifically moral judgments in themselves, are motivating or motivational (components of or reflective of motivations). These are not judgments of objective facts, which are motivationally inert. I will disagree with the claim that moral judgments always express motivations, but I will argue that certain other evaluative judgments do. And of course I agree with the crucial thesis that objective facts in themselves provide no reasons and rationally require no motivations.

I share Hume's skepticism about objective values, and therefore I am skeptical of external reasons as well. Reasons are states of affairs and not desires, but they depend on subjects' motivations, including their deepest and broadest concerns. This account fits well with a plausible analysis of desires themselves. Suitably amended and expanded, as it will be in the chapters to follow, Humean internalism provides our most economical and unified theory of practical reason. This theory informs us that, although reasons for action are states of affairs in the world, what makes them reasons lies within valuing subjects.

2

Reasons and Rationality

I. Reasons Defined

"Ninety percent of this game is half mental."

In the introductory chapter it was noted that practical reasons, reasons for actions, are what we deliberate about and what explain and justify our actions. Some philosophers divide normative or justifying reasons from explanatory reasons. Indeed, there are senses in which the two are distinct, in which explanatory reasons may not justify and justifying reasons may not explain. The sense in which reasons may be only explanatory is the sense in which "reason" is synonymous with "cause". "The reason he did it is that he was drunk (he did it because he was drunk)." In this sense we can also say, "The reason the engine stalled is that dirt got in the carburetor". Clearly such usage has nothing essentially to do with practical rationality. Just as explanatory reasons in this sense can fail to justify, so justifying reasons can fail to explain when not acted on. "He had every reason to attend the meeting, but he played golf instead." Such justifying reasons would explain actions if acted on, but they cannot explain what does not happen.

Although the explanatory can thus come apart from the justificatory, these two aspects of reasons normally go together, since normative reasons are what motivate or explain the actions of rational agents, and most of us are rational most of the time. Reasons must be normative and not simply explanatory if we can fail to act on reasons we have. If I had a reason to attend the meeting but did not, then this reason can be only normative. But reasons must be explanatory and not simply normative if we ever do act on them. And they cannot be normative unless they are also potentially explanatory, since there is no point in telling people they ought to act on certain reasons unless they can act on them, unless the reasons are able to motivate them.

When we deliberate, we consider states of affairs that would justify acting in certain ways, but we deliberate in order to decide which such normative reasons to act on, to determine which will explain our actions. We normally cite reasons on which others acted in order to explain their actions, but we give reasons to others for having acted as we did in order to justify our actions. If we take others to be rational, as we do almost all the time, then the reasons we cite to explain their actions also rationalize or justify them from the rational (not necessarily moral) point of view. And if we succeed in justifying our actions to others, we will also have explained those actions to them. The actions of rational agents are explained by reasons that also justify the actions, and most of us are rational in our actions. Reasons motivate us precisely by justifying our actions in our own eyes, and if they motivate us, they enter into the causal explanations for our actions. Thus reasons are normally both justifying and explanatory.

I also noted in the previous chapter that reasons are states of affairs or facts, such as a tennis racquet's being on sale or its raining outside, that count for or against certain actions, such as going to the sports store or having a picnic. On the internalist view, they count in favor of certain actions because they indicate how those actions will tend to satisfy our desires. If reasons in the full sense of justifying and explaining reasons are states of affairs or facts, they are not desires or beliefs (or combinations of them). They are not even half mental. If one thinks only of explanatory reasons, then desires and beliefs can seem to be reasons since they can explain actions, being parts of the causal chains that lead to actions. Facts or states of affairs are also parts of those causal chains since they give rise to the beliefs that cause the actions when paired with the relevant desires. That a racquet is on sale causes me to believe there is (via a newspaper advertisement), which causes me to go to the sports store when combined with my desire for a racquet. Which part of the causal chain is cited in an explanation is a pragmatic affair. Always only that part of a causal chain on which interest is focused gets cited in an explanation. Thus, externalists are right that we do not necessarily need to cite additional elements when citing factual reasons as explanations, but wrong if they think this implies that desires are not also necessary parts of the relevant causal chains. And traditional Humean internalists are also right that we can explain actions by citing desires and beliefs, other parts of the causal chains.

But, as noted earlier, desires and beliefs are not typical objects of deliberation, and they do not in themselves justify actions. If I wake in the morning, desire to go back to sleep, and believe that I can, I still may have no reason to do so and many reasons not to, given my concerns and busy schedule for the day. I could not justify, even begin to justify, additional sleep to myself or others simply by pointing out that I felt a desire to go back to sleep and knew I could. To such an attempt at justification my first missed appointment could certainly reply quite literally and truthfully, "That is not a reason at all". The internalist must then explain why some desires create reasons and others do not, and I will do so in the next chapter.

As noted, reasons motivate, and desires are states of being motivated. Moral reasons, for example, are not desires plus beliefs, but states of affairs that result from actions (consequences, such as that an action will be harmful to others) or facts that actions are of certain types, for example the breaking of a promise. Once more this leaves it open whether such facts or states of affairs are reasons only for those with moral concerns or motivations. I will argue for this thesis in the fourth chapter. That certain facts are reasons seems more obviously relative to background concerns in other cases. That a grant is available is a reason for me to apply only if I desire to have one, or ought to have that desire given my other concerns, or would desire it if I knew of the availability; only if I desire one and know what having one entails or would desire one if I did know, and only if having one fits my deeper concerns instead of frustrating them, not, for example, if I care more about teaching than research. Such concerns are backgrounded in deliberation, but the availability of a grant is a reason to apply only relative to them. In this sense more than ninety percent of reasons are half mental.

Questions will arise for some of these claims from apparent counterexamples. First, it seems that some desires in themselves justify actions and that my generalization that desires are not reasons from the alarm clock example was therefore illegitimate. My desire for chocolate ice cream seems to justify my trip to Ben and Jerry's, for example. Second, it seems that beliefs too can count as reasons, ironically most apparently in those cases in which the beliefs are false. "The reason he spoke up at the meeting was to increase his chance at promotion, but his comments had the opposite effect." Here it seems that his reason for speaking was his false belief that this would lead to a promotion. The reason cannot be the fact that his speech would make a promotion more likely, since there was no such fact. In the absence of a fact or state of affairs that could count as a reason, must we not appeal instead to a belief? Certainly the belief in the example explains his action. Does it also justify it, and if so, does it it count as a reason in the full sense I have so far indicated, as what justifies and explains action?

I have denied that desires and beliefs in themselves count as reasons. I will postpone discussion of the apparent counterexample involving the desire for ice cream until the next chapter, when we will examine at greater length the relation of desires to reasons. But the claim that beliefs are sometimes reasons can be answered now. When an action is based on a false belief about a reason, I think it is generally better to say that the agent had no reason, but only thought he had one, instead of saying that his belief was his reason. So the employee who spoke up at the meeting had no reason to do so and a good reason not to, namely that his speech would decrease his chance for promotion. If his belief that his speech would be beneficial to him was itself irrational or not based on any evidence, then his speaking up was also irrational. But suppose that his belief that speaking would increase his chance of promotion was itself justified, say by his knowledge that others had been promoted after making similar speeches. Would not that justified belief then justify his acting as he did, and therefore count as a full-fledged reason in both explaining and justifying his action?

In such a case I still think it better to say that the fact that justifies his belief also justifies his acting as he did. That others were promoted after speaking up can be his reason for acting as they did. Given that he acted on his knowledge of this reason, his act was rational even though his belief that it would benefit him was false. This construal allows us first to maintain a more unified account of reasons, instead of giving one account when underlying beliefs are true and another when they are false. Since we must often speak naturally of states of affairs or facts as reasons, it is more coherent to stick to that account when it is available as an alternative to counting false beliefs as normative reasons. Second, there is the fact that reasons are what we deliberate about, and in deciding how to act we do not deliberate about our beliefs (we do so only sometimes when deciding what to believe).[1]

When I take an agent to have acted for good reasons, I will appeal to those reasons in explaining her action, and I will agree with her in taking those reasons to be normative or justifying. When I take her to have acted without good reason, I will appeal in explaining her action to her beliefs about reasons she had, beliefs I will take to be false. The state of affairs to which these beliefs refer may or may not exist. If Sue acted as she did because she thought Tom had insulted her, and I, the appraiser of her action, do not think she acted with good reason, this may be because I do not think Tom insulted her or because I think he did but the insult did not justify her response. In either case her belief that he had insulted her and that this warranted her response explains her reaction, but is not a reason for her to have acted in that way in my eyes.

Once again, however, if her belief that Tom insulted her was justified by her evidence even though false, then her evidence, the fact that he said what he did (while not intending it as an insult and not realizing that she would reasonably take it that way), should be recognized by me as a valid reason for her to have reacted as she did. She would then have been rational in acting on a full-fledged reason, even though she had a false belief about the reason for which she acted, a false belief that he had actually insulted her (assuming here that insults must be intentional). More on rationality below. Here the point is that what we take to be full-fledged reasons are always normative from our point of view, and beliefs along with desires that explain actions do not fill that bill. Some philosophers would count justified but false beliefs as subjective reasons, as opposed to objective ones. I prefer to count only objective reasons of which subjects are aware or on which they act as their subjective reasons. This once more allows us to recognize only facts or states of affairs as reasons.

We may summarize in order to propose more formal definitions. Reasons justify actions and explain the actions of rational agents by motivating them

---

[1] We could also say alternatively that the possibility that the speech would increase the chance of promotion was a reason to make it. But this would again increase the metaphysics of the account, so that once more the economy of the account I propose makes it preferable.

to act as they do. But they will motivate agents only if they have the proper background concerns or motivations. This last claim is the internalist's thesis. If we define reasons as states of affairs that motivate rational agents, we had better not define rational agents as those who act on reasons. The latter definition, although accurate, would combine with the former to make a circle so tight as to be totally unenlightening. I shall instead define a rational agent as one who acts on coherent and relevantly informed desires or motivations. These include both the background motivations that constitute the reasons as reasons and those motivations that are induced by the reasons themselves, specific motivations to act in various ways.

I then propose the following two definitions:

(1) *There is an F (moral, prudential, religious, aesthetic . . .) reason R to do act A = If and only if a subject S is F-minded, then S, if rational, would be motivated by awareness of R to do A.*

(2) *S has an F reason R to do act A = S is F-minded, and because of that, if rational, would be motivated by awareness of R to do A.*

Thus, there is an aesthetic reason to not wear a brown tie with a purple shirt if and only if an aesthetically-minded rational person would be motivated not to wear them together. A person has such a reason if and only if he is aesthetically-minded.

Reasons motivate rational agents because they indicate how certain actions, actions in light of those facts, will tend to satisfy their desires. This suggests an alternative definition of reasons in those terms, as facts that indicate or explain why actions for which they are reasons tend to satisfy desires.[2] But that definition in turn suggests that all desires are capable of generating reasons that indicate how to satisfy them, a claim I reject. It is preferable because clearer to define reasons in terms of rationality and then analyze rationality in terms that do not include appeal to reasons. First, this emphasizes that what makes a state of affairs a reason is nothing intrinsic to that state of affairs, as objectivists about value would have it. What makes something a reason is that it motivates rational agents by relating to certain of their desires or concerns.

---

[2] Mark Schroeder, *Slaves of the Passions* (Oxford: Oxford University Press, 2007), defines reasons in that way, p. 59.

Second, our analysis of rationality will imply an answer to the question of when desires generate reasons. For an agent to have a reason, it is not necessary that she be motivated to act on it. But neither can it be entirely independent of her motivations. She will be motivated if rational and aware of the reason. "If rational" means if informed and coherent in her motivational states, as I will spell out below, so that an agent can have a reason if required to be motivated by it or by her other motivations or concerns on grounds of coherence. Hence third, our analysis of rationality will show clearly how this central normative concept reduces to the non-normative concepts of coherence and information. To reverse the order of explanation and define rationality by saying that rational agents are moved by reasons they have fails to provide an adequate analysis of rationality, since there are other ways of being irrational besides failing to be moved at all by one's reasons. Thus it is preferable to analyze reasons in terms of rationality instead of the converse.

Several more clarifying comments on the above definitions are in order. First, the reference to awareness in both definitions indicates that agents can have reasons of which they are unaware. I can have a reason to apply for a grant given my desire for research support, but if I am unaware of the availability of the grant, I will not be motivated to apply for it. Obviously, lack of awareness of reasons can prevent being motivated by them. At the same time, I can be motivated by reasons of which I am unaware at the time—as emphasized in the previous chapter, we often act automatically without focusing on our reasons. But if rational, we must be motivated by reasons we have of which we are aware. Thus the test of whether some fact is a reason is whether awareness of it motivates a rational agent. A rational subject's objective reasons are all those that would motivate her if she were aware of them, and her subjective reasons are those of which she is aware or on which she acts.

Second, the requirement that rational subjects be motivated by reasons they have is not a requirement that these motivations are always strong or result in action. We must not interpret motivations too strongly here. They cannot always override others or result in action if agents can have conflicting reasons. Being aesthetically-minded, I have reasons to go to concerts and museums, and I am motivated to do so. But obviously, given my many other concerns and time limitations, I do not go to concerts or museums constantly. Nor do I feel an urge to go to one every day.

What I do have is a long-range disposition to go on occasion when I am not more motivated to do something else. I also occasionally have pleasant thoughts about going to a concert or museum, especially when the opportunity to hear a favorite piece or see a new exhibit arises. This disposition and occasional pleasant direction of attention is sufficient to ascribe motivation in the relevant sense. Given that rational agents can have conflicting reasons, reasons to do things not all of which can be done at the time, it is clear that rationality or coherence does not exclude conflicting sets of motivations. What it does exclude and demand will be clarified below.

The difference between the two definitions and the reference to being F-minded indicate that not all reasons there are, are reasons that particular agents have, reasons for them. There are no objective reasons that require motivations from all agents regardless of their concerns. This might still allow that there are concerns that all rational agents must have—for example, moral or prudential concerns—but I will argue against this possibility later. Reasons require motivation only when they are a subject's reasons, and they are a subject's reasons only when they connect to her prior informed and coherent motivations. There are good reasons to hit a tennis ball with topspin, but they are reasons only for those concerned to play tennis at a high level. There are religious reasons to do or not to do various things, but they are not reasons for me, since I am not religious and have no concerns that require me to accept religious reasons. (If, for example, I were concerned about relations with my mother, and if she were religious and intolerant of unobservant atheists, then I might have reasons to obey some religious laws, at least in her presence.)

The distinction between these definitions allows us to be externalists in at least an attenuated sense about what reasons there are and strong internalists about what reasons agents have. The externalism is attenuated or weak because the first definition still makes reference to motivation in two places, and because we would not recognize any reasons as such unless at least some people were relevantly concerned and therefore motivated by them. If no one were sensitive to beauty, there would be no aesthetic reasons. If no one ever cared about the interests or needs of others and had no prudential concerns that required such moral concerns, there would be no moral reasons. But the distinction between reasons there are and reasons particular agents have will allow us to accommodate some of the premises in the arguments of externalists without accepting their conclusion. For example, we can admit that there may be moral reasons or obligations to do certain things and yet deny that it would be irrational of a particular agent not to do those things.

The thoroughgoing externalist will deny that reasons are relative to agents' concerns in the way my definitions indicate. I claim that it is my interest in improving my tennis game that gives me a reason to go to the store where a racquet is on sale. An externalist will say that it is not my desire to improve my game that gives me the reason, but instead the enjoyment that I would derive from doing so, enjoyment that is objectively good. And he will deny that religious concerns give us religious reasons; instead he will claim that all people have such reasons if being religious benefits them or others. In my view this move only puts off the relativity to desire or concern one step, since I would not derive enjoyment from improving my game unless I were interested in tennis, or unless I were the type of person who is disposed to enjoy such activities, as others are not; and my enjoyment would not support a reason unless I cared about experiencing this kind of enjoyment. Similarly, even if religion benefits religious people or others with whom they interact, this would not generate religious reasons for those people unless they were concerned about their own or others' welfare.

The externalist will reply that all rational agents must be concerned about their own and others' welfare, a claim that I will deny at greater length in the fourth chapter. He will also say that I have a reason for caring about enjoyments I might have, namely, what it is like to experience those enjoyments. But I reply that I am not rationally required to care about every enjoyment I might experience, and that those I do not care about give me no reason to pursue them. If an externalist admits that not even all those who might somewhat enjoy tennis have a reason to take up the game, then she will not be so thoroughgoing: she will want to distinguish reasons that are relative to interests in such activities as tennis from those that depend on what she considers objective values, such as moral reasons that are held to depend on the value of satisfying other people's needs and interests. Later chapters will challenge the idea of objective values and rationally required concerns based on them.

Reasons motivate rational agents when they are aware of them. If an agent fails to be motivated by some reason there is of which he is aware, then either the agent is irrational or the reason is not a reason for him, not a reason he has. Irrationality is rare and, I will argue, consists in incoherence or self-defeat. Even if this analysis is not accepted, it still must be admitted that the concept of irrationality as ordinarily applied is instantiated only in rare or abnormal cases. For most reasons that fail to motivate particular agents aware of them, it will be difficult or impossible to make the case that they are irrational or incoherent in their desires and actions. Therefore, most agents who are not motivated by reasons of certain kinds do not have reasons of those kinds.

Thus my definitions, reflecting internalism about reasons, imply that only F-minded people have F reasons. Non-philosopher readers (of whom I hope there are some) might be impatient with my reference to F reasons and F-mindedness. This is not an abbreviation for an expletive, but, as the parenthetical modifiers in the definitions indicate, a reference to broad categories of deep concerns that people have. Deep concerns that sit at the base of an agent's motivational system are often called the agent's values, and they ground many more specific and superficial desires. Motivations typically nest in hierarchical structures. My concern for my welfare, my being prudentially-minded, spawns a concern for my health, which spawns an interest in exercise, which spawns a desire to play tennis, which spawns a desire to have a good racquet, which spawns a desire to go to the sports store, which spawns a desire to avoid the rush-hour traffic, and so on. My concern to have something to live for or devote the bulk of my time to and to have a means of support spawns a choice of and an interest in a particular career, which spawns many other interests and concerns involved in that career. My natural interest in the welfare of certain others close to me becomes broadened into a moral concern for many others and specified in terms of the desire to meet more specific demands that I accept as part of morality. Values or broader concerns typically give rise to more specific desires when certain states of affairs are recognized as opportunities, thereby becoming reasons for the more specific desires. For example, I see an advertisement for a tennis racquet and thereby come to desire to go to the sports store. The availability of the racquet is an opportunity for me to get one and a reason for me to go to the store. I acquire a desire to go to the store because of my broader concerns that will be satisfied by doing so.

I have provided examples of broader concerns generating more specific desires for which they provide reasons. One could still question why more generally these broader concerns must be seen as deeper and why they should be seen as giving rise to the more specific desires instead of the other way around. I characterize broader concerns as deeper because they connect to many others for which they also provide reasons, while the more specific desires are relatively isolated. If one did not have the broader concerns or dispositions, the more specific desires would be ungrounded, would exist as mere whims or urges. The broader concerns can be seen as giving rise to the more specific, because if one did not have the former one would not have the latter, while the converse is not true. If one did not have the disposition to enjoy outdoor sports, for example, one would not specifically desire to play each of these sports, while if one did not desire to play golf, for example, for some specific reason, one might still have the general disposition. The disposition together with other elements to be spelled out in the next chapter counts as a broad concern or general desire because the dispositional component is central to desire and the other elements will presumably be present as well (for example, occasional pleasant thoughts about outdoor activities).

That broad and deep concerns lie at the base of one's motivational system removes the initial implausibility of the claim that an agent's reasons must always relate to prior motivations, those already in the agent's system. This claim might prompt the questions how we could initially have reasons to do anything and how we could acquire new motivations. The answer is that we begin life with certain very broad dispositions and instinctual concerns that become more specific in countless ways over our lifetimes. We begin with instinctual concerns for ourselves (although not yet conceived as individual subjects) and feelings for others in our vicinity. We begin with dispositions to want nourishment and warmth, to avoid pain and discomfort, which I am interpreting as concern for ourselves, dispositions to react to the distress cries of others, to be attracted visually to certain objects or colors, to find certain sounds unpleasant and others pleasant, and so on. Such dispositions lead eventually through continuous stimulation and interaction to prudential, moral, and aesthetic concerns that gradually develop in different specific ways in different people.

At the deepest level our concerns need no reasons for support but generate reasons for many other desires. We need no reason to care for ourselves or others, to love our children (the very suggestion of reasons is offensive), to react positively to beauty, to want projects to which we can commit ourselves, and so on. We could have reasons even for such concerns—we might care for ourselves in order to preserve ourselves for some other cause or love our children because they are so admirable (mine, not yours)—but we need no such reasons. This does not mean that our deepest concerns must be mysterious to us. We can be aware of them even though they are not often at the forefront of our consciousness. And we can assess them in terms of coherence with each other and with more concrete desires that specify them (to be spelled out in the next section). But their positive assessment is grounded in coherence with desires for which they provide reasons, not the other way around.

Being F-minded then stands roughly for being morally-minded, prudentially-minded, aesthetically-minded, sports-minded, and so on. Only roughly, because often these categories will have to be specified in a more finely grained way for particular subjects. Most people who are sports-minded care only about particular sports and not others. If mature aesthetic judgments are irreducibly relative to tastes, then we would have to further specify being aesthetically-minded in terms of different tastes. A feature of an artwork that gives a lover of the baroque a reason to approve of the work might not give those who prefer minimalism a reason to approve. Similarly, if moral judgments are relative to different moral frameworks, then, for example, a libertarian who is morally-minded might not have a reason to promote equality, while an egalitarian obviously would have a reason to do so. If instead moral relativism is false, then it might seem that a libertarian who is morally-minded would have a reason to promote equality if properly informed of this genuine moral requirement.

The situation, however, is somewhat more complex than the last sentence indicates. Even if the content of morality is somehow univocal and fixed, most of us are only partially morally-minded. I am only mildly abashed to admit that, although I am convinced by the moral arguments of vegetarians, I am unmotivated by them. I feel no qualms about placing gustatory pleasure ahead of my cerebral recognition that it is wrong to kill animals for the way they taste. It is not just that the one motivation overrides the other: I am not motivated at all to avoid eating meat on moral grounds, hence really feel no qualms. If I am correct that I am morally wrong in this attitude and practice, then I am also inconsistent or incoherent in my moral attitudes. I treat humans one way and animals another in regard to killing them for gustatory pleasure without being able to find a morally relevant difference between them in this regard. But although this is morally inconsistent and hence wrong, it does not strike me as a defect of rationality. It does not lead to a defeat of my own aims or concerns as genuine irrationality does (to be further described below). I am simply only partially concerned about moral matters, as I suspect are many others, partially morally blind or insensitive in ways more or less culpable.

Thus the moral-mindedness of individuals has to be specified in a more finely grained way irrespective of the truth of moral relativism. Similarly, I am only partially aesthetically-minded by my own lights, since intellectually I recognize great works of art that I do not appreciate, that do not engage me on other levels. I am not motivated to seek them out or attend to them fully, as appreciation requires. Again this is not a failure of rationality. I am not acting against my own aesthetic interests, as I would be if I never summoned the energy for a trip to a museum, but instead recognizing that those interests are not as extensive as they might be. That is an aesthetic shortcoming, aesthetically culpable perhaps as a lack of sensitivity to certain great works, but not unreasonable or irrational. It is not that I fail to act on reasons I have; it is simply that not all the aesthetic reasons there are, are reasons for me, reasons I have.

To count as morally- or aesthetically-minded, one must have concerns that are publicly recognized or acknowledged to be moral or aesthetic. This does not mean that one has to recognize them oneself as such. If I am F-minded and therefore motivated by F reasons, then I will be motivated by the F-ness of the reasons, although I might not conceive them as such. By his own lights Huckleberry Finn was not morally-minded. He declared that he was washing his hands of the whole morality business after deciding that he could not return his friend Jim to his slave-owning aunt, which act he considered a genuine moral demand. But being concerned for Jim's welfare and for what we recognize as justice, Huck was in fact morally-minded. He was not motivated by his moral beliefs or (what he took as his) moral judgments, but he was motivated by genuine moral matters. Conversely, many "value voters" today take themselves to be strongly morally-minded, while they do not strike us as being genuinely so. Or perhaps they are just differently morally-minded (not!), again to be specified more narrowly.

Objectivists or externalists will view the domains of morality, aesthetics, and sports, for example, differently. They will see objective reasons to be morally-minded, so that one is rationally required to be so; they will probably think that we can all derive enjoyment from aesthetic appreciation and that we therefore all have an instrumental reason to be aesthetically-minded; and they will think that only those who do enjoy watching sports will have an objective instrumental reason to do so. I began to answer the appeal to enjoyment or pleasure above, and I will return to the subject in Chapter 5. I will also deny even in the case of morality that we are rationally required to be morally-minded. In all domains the reasons we have depend on our concerns or motivations. The precise way that they do remains to be clarified in the next chapter.

A final distinction must be drawn here between objective and subjective reasons, although we must be very careful in how we draw it. Objective reasons are not those that demand motivation independent of subjects' background concerns: there are no such reasons. Subjective reasons are not mental states such as beliefs and desires: all reasons are facts or states of affairs. And subjective reasons are not merely apparent reasons: merely apparent reasons are not reasons but states of affairs, existent or non-existent, falsely but often justifiably believed to be reasons. Finally, the distinction is not the same as the difference between reasons there are and reasons one has, reflected in the two different definitions. The distinction I presently wish to draw is very simple. Subjective reasons are those subjects have of which they are aware or on which they act. Such reasons are not exclusive of or weaker than objective reasons, but form subsets of objective reasons, those of subjects who are aware of them or act on them. As noted earlier, subjects may also have objective reasons of which they are unaware.

This distinction allows us to escape accepting an inconsistent triad of propositions (such sets of individually plausible propositions make up some of the juiciest philosophical puzzles). The triad is the following: (1) A rational person must act on the strongest reasons he has. (2) One can have strongest reasons of which one is unaware. (3) One cannot be irrational for failing to act on a reason of which one is unaware. Considered separately these propositions seem correct, but they are inconsistent. If the strongest reasons one has can be reasons of which one is unaware, then either proposition 1 or proposition 3 is false. One might question proposition 3 on the ground that one could be irrational in failing to be aware of a reason. But this claim is both compatible with proposition 3 and in my view not quite correct. What it should say is that one could be irrational in failing to investigate whether there is a reason of which one is unaware. One could also be self-deceptive, a form of irrationality, in hiding a reason from oneself. But in that case it is plausible that one is aware of the reason on some level. I argued for proposition 2 earlier. Another example that it captures is that of a person who is allergic to peanuts but unaware of that fact. It certainly seems that she has a strong reason not to eat them without knowing of the reason.

The simple solution is to alter proposition 1 so as to claim only that a rational person must act on the strongest subjective reasons he has, on the strongest reasons of which he is aware. Once the distinction is drawn between subjective and objective reasons, proposition 1 no longer seems plausible, although in the absence of the distinction it may seem the most plausible of the three. A rational person can act on reasons he is not aware of at the time, if he acts automatically (as described in the first chapter) without thinking about the reasons on which he acts. Proposition 1 must then also be amended to allow the unusual case in which a person acts automatically on a reason stronger than opposing reasons of which he is aware. (As we will see later, this is true of Huckleberry Finn.) Given the rarity of this case, I will not bother to restate the proposition to capture it. Reasons that prompt automatic actions are still available to a subject through introspection. One cannot be motivated by external states of affairs that one has never encountered even indirectly, even though they can be reasons for one. If I am allergic to peanuts, I have a strong reason not to eat them; but if I am unaware of the allergy, I will have no subjective reason not to eat them. I would not be irrational in eating them. The distinction between subjective and objective reasons will also be useful in further clarifying the nature of rationality in this chapter, while the distinction between reasons there are and reasons one has will be crucial in answering some of the purported counter-examples to internalism to be considered in the fourth chapter.

In closing this section, I will briefly discuss a counterexample to Bernard Williams' analysis of internal reasons, as doing so will clarify the difference between Williams' analysis and mine. His partial account is the following: "A has a reason to ϕ only if there is *a sound deliberative route* from A's subjective motivational set to A's ϕ-ing."[3] For Williams it is also true that, if R is a reason for S, then, if S deliberates rationally from present motivations, then S will be motivated by R (S need not act on R if there are equally strong motivations to do something else). The counterexample derives from Elijah Millgram.[4] Millgram's character Archie is insensitive but desires to have friends. His insensitivity gives him a reason not to go to a meeting where he will hurt people's feelings and lose friends. He cannot grasp this reason because he is insensitive. If he were capable of rational deliberation from his present motivations to a grasp of this reason, he would already have to be sensitive and so would not have this reason or be motivated to act on it. Thus he has a reason although there is no deliberative route from his present motivations to his acting on it. Williams' analysis is refuted as it stands.

My analysis is different, because being capable of rational deliberation from present motivations is not the same as being rational *tout court*; that is, coherent in one's motivations and relevantly informed. The information requirement is more relevant here. In my view, to be spelled out and

[3] Bernard Williams, "Some Further Notes on Internal and External Reasons," in Elijah Millgram (ed.), *Varieties of Practical Reasoning* (Cambridge, MA: MIT Press, 2001), p. 91.
[4] Elijah Millgram, "Williams' Argument Against External Reasons," *Noûs*, 30 (1996): 197–220, p. 203.

defended in the next section, to be relevantly informed is mainly to know what it would be like to act on a purported reason and what it would be like not to act on it. In the example, if Archie were informed of what it would be like not to attend the meeting (keeping his friends) versus what it would be like to attend (losing his friends), he would be motivated to act on the reason not to attend. So the example is not a counterexample to my analysis. As I suggested earlier, one could be rational without ever deliberating, perhaps without even being capable of deliberation if, for example, one always did the rational thing automatically. Millgram might still maintain that counterexamples to my analyses will exist when one's reason to do something would not exist if one were rational, when, for example, one has a reason to become rational. I believe, however, and will argue further below, that the moral to be drawn from the fact that one cannot grasp reasons unless one is rational is that one cannot have a reason to be rational. I will then leave it to Millgram or others to propose other counterexamples to my analyses.

II. Rationality: The Information Requirement

"If you don't know where you're going, you might not get there."

It remains in this chapter to clarify the nature of rationality to which appeal was made in defining reasons. Being rational, it was claimed, consists in being relevantly informed and coherent, which allows one to avoid self-defeat of those concerns on which one acts. The internalist does not claim that whatever motivational states we happen to have are normative or create reasons that rationalize our actions. That claim would imply that whatever we do is rational, or that there is no rationally right or wrong when it comes to actions. But clearly internalists must allow for irrationality, not only in action and belief, but in motivations themselves. Hence the emphasis on coherence and relevant information. In this section I will clarify the information requirement, and in the next the coherence requirement. There are three main questions in regard to information. First, why is information required? Second, how much information is required, or which information is relevant to determining reasons or rationality? Third, does relevant information reveal what is presently rational for an agent to do (what her subjective reasons are) or what objective reasons she has?

According to my definitions of reasons, they motivate rational agents, and rationality consists in being relevantly informed and coherent. Conversely, motivations or desires create reasons when and only when the desires or their subjects are relevantly informed. There are two sides to this last claim. First, an agent will have the reasons he would have if, counterfactually, he were relevantly informed. These may be objective reasons of which he is presently unaware. If so, they will not affect what it is presently rational for him to do, which depends on his subjective reasons. Second, an agent will lack reasons based only on desires that are not relevantly informed. These will include seeming subjective reasons that are not reasons and so will reveal that what might have seemed rational to do is not. Information can either reveal reasons one has of which one is unaware or remove seeming reasons on which it is irrational to act.

Externalists will question the implications for internalism of this claim that only informed desires create reasons. If an agent is motivated to pursue some object in the absence of information about its nature, why should his reasons depend on a set of hypothetical desires he would have but does not, instead of depending on his actual desires? The externalist will claim that this could be only because the information in question reveals the true or objective value of the objects desired, or because there is some objective value to the truth itself or to acting on the basis of true belief.[5] In either case it will be claimed that the information requirement rests upon appeal to some objective value and therefore takes us beyond the resources of internalism.

My reply is that information is required not to reveal or reflect objective value, but in order to avoid self-defeat, the essence of irrationality according to the internalist. Ignorance of the nature of the objects one takes oneself to desire, or of the likely outcomes of satisfying the desires, or of the real origins of the desires, or of the relations of these seeming desires to one's deeper concerns, likely hides either the fact that one does not really desire

---

[5] The first claim is made by Warren Quinn, *Morality and Action* (Cambridge: Cambridge University Press, 1993), p. 245.

the objects in question, or the fact that attaining those objects will likely defeat some of those deeper concerns. As for the value of true beliefs, in their roles as guides to action, true beliefs are instrumentally valuable in allowing us to obtain what we really desire. Given this instrumental value so fundamental as to be necessary for survival, it is clear why we would come to value truth in itself. This is a case in which intrinsic value (what is valued in itself) is dependent on instrumental value (what is valued as a means). But despite being valued in itself, in this context information or true belief is required to generate reasons from desires. It does so not by tuning the desires into objective values, but by showing what is really desired or what is likely to cohere with other concerns. Lack of relevant information likely leads to self-defeat, and that is why it is often irrational to act without such information. (The exception is when one must act immediately and therefore on whatever information one has.)

To see this more clearly we may return first to our earlier example of a desire based only on a false belief about its object or about the outcome of fulfiling it. False belief is not always the same as ignorance or lack of information (false belief implies ignorance or lack of true belief, but lack of true belief does not imply false belief), but in this context their effects are likely to be the same. We earlier considered the case of an employee who spoke up at a meeting under the false belief that this would enhance his chance of promotion. I argued that, if he lacked evidence for the truth of this belief, he had no reason to speak up and a good reason not to. This was true despite his desire to speak up: thus the desire that itself was based on a false belief generated no reason. A similar example that has cropped up in the literature several times is that of someone who desires to drink a glass of clear liquid in front of her under the belief that it is vodka, when in fact it is gasoline. Once more it seems clear that the person lacks a reason to drink the liquid based only on her false belief (if she has a reason, it is some fact such as that the liquid looks like vodka and is in a glass on a bar).

One plausible interpretation of this situation is that the person does not really desire the object in question, that is, the gasoline in the glass. Another is that despite her desire to drink the liquid in the glass (picked out under that description), the desire generates no reason for her to do so. She has an objective reason not to drink the liquid of which she is unaware and perhaps a desire to drink it that nevertheless creates no reason. Relevant information would both reveal the objective reason and perhaps eliminate a seeming subjective reason, for example that it would make her feel good, which is reflected in her desire (under that interpretation). It is clear that she does not desire the likely outcome of acting on her desire or false belief and that the desire, if there is one and not simply the illusion of one, depends on ignorance of that likely outcome.

I think we can generalize from these examples that desires based only on false beliefs about their objects or about the outcomes of fulfiling them generate no reasons to act on them. But if desires based on false beliefs generate no reasons, then desires based on lack of information or ignorance generate no reasons either, having similar likely effects. If the employee had no reason to speak up based on his false belief that doing so would enhance his chance of promotion, then he would have had no reason if he simply had no idea or information about the effect of his speech on his chances, and if the speech in fact would decrease his chances. If the person had no reason to drink the gasoline based on her false belief that it was vodka, then she would have had no reason to drink it if she had no idea what was in the glass or no information about the probable outcome of drinking it and if in fact drinking it would conflict with her other concerns. In the first case ignorance still leads to defeat of the deeper desire for promotion, and in the second leads to frustration of the concern to remain healthy. In general, if one's immediate and informed desires tend to cohere with one's deeper concerns, often having developed as specifications of them, and if acting on uninformed desires often leads to outcomes different from those that would be achieved with more information, then actions based on uninformed desires will tend to be incoherent with one's deeper concerns; that is, will likely be self-defeating. Furthermore, when an agent lacks relevant information she will have objective reason to do what she would desire to do if she had that information, since that hypothetical desire will again tend to cohere with her deeper concerns.

Sometimes it is rational to act in the absence of information, but that will be in cases in which one must act and cannot acquire the information. One's reason for acting is then that one must act and cannot acquire relevant information. In the absence of such a reason, it will not be rational to act in the absence of relevant information, information that might show that one's desires or seeming desires create no reasons. There might seem to be situations in which it is rational, at least not irrational, to act without information and without being virtually forced to act by circumstances. Suppose I am in a restaurant of a nationality I have never sampled before. Is it not rational of me to want to try some dish having no idea what it will taste like? Yes, but this is because I do have the information I need as to what it would be like to act on the desire. I know that since the dish is served in a restaurant, it is likely to be edible and not to taste exactly like lye or turpentine or mud, for example. I can also infer from past experience in restaurants that it will likely be worthwhile to taste the new dish.

The question then becomes pressing which and how much information is relevant or required to rationalize desires and actions based on them. We cannot define relevant information as awareness of all the reasons to act or not act on the desires. We have defined reasons in terms of rationality (what motivates rational agents), and rationality partly in terms of relevant information. Again the circle would be too tight if we then defined relevant information in terms of reasons. Nor can we demand omniscience to determine either the reasons one has or what it is rational for one to do, that is, to reveal either objective or subjective reasons. Rational desires and actions cannot be those that would be had or done by an omniscient agent.

First, there are examples of information that can lead to irrational actions or failure to act on overriding reasons that one has. Such information available to an omniscient agent distorts instead of revealing his reasons. In questioning a full-information account of rationality, Allan Gibbard gives the example of vivid knowledge of people's digestive systems preventing him from going to dinner parties or eating meals with other people.[6] In the language of reasons, it seems clear that he might have reasons to attend a dinner party and no reasons not to, even though if he had full knowledge of what the guests' intestines were doing at the party, he would not attend. Hence the information would make him act irrationally. If such knowledge would give him reasons not to attend, they would be reasons that he does not now have and should not have. Informing his present motivational set in this way would not bring out the reasons that it generates. It would not turn objective reasons he has into subjective reasons by making him aware of them, but would create entirely new reasons he does not now have and that remain irrelevant to his actual situation. He

---

[6] Allan Gibbard, *Wise Choices, Apt Feeling* (Cambridge, MA: Harvard University Press, 1990), p. 20.

does not now have an objective reason not to attend a dinner, although he might have reasons, such as avoiding nausea, if he knew of the guests' digestive systems.

Gibbard gives another example of a civil servant who would lose his determination not to take bribes if he dwelled on all the good things he could buy with the money.[7] In the language of reasons, he might have overriding reasons not to take the bribes but would allow reasons in favor of taking them to override if the desires that generate the latter reasons were fully informed. Gibbard seems to think these examples are similar, but for us they are relevantly different. In this one the civil servant does seem to have reasons to take the bribe, although not overriding ones, while in the last one Gibbard did not have reasons not to attend the dinner party. The examples will be treated differently below.

Both examples seemingly show that we can have overriding reasons to do what we would not do with full information we presently lack. Second, we can also have overriding reasons to do what it would not be rational to do if we had full information in cases mentioned earlier in which we must act but cannot acquire the information in question. Gibbard gives the example of being lost in the woods and needing to get out without a map or directions.[8] Modifying his example somewhat, we can imagine that a path on the left is the way out, but that a path on the right appears straighter, so that the rational thing to do is to take that path. More generally, there are many situations in which it is rational to make bets or play the odds, but in which one would not have reason to do so if one had full information about the outcomes. Once more rationality is not determined by total information or omniscience. Omniscience can reveal objective reasons one has that are not relevant to rationality in the present circumstances, rationality being determined by subjective reasons, or it can give one reasons one does not presently have, hence once again being irrelevant to one's present rational choice. We want to know both what information will reveal all the reasons one has and what information will eliminate certain desires from the set that creates reasons, or eliminate apparent subjective reasons.

Third, others have pointed out that omniscience in regard to all the information that might seem relevant to important life choices is impossible

---

[7] Ibid.   [8] Ibid. 18–19.

not just because of limitations of time and brain space, but in principle. It seems impossible to appreciate fully what it is like to lead one kind of life in full knowledge of certain other kinds. One who knows the life of an investment banker cannot fully appreciate the life of a samurai warrior.[9] Then too, in order to live the life of a samurai warrior, the banker would have to be a completely different person. Even if an omniscient agent would choose a life like that, it seems implausible that this fact could give the banker a reason to do anything. Our limited experience and knowledge help to define who we are, and who we are helps to determine the reasons we have. Hence the vantage point of an omniscient agent, were one possible, seems irrelevant to assessing the reasons of real agents.

Nor, for all these reasons, can the criterion of relevant information be whatever information would effect a change in our present motivations. The examples that show that total information would not rationalize our present desires, would not make them reason generating desires or desires that result from reasons, all involve information that changes present desires. It changes them for the worse in terms of introducing irrelevant reasons that agents do not have, instead of bringing out reasons that agents have or revealing what it is rational for them to do. Information about the invitees' intestines would change my reasons and desire to attend the dinner party, but such information is still not relevant to the reasons I now have. If then relevant information is neither total information nor that which changes present desires, the question remains which and how much information is relevant to rationalizing desires.

The answer is that relevant information is mainly information about what it would be like to act on one's present desires, what it would be like to fulfil intentions based on those desires, and what it would be like not to act on the desires. Such information will include other facts that seem to be relevant to determining whether desires create reasons. What it is like to act on a desire includes whether acting on it will frustrate other deeper concerns of the agent. This is part of what it is like since such frustration will be felt as such. Similarly, it includes whether acting on a desire actually satisfies it, whether the desire is satisfiable in the circumstances in which one would act on it. It may not include knowledge of the full nature of

---

[9] David Sobel, "Full Information Accounts of Well-Being," *Ethics*, 104 (1994): 784–810; see also Connie Rosati, "Persons, Perspectives, and Full Information Accounts of the Good," *Ethics*, 105 (1995): 296–325.

the object desired, but features of the object are relevant only in so far as they affect what it is like to acquire it. It will also not include information about how the desire originated. Some philosophers hold that it is not rational to act on desires that originate from some objectionable kind or programming, that such desires create no reasons. But the fact that a person continues to want to act on a desire when informed of what it is like to act on it seems to rationalize acting on it (in the absence of incoherence), whatever its origin. I do not want to insist on that claim, however, so that information about the origins of desires might be added as also relevant. But information about what it is like to act and not to act on a desire remains at the forefront of relevance. Certainly when I get what I desire or what I thought I desired and am nevertheless disappointed by the outcome, that is typically because I did not know what it would be like to act on the desire.

In order to see better whether such information is what we need to rationalize choices based on desires, we may return to our examples and match intuitions about reasons and rationality with applications of the suggested criterion. Once more the information may reveal objective reasons of which the subject is not aware, showing all the reasons she has but not affecting the rationality of her action in the actual circumstances of limited knowledge, or it might remove seeming subjective reasons, affecting the rationality of choice in the absence of other subjective reasons.

In the case of the dinner party, knowing what it would be like to act on one's present desire to attend, as opposed to omniscience, does not affect any subjective reasons or reveal any reasons one has of which one is unaware. What it will be like will not involve the guests' intestines at all. Hence, having this information of what it will be like to attend, it remains rational to attend and irrational not to. This verdict matches our intuition. In the case of the employee's meeting, he intends to increase his chance of promotion by speaking up. But knowing what it will actually be like to act on that intention will reveal that his chance will not be increased (he will, for example, see the frowns of the executives), revealing an objective reason not to speak of which he is unaware. If his only seeming reason for speaking is the purported fact that doing so will enhance his chance, then this seeming reason is eliminated by informing his desire, and his speaking up is not rational. But if he has independent evidence that speaking up will have the positive effect, then speaking is rational although unfortunate in its outcome. He will have an objective reason not to speak, but this will not affect the rationality of speaking, which depends only on subjective reasons.

The case of the peanuts is similar. Knowing what it would be like to eat them would once more reveal an objective reason of which the allergic person is unaware. If she has other subjective reasons to eat them, for example the fact that they taste good, then her eating them would be rational unless she has reasons to suspect an allergic reaction, perhaps other allergies she knows about. The vodka-gasoline case is also similar. If the person who desires to drink the liquid has evidence that it is vodka, say that it looks like vodka and is sitting on a bar, then what it would be like to drink it does not contradict those facts or eliminate them as subjective reasons for drinking. It only reveals a much stronger objective reason not to drink it. Such cases do not indicate irrationality in acting on present desires, but they do indicate that in general we have some reason within time constraints to find out what it would be like to act on our desires before we do so. We should have some evidence of what it would be like in virtually all cases. In the example, if the glass of liquid is sitting on a garage shelf, providing no evidence that it is potable, then it would not be rational to drink it.

We might yet again analyze the lost-in-the-woods example in the same way. We might say that the person has objective reason to take the left path revealed by what it would be like to take the right one (not getting out of the woods), but subjective reason to take the right one (its looking straight). But my intuition is that this case differs from the peanut and gasoline cases. In those cases it sounds right to say, "You had a reason not to eat (or drink) the stuff; unfortunately you did not know it." In the woods case it does not sound right to me to say, "You had a reason to take the left path." It seems instead that the person had no reason to take that path even though in fact it was the way out of the woods. Can the suggested criterion of relevant information capture this difference between the cases? It can, but showing that it can requires a subtle clarification of the criterion.

The criterion once more is that relevant information for determining reasons is information about what it would be like to act or not to act on present desires. In order to act on a desire, one must act on an intention formed in response to the desire. Thus, relevant information extends only to what one can intend. One can intend only what is largely within one's power to bring about.[10] It is not largely in the power of the lost person to get out of the woods, in contrast to the persons who can eat the peanuts or drink the liquid. Thus, the lost person cannot literally intend to get out of the woods, but only to try to do so or to take one path or the other. Similarly, a person cannot literally intend to win a game or a bet, but only to play or to make one. Athletes sometimes say, "I intend to win this game," but that is hyperbole intended to pump them up. Literally, they can intend only to try to win or to play hard. Thus, information about what it is like to make a bet is information about what it is like to act on the intention to make the bet and does not include the future fact of winning or losing. Similarly, since one cannot intend to get out of the woods, but only to take one of the paths and try to get out, information about what it is like to act on that intention does not include the fact of succeeding or failing. Thus, in our example, informing the desires on which the person can act does not reveal any reason he has to take the left path. Nor does it affect the rationality of taking the right one.

In the bribery example, Gibbard argues that, if the civil servant dwelled on all the good things he could buy with the bribes, he would act irrationally and take them. That he would act irrationally in accepting the bribes assumes that he has stronger reasons not to take them. We may accept that assumption, although for us it will be true only if the civil servant is morally-minded or prudentially concerned about the consequences of being caught. Let us assume that our civil servant is the rare politician strongly concerned in both ways but also subject to temptation or weak willed. Gibbard, as noted, uses the example in an argument against full information accounts of rationality, but it also seems to apply to our criterion, since information about what it would be like to accept the bribes produces knowledge of all the good things that could be bought and enjoyed with them.

Here, however, the information neither reveals objective reasons of which the subject is unaware nor eliminates seeming subjective reasons from consideration. It simply makes some of his subjective reasons, the

---

[10] Only largely within one's power, because, for example, I can intend to meet you for lunch even though it is not entirely in my power to succeed: you must show up as well.

weaker ones, more vivid, leading to an irrational yielding to temptation, a surrender to an urge at the expense of an evaluative judgment reflecting deeper concerns. One answer for the victim of weak will might be not to dwell too intensely on his potential purchases once he is aware of them. This may involve a different kind of irrationality, namely, self-deception in hiding truths from himself. A better answer is to dwell more intensely on the prospect of exposure, on the effect on his moral character, or on the unfairness of taking the bribes, also included within the information of what it will likely be like to accept them. It will be acting immorally and feeling the guilt or the shame of exposure, overriding considerations for the morally- and prudentially-minded civil servant. Dwelling equally on all the aspects of what it would be like to act on the desire to accept the bribes reveals the true weight of all the reasons the agent has. Either his taking the bribes is not irrational after all or the information of what it would be like to take them will reveal it to be irrational. So the example is not a counterexample to the criterion of relevant information proposed here. Rational action on a desire is action with full information of what it will be like to so act. The danger for the civil servant lies in thinking only of the positive aspects of what it will be like to the neglect of the negative.

We might want a clearer example than the previously considered one of the talkative employee of relevant information that eliminates a merely apparent subjective reason and thereby shows an intended course of action to be irrational. Such examples are not hard to find. You might have the talent for and desire the life of a professional tennis player or that of a philosopher, thinking that the first is glamorous and the second worthy of great respect. But if you lack information about what it is like to travel constantly and to strain physically to the point of certain injury (not very glamorous), or information about what it is like to fail to get the respect that you think you deserve (I said you, not me), then it will not be rational to act on those desires. You might desire to marry Mary, thinking that (fill in activity) with her for the rest of your life will be wonderful. But if you lack information about what it would be like to (fill in activity) with her for the rest of your life, it will not be rational to act on that desire.

This last example raises another possible problem. Just as we noted the impossibility of simultaneously having full information about what it would be like to lead every conceivable kind of life, so it might be impossible to imagine what it would be like to pursue certain goals or engage in certain activities over very extended periods of time.[11] One perhaps cannot imagine in advance what an entire lifetime of philosophical reflection will be like. In this case, however, unlike information about every conceivable life style, the information about what it would be like to act on one's desires remains relevant to the determination of objective reasons one has. The conclusion is simply that one will not know in advance what all these reasons are; they will not be subjective reasons that determine the rationality of one's choice. Life may require gambles not only when one has no reasons to go one way or another, but also when one has reasons of which one cannot be aware.

On the up side, you may lack information regarding good aspects of acting on your desires, so that acting on them would be better than you presently think. Such information might again reveal objective reasons of which you are unaware, or it might remove seeming subjective reasons, this time about apparently negative aspects of acting on your desires. If you desire to become a philosopher, you might think that you will have to spend countless hours reading tedious journal articles, but it might be instead that you would find most of the articles scintillating. In general, what you have most objective reason to do might depend on the balance of unanticipated good and bad features of what it would really be like to act on your desires. The rationality of what you do depends, by contrast, on what you have subjective reasons to do.

Finally, I have claimed that a person's reasons depend on informing only her present desires. Two potential problems remain to be briefly discussed. First, it seems to follow that a person cannot have reasons to totally transform herself into a different character pursuing a different kind of life. But could not there be such reasons? Could not a hardened criminal who presently desires only to continue in his ways nevertheless have reason to repent? Yes, but once more it depends on his deeper and broader concerns. If, for example, a person's deepest and broadest concern is simply to be content and coming to lead a different kind of life would make him overall more content, then he has an objective reason to radically transform

[11] The problem is discussed in Dan Egonsson, *Preference and Information* (Hampshire: Ashgate, 2007), p. 34. This section is indebted to my reading of his book-length discussion of the topic. At some points he suggests the criterion of relevant information defended here, and at others he suggests that relevant information is that which would change present desires, a criterion I reject.

himself. For most people, however, these conditions are unlikely to be met. What makes most people happy is the satisfaction of other deep concerns that they have, defining of who they presently are. Also relevant are the high psychological transaction costs involved in radical transformations of the self, where such transformations are possible.

Second, our criterion of relevant information seems to imply that people cannot rationally desire things if they have not experienced anything like those things before. Without such experience they would have no information regarding what it would be like to act on those desires or acquire those things. They might have objective reasons to pursue those objects, but they would not be aware of those reasons, and so they would not be subjective reasons making it rational to pursue them. But cannot we desire entirely new experiences? Yes, but a proper understanding of "entirely new" that is not hyperbolic shows that this answer is not incompatible with the implication that is this time genuine and not merely apparent. Once more the antecedent condition is unlikely to be satisfied. By a certain age almost all people have experienced something like whatever else they desire to experience. It follows only that young children are likely to have fewer rational desires, but this is an acceptable implication. Since, as I have emphasized, persons' desires include their deepest and broadest concerns, it is not implausible that rational choices and actions result from informing them of what it would be like to satisfy or to try to satisfy those concerns in various more specific ways.

III. Rationality: The Coherence Requirement

"I'd give my right arm to be ambidextrous."

As indicated earlier, coherence in my view is the avoidance of self-defeat in the domains of both theoretical and practical reason, in regard to both action and belief.[12] Just as rationality or coherence can require certain beliefs given other beliefs or evidence, so it can require certain desires or motivational states given other desires or concerns. A belief in itself is

---

[12] Others who have spoken of irrationality as self-defeat include Philippa Foot, "Morality as a System of Hypothetical Imperatives," *Philosophical Review*, 81 (1972): 305–316; Michael Slote, *Morals from Motives* (Oxford: Oxford University Press, 2001), ch. 7.

not a reason to believe it true, and a motivation is not a reason to be motivated or to act, but beliefs can require other beliefs they imply in order to maintain coherence, and desires can require other desires. We can see how the latter works first in relation to a practical rational requirement that all philosophers on both sides of the debate agree on, the demand to desire or to adopt means to the satisfaction of those ends that we rationally have.

If we rationally desire an end, then, if there is no reason not to desire or adopt the means to achieve the end, we are rationally required to desire the means. The antecedent clause posits that we rationally desire the end, since ends that are irrational do not generate reasons to adopt means to their fulfilment. If there are reasons on balance against desiring or adopting an end, there will be no reason deriving from that end to adopt the means to its achievement. We are not required to desire any ends except, as we shall see, those required if we are to fulfill broader or more abstract ends that we have. But in the absence of independent reasons for or against various ends and means, we must desire either both the ends and the known available means to fulfil them, or neither the ends nor the means.[13] Cannot we, however, rationally desire that someone be dead without desiring to kill that person? Can't we desire to have sex with someone or to have someone's fortune without desiring the only means that might succeed? Yes, in all three cases, but that is because we have reasons here not to desire the means, especially if we are at all morally-minded. The requirement of instrumental reason still stands as stated above.

In expanding on this requirement, we may first ask why it is a genuine demand of rationality and then see whether the reason for it implies other rational requirements as well. The nature of the requirement of instrumental rationality is most obvious at the stage of translating desires into intentions. If we intend an end, then, if rational, we must intend some means to bring it about. To intend an end is to intend to do something, perhaps at first unspecified, that will bring it about. Not to intend some means to bring it about is therefore to be incoherent or self-defeating: not to intend to bring about what one intends to bring about. There is a close parallel here to the logical requirement of *modus ponens* in the domain of

---

[13] For further discussion of the requirement see John Broome, "Are Intentions Reasons? And How Should We Cope with Incommensurable Values?" in C. W. Morris and A. Ripstein (eds.), *Practical Rationality and Preference* (Cambridge: Cambridge University Press, 2001).

theoretical reason, the domain of belief. If I believe that p implies q, I cannot coherently believe p and not-q, because then I would believe, or believe to be true, what I implicitly believe is not true (namely not-q). Since believing is believing to be true, my belief in not-q when I believe that p and that p implies q would be self-defeating. It would defeat the aim of belief. I may not have any reason to believe p, and hence no reason to believe q, but I must believe either both or neither if I believe that p implies q. Similarly, I must intend either both ends and means to them or neither.

Like the demand to believe implications of what we believe, the demand to desire or intend means to ends that we rationally desire is a demand to avoid self-defeat, the defeat of the very end intended. We need not ask why we should desire or intend to avoid self-defeat. We can desire without intending to act on the desire. We can also desire what we desire not to desire, especially when the original desire is opposed by other first-order desires. But it is impossible to intend what one knows one intends to ignore or frustrate. We cannot intend to defeat our own intentions. The closest we can come to that is simply giving up an intention. Similarly, we can hide evidence from ourselves, but we cannot consciously believe what we consciously believe is not true. Various kinds of irrationality or self-defeat are possible, to be more fully described below, but they are more indirect, involving interfering factors and not the direct intention to defeat our own intentions or the concerns from which they derive.

Stephen Darwall has a different view.[14] According to him, we are not automatically motivated to avoid self-defeat. Instead, to be rational we must accept norms of inference in both the doxastic and practical spheres that take us from premises to logically or practically implied conclusions. He argues that just as belief in *modus ponens* (believing that if p, and if p then q, then q) will not in itself get us to conclude q from p and if p then q—only accepting and being guided by *modus ponens* as a norm of inference will get us to conclude q—so to be motivated to adopt means to one's ends, one must accept a practical norm of instrumental rationality. It takes an application of *modus ponens* and not just belief in it to get from premise to conclusion at any level, and similarly it takes application of the practical

[14] Stephen Darwall, *The Second-Person Standpoint* (Canbridge, MA: Harvard University Press, 2006), pp. 154–6.

norm to get from desire for an end to adoption of the means. Application requires acceptance of the norm as a guide to practice.

The implications of this argument are damaging to internalism about reasons and rationality, our central thesis. Since according to this view, we must accept independently of our desires these norms of rationality requiring coherence or avoidance of self-defeat, our reasons derive ultimately from these independent norms and not from our motivations or concerns. If these norms of theoretical and practical reason are independent of our aims and motivations, then there are ultimate or irreducible normative facts or values to which rational practice must conform.

My reply is implied above. There it was pointed out that we cannot intend to frustrate our own intentions. While we can have a second-order desire to eliminate some first-order desire, to be motivated on any level is to be motivated to avoid the defeat of that motivation. That is why in the case in which I desire not to have a certain desire, for example a desire for my next cigar, the first-order desire is in genuine conflict with the second-order desire, and I feel genuinely torn. To be motivated is in part to be disposed to act on that motivation. We therefore do not need to accept an independent norm in order to act so as to avoid self-defeat or achieve practical coherence. To accept such a norm would be to intend to believe or to desire in accordance with it. But we cannot intend to believe or to desire at all, because we do not choose to do these things. We form intentions only when we choose to act in one way or another.[15]

Both the premise in Darwall's argument and his inference from it should be rejected. The premise relates to *modus ponens* and belief. Lewis Carroll notwithstanding, the premise that we need to accept an inference guiding norm *independently of our beliefs and motivations* in order to infer correctly in the form of *modus ponens* should be rejected. The aim of belief, as we and many others have noted, is truth: in believing any proposition, we are motivated to believe or accept only what is true. It follows that if we not only understand but believe that q must be true if p is true, and we believe that p is true, and we connect these propositions and have them in mind, then we will be motivated to believe q. Various factors may interfere and prevent our drawing the inference, but we need accept no independent

---

[15] Compare Philip Pettit, "Preference, Deliberation, and Satisfaction," in S. Olsaretti (ed.), *Preference and Well-Being* (Cambridge: Cambridge University Press, 2006).

norm in order to draw it. The case is indeed parallel to the practical sphere of instrumental rationality. I will have more to say below about the aim of action that parallels the aim of belief. Here it suffices to say that if Darwall's premise regarding belief were true, which it would be if belief had no aim or motive, motivations in the practical sphere would render that case different. Once more, if we are motivated, then we are motivated to avoid frustration or defeat of that motivation, even though it may be opposed by a stronger motive that leads us to want overall to defeat it. And we do not choose or intend to have the motivations we do have.

Thus, to repeat, we need not ask why we should want to avoid self-defeat. We can certainly ask, however, whether the demand to intend means to our intended ends, deriving from the requirement to avoid self-defeat, implies rational requirements beyond that of instrumental rationality. And the answer is clearly affirmative. One clearly related requirement is to specify broad concerns more concretely. Such specification must occur in two ways. First, we must specify which aspects of the broader concern we will pursue. If I desire a successful career, how do I more narrowly define success: in terms of fame, money, power, prestige, interesting work, or some combination of these? Seeking all of these may be beyond my capacities, but clearly some may be more important to me than others. And some, such as fame, might conflict with other things I value, such as privacy. Second, having narrowed my goal, I must specify how I propose to pursue it. If it is money I am after, I had better settle on a career in business or law or medicine, but not philosophy. If I'm after work that interests me, I had better settle on philosophy, but not business or medicine. But clearly, if I am not to defeat my own broader concern to have a successful career, I had better settle on some such option and get down to its pursuit.[16] Broader concerns become more specific over time as one learns from experience what it would be like to try to satisfy them in various ways. Informing desires goes hand in hand with specifying and coordinating them.

Thus, avoidance of self-defeat involves both specifying broad or abstract ends and adopting means to their fulfilment. These are different although closely related requirements. Pursuing a career in medicine is not a means to pursue a successful career, but it *is* such a pursuit or a way of doing it. At

---

[16] For elaboration on the requirement for specification, see Henry Richardson, *Practical Reasoning about Final Ends* (Cambridge: Cambridge University Press, 1994), ch. 4.

the same time the distinction between means and ends is not a hard and fast one. First, in considering which means to adopt, we must consider how they would affect other ends that we have, whether they would tend to facilitate or frustrate those other ends. The best means might be not those that would most efficiently and easily achieve the specific ends at which they aim, but those that promote the achievement of several ends at once. I might, for example, initially want to choose a restaurant with the aims of taste and value in mind, but then might find one close to my office, where I have to go after dinner. Choices and actions are more coherent with my overall motivations when they serve several at once. On the other side, means that most efficiently achieve an end might be unacceptable because of the way they interfere with the achievement of other ends.

Second, means become ends themselves, and ends become means to other ends, some of which emerge as new opportunities arise in the course of pursuing the former ends. What is pursued only as a means would not be pursued if it were not believed to contribute to the satisfaction of a distinct end; what is pursued as an end in itself would continue to be pursued in the absence of any collateral benefit. But what is at first pursued as a means can become an end in itself. Thus, a student might initially read philosophy books as a means to passing a college course, come to read them as an end in itself, that is, continue to read them outside the course, and then find that doing so can be a means to a successful career, when she learns of the availability of lucrative teaching assistantships (fictional example). Means can require further means, whether or not they become ends. I might play tennis as a way of specifying exercise as a means to good health, but in order to play tennis I might need to join a club, buy a racquet, and so on. What we find are hierarchies of ends and means, as means become ends and ends become means to further ends.

All this is quite commonplace, but it reflects a complex picture of relations between motivations and actions that requires coherence on many levels, a requirement far exceeding the simple instrumentalist view of practical reason. In further spelling out the full requirement we can first make explicit what was implicit above. Our broad concerns must generate more specific desires. Our desires must be translated into goals or ends. These goals or ends may be outcomes desired or actions themselves: winning a tennis match or simply playing tennis. The ends must in turn create desires for means to pursue them. Standing desires or long-term dispositions must produce occurrent desires when the suitable occasions arise for their satisfaction, and those desires must produce intentions to act. Finally, these intentions must actually produce the actions intended. The bad news is that for us of weak will and frequent procrastination, pitfalls lie along each of these stages. To succumb is to fall to irrational self-defeat of the initial motivations. The good news is that we normally progress from one stage to the next automatically when opportunities arise.

Deliberation occurs, as pointed out in the first chapter, when opportunities for actions connect to conflicting motivations. Motivations or ends deriving from them conflict when they cannot be simultaneously satisfied or achieved. Some conflicts involve impossibility of joint satisfaction and are intrinsic to the nature of the desires: I cannot be both a great liar and thief and a moral person. Similarly, some means by their very nature defeat the very ends at which they are aimed: I cannot literally give my right arm to be ambidextrous (although I could figuratively do so, as played on by the quotation). Other means interfere with means or ends external to them: working very hard leads to career success but can damage health and family relations. Some conflicts involve merely improbability of joint satisfaction and result from the way the world happens to be at a time and place: it is unlikely that I can be a philosopher and be rich, given the unfairness of the free market. And some desires that cannot be jointly satisfied simultaneously can be jointly satisfied over time: I cannot read philosophy and play tennis at the same time (unless I am in a Monty Python skit), but I can certainly do both over time.

In regard to the latter partial conflicts, coherence is achieved by prioritizing at given times, subject to reversals later, and coordinating over time, taking organic effects into account so as to achieve a near-optimal mix. By "organic effects" I refer to the ways activities affect each other and the values they have in non-cumulative ways. Some exercise helps one later to concentrate on work; too much makes one too tired to work. Some exercise is good in itself and good for health; too much is not. But we cannot simply aim at the optimal amount of each activity we desire. Instead, given time and budgetary constraints and limited abilities, we must aim at the optimal mix achievable, once more taking into account effects of these activities on each other.

This might begin to sound like a hopelessly complex task of calculation, but, as also emphasized in the first chapter, acting more or less automatically often accurately reflects priorities at various times for achieving the mix of activities that best reflects our motivations. When we do deliberate, as noted, it is normally not a matter of deciding whether to satisfy a particular desire or even to initiate a particular action, but is instead a matter of choosing between options each of which satisfies certain desires and frustrates others. Just as the best choice of means is not always that which most efficiently achieves the specific end at which it aims, so the decision most coherent with one's prioritized set of motivations is not necessarily the one that best satisfies the most important specific concern. If I must choose between philosophy and another more lucrative career, if interesting work is more important to me than being rich, philosophy would afford me the most interesting work, and I have the skills to succeed in it, the choice of a career in philosophy might nevertheless not be the right one. This is because I might find another line of work that allows me to use analytical skills in only slightly less interesting projects, which I might find more interesting as I become involved in them, and which are far more lucrative. Once more the option that will achieve an optimal mix of desire satisfaction may not be the one that maximally satisfies a particular desire with highest priority. Particular desires, such as those for money or interesting work, are specifications of deeper concerns, for successful careers for example, and the deeper concerns may be better satisfied by an option that mixes or coordinates satisfactions of the more specific desires.

The most important concerns are not necessarily those most strongly felt, but those broadest and deepest concerns that connect with many others and may be specified in different ways. If we say that a rational agent acts on her strongest reasons at a time, we must recognize first that strongest reasons are those which, if acted on, will produce the optimal mix of desire satisfaction over time; and second, they are those that derive not from the most urgently or strongly felt desires, but from the most deeply embedded. A student who refuses to run through a snowy street in his underwear for a fraternity initiation might feel most strongly averse to being laughed at, but his strongest reason to refuse might well be the risk of pneumonia that would lose him a semester and frustrate many of his other plans and desires. Options are to be preferred when they can be predicted to maximize the satisfaction of one's deepest and broadest concerns over time.

Then too, one can rationally choose a less preferred option because there is far less probability of achieving the more preferred. The lower probability most often reflects the limitations of the agent himself, and a rational agent must take his own limitations into account in seeking to optimize the satisfaction of his concerns. If I know I am very unlikely to complete a project by a deadline, I might do better by refusing to undertake it, even though my completing it on time would be the best outcome, and there are no external factors preventing me from doing so. Nor is rational choice always a matter of maximizing expected utility, since different attitudes toward risk may be all rationally acceptable. Given the astronomically high utility of becoming a superstar in philosophy, there might be more expected utility in attempting to become one despite the very low probability of success (where expected utility is the product of the utility and the probability of achieving it) than in attempting to become a good lawyer. But I may rationally not want to take the gamble at such low odds and opt for the career in law instead, especially if the utility from the philosophical life drops below that of law at lower levels of success (the total expected utility may still be higher for philosophy, given the surge at the high end: total expected utility is the sum of the expected utilities for each possible outcome).

Avoidance of self-defeat requires not defeating one's own most important concerns. But spelling out what this requirement of coherence involves is complex and subtle. Coherence among motivations and actions requires not simply acting on one's prioritized first-order desires at a time, but coordinating actions and desires over time, coordinating them with those of others whom one is concerned about, and with one's second-order desires as well. If you care deeply about other persons and their welfare, then you must care about what they care about. You must take the concerns of these others as both limitations on your aims and as additional goals to be pursued. If my wife cares deeply about pursuing some project, say saving the deer from the vicious hunters in my neighborhood, then, if I care for her, I must care about the success of that project as well, even though I would otherwise care little about what happens to the deer (I have already admitted to moral blindness in this area). If the concerns of others become one's own, then these will include their altruistic concerns, so that there will tend to be convergence of concerns among mutually caring persons.[17]

---

[17] For expansion on this point, see Graham Oddie, *Value, Reality, and Desire* (Oxford: Clarendon Press, 2005), ch. 4.

I shall have more to say about coherence over time later in this and in the fourth chapter. I turn here to those second-order concerns that help to coordinate first-order desires and to determine which will be translated into actions. These include judgments about what kinds of desires one wants to act on, what kind of person one wants to be, what kind of life one wants to lead. Coherence requires that one acts only on desires that one wants oneself to act on, that, so far as opportunities allow (a big qualification), one leads the kind of life one wants to lead. A person at odds with her own vision of herself is a divided person, a person who is defeating her own aims for herself, and this conflict between first-order desires and actions that flow from them and broader second-order aims and judgments is a deeply tragic kind of practical incoherence. Most people these days must divide time between conflicting concerns, typically family and career, but genuine incoherence occurs only when the requirements of one come to dominate the other in opposition to a person's preferred vision of herself and her settled judgment of the proper priority (more on such incoherence below).

Even deeper in one sense than these second-order concerns for oneself are the most basic and natural aims of belief and action, that at which all belief and action aims, that which regulates both the rational formation of beliefs and the rational choice of actions. These basic aims determine both what counts as reasons for beliefs and actions and indeed what counts as beliefs and actions. J. David Velleman therefore calls them constitutive aims of belief and action. Beliefs and actions are defined as beliefs and actions by the most basic goals at which they naturally aim. The case of belief is quite straightforward. Belief, as we noted, aims at truth. It is a psychological state that can be successful or not, and it is so when true, when it represents the world as it is.[18] Believing is believing true: if I believe some proposition, then I believe that it is true. Unlike assuming or wishing, which are also the same as assuming true or wishing true, belief aims to track the truth, to exist only when actually true.

We can speak equivalently here of a basic aim or a natural function. Thus, we may say that the natural function of belief is to represent the world as it is, so as to be capable of guiding action. Successful action

---

[18] Bernard Williams, "Deciding to Believe," in *Problems of the Self* (Cambridge: Cambridge University Press, 1973), pp. 136–7.

REASONS AND RATIONALITY 67

generally requires accurate information about the environment in which it takes place, and true beliefs store such information. We may define a function as follows. Roughly, it is the function of x to do or produce y when x is designed or selected for its capacity to do or produce y.[19] Functions are capacities that contribute to higher-level capacities of the systems to which they belong.[20] Thus, organisms (systems in which beliefs function) with psychological states that store accurate information about the environments in which they live (true beliefs) are better able to act and survive (higher-level capacities) in those environments. This explains why truth is a *natural* function or aim of belief. Organisms with brains capable of true beliefs would be naturally selected.

While none would deny that truth constitutes a norm for belief, some might contest that truth is a natural aim, as I have just claimed. They would point out that false beliefs can have useful functions too. Believing religious myths can give us mental strength in the face of adversity, and even on the perceptual level, exaggerated contrasts at boundaries of objects can aid in their rapid identification. But while such inaccuracies can be useful, it remains true that successful behavior, including the acquisition of food and avoidance of dangers necessary to survival, requires mostly accurate perceptual beliefs about one's environment. Again, almost all would agree when it comes to perception or the acquisition of perceptual beliefs, but some might contest the extension of the claim beyond perception. But it is just as obvious that truth is required for inferential beliefs about the immediate or near future, without which successful action is once more impossible. To survive we must know what will threaten and what will nourish: we must make accurate predictions. According to one currently popular neurological theory, the brain works by making functional equivalents of inferential predictions even in perception.[21] Thus, even if the truth of more remote and theoretical inferences is not necessary for survival, the aim of truth even for such inferences can be seen as a natural extension or byproduct of the selection of creatures with brains capable of such truth-preserving forms of inference.

---

[19] Robert Nozick, *The Nature of Rationality* (Princeton: Princeton University Press, 1993), pp. 117–19.
[20] Paul Davies, *Norms of Nature* (Cambridge, MA: MIT Press, 2001), p. 3.
[21] Christopher Frith, *Making Up the Mind* (Oxford: Blackwell, 2007).

If communication among creatures with as poor physical senses and capacities as we have is also necessary for survival, then there is another plausible just-so story to be told as to why truth is the natural aim of belief. Since the meanings of our assertions are given by truth conditions, if truth were not the natural aim of belief, we could not grasp each other's meanings or interpret each other's assertions. Communication would be impossible. Furthermore, testimony, a primary source of knowledge, would be useless. If truth were not known to be the aim of belief, we could not infer to states of the world from others' expressions of their beliefs. Facts could not be communicated because assertions would not be regularly enough correlated with those facts. Communication would be useless even if possible. Once more we would not have survived if we did not aim at truth for all beliefs. This, together with the fact that belief is universal in our species and that belief cannot be maintained in the face of known falsity, is sufficient to establish that truth is its natural aim. This allows that people can be self-deceptive about the means to acquiring true beliefs. Such self-deception can be useful too, but it is far less likely that the capacity for it was a product of natural selection.

The aim of truth determines what counts as success for belief, and it therefore determines what counts as reasons for belief. It is trivial that we ought to believe what we have most reason to believe. Reasons count in favor of beliefs or actions because they indicate ways of succeeding in believing or acting. Reasons for belief are indications of truth or, in other words, evidence. It is irrational not to believe on the basis of known evidence or indications of truth. It is also irrational not to seek out evidence for one's beliefs, given time constraints (an information requirement similar to that for desire described in the previous section). Irrationality is incoherence, and incoherence is self-defeat. Not to believe on the basis of known evidence and not to seek out evidence are self-defeating of the basic aim of belief, as is believing contradictory propositions, not all of which can be true. The demand for coherence in the form of consistency follows from the aim of truth, since inconsistent beliefs cannot all be true. But coherence is broader than consistency, since avoiding self-defeat requires avoiding any practice likely to defeat this basic aim, such as ignoring evidence. Finally, it is impossible to believe what one thinks is not true, and impossible not to believe what one thinks is true, although one can irrationally deceive oneself about the evidence or about what one believes.

We may note the parallels here between belief and action. The demand for coherence or the avoidance of self-defeat defines rationality, I have claimed, in the case of practical reasons for actions as well. If self-defeat is ultimately defeat of the basic natural aim of belief in the theoretical realm, is there a parallel natural aim in the case of action? This basic aim would determine what counts as successful action, would determine what counts as reasons for actions, and would be definitive of actions as such. It would be impossible to act in conscious and intentional violation of this aim. Velleman, who proposes such an aim, emphasizes what is definitive of "full-blooded" action, as opposed to mere goal-directed behavior.[22] The crucial contrast for him is that between self-conscious action under the conscious control of the agent versus behavior aimed at a goal that is nevertheless automatic and not consciously controlled by the agent. With this contrast in mind, he proposes that the constitutive aim of action is autonomy or self-knowledge. The fully autonomous agent controls her actions in full knowledge of what she is doing, while the person who merely reacts automatically to some stimulus does not.

There are serious problems, however, with this idea of the constitutive aim of action generally. The problems result precisely from thinking that the constitutive aim of all action is what distinguishes self-conscious human action from automatic responses or the behavior of other higher animals. What distinguishes human action from the behavior of other animals is not its constitutive aim, but the way that aim is often satisfied, namely, with self-awareness. Autonomy or autonomous action might be defined as action under the self-conscious control of an agent who is fully aware of what he is doing, who acts in full self-knowledge. But autonomy and self-knowledge seem to be neither the criterion of success for action generally nor to determine what counts as reasons for actions generally. Several points confirm this doubt.

First, as argued in the introductory chapter, a person can be acting rationally, acting from reasons or responding to them, even when acting more or less automatically, without deliberation, self-conscious control of

---

[22] J. David Velleman, "The Possibility of Practical Reason," in *The Possibility of Practical Reason* (Oxford: Oxford University Press, 2000), pp. 189–91.

each movement, self-awareness, or awareness of the reasons for which he acts. He might become aware of his reasons only if he is made to reflect on his action. And, conversely, an agent can self-knowingly act on impulse and not reason. Thus, self-awareness or self-conscious control is neither necessary nor sufficient for acting in response to reasons.

Second, self-knowledge or full awareness of what one is doing is neither necessary nor sufficient for success in action. Automatic actions can certainly be successful, and even more obviously, an agent can be fully aware of what she is doing and yet fail in her action. It is arguable that we gain self-knowledge more from our failures than from our successes. It is true that we often gain knowledge of our own deepest concerns and motives through our important choices and the actions that flow from them. We do achieve self-knowledge when such actions are rational and successful. For some of us, it may be that only when faced with such choices do we come to understand through our actions what matters most to us. But self-knowledge does not seem to be the motive behind most actions or their primary aim. We aim to satisfy other motives, not to reveal them to ourselves, even if we do reveal them through our actions.

Third, Velleman's proposal does not maintain another parallel with the constitutive aim of belief, as his discussion suggests it should. The aim of truth does not distinguish fully reflective beliefs from those more immediately acquired. All beliefs aim at truth, and in fact our more immediately acquired perceptual beliefs achieve it more often. My belief that there is a computer before me, immediately and passively acquired as I look at it, is more likely to be true than my highly reflective belief in some philosophical proposition, for example that mental states are distinct from physical states. It well may be, as in the case of beliefs, although I have no hard evidence, that our more automatic actions are also more often successful than our more reflective and consciously controlled actions. Less controversially, all true beliefs are successful, while some autonomous and self-conscious actions are not.

Thus, autonomy and self-knowledge do not separately or together comprise the constitutive aim of action that parallels truth as the constitutive aim of belief. John Searle argues that there is nothing that stands to intention and action as truth stands to belief. He makes this skeptical claim based mainly on the premise that intentions and actions aim at diverse goals with nothing necessarily in common, while all beliefs aim at the single goal of truth.[23] But he is simply thinking in more general terms in the one case than in the other. The constitutive aim of action is more general than Searle envisages and more basic and simple than Velleman proposes. It helps here to remember that we are speaking of a second-order aim or concern. Just as beliefs aim directly at different contents that express different satisfaction conditions for different propositions, but aim also at truth as the second-order condition for the success of each of these beliefs, so actions aim at different goals but can share a single second-order condition for success. Philosophers seem to miss this condition or constitutive aim because it is right before their eyes. Actions are successful when they fulfil the motivations that prompt the actions. Moreover, just as it is impossible to believe without thinking that what one believes is true, so it is impossible to act without being motivated to act and without trying to satisfy the motivations behind the action.

If we believe, we are concerned about truth; if we act, we are concerned about satisfying the desires that prompt the action. This is so even if we are typically focused on the objects of our desires and not on the desires themselves. Achieving the object is fulfiling the desire, so that if one aims at the object, one is indirectly, even if not consciously, concerned to satisfy the desire. This criterion of success for action does not distinguish the merely intentional or reactive types from the fully autonomous or reflective types, but then, as pointed out, neither does the criterion of success for belief distinguish automatic belief acquired in perception from its fully critical and reflective versions. Reflection in both realms may or may not increase the chances of success, depending on the context and type of belief or action, but it is not necessary for success.

The proposed criterion of success should be uncontroversial. Does the proposed aim also define what it is to be an action, is it a natural aim, and does it determine what counts as reasons for actions? That it is constitutive of what it is to act seems equally uncontroversial. Believing is what we do when we want to arrive at the truth; acting is what we do when we want to satisfy our desires. Since desires are as natural to us as beliefs, and since as motivations they aim to be satisfied, this aim is a natural constitutive aim. That this basic aim of action determines what counts as practical reasons, reasons for actions, will be more controversial, since accepting this claim is

---

[23] John Searle, *Rationality in Action* (Cambridge, MA: MIT Press, 2001), p. 137.

accepting the internalist's thesis. But the plausibility of the proposed basic aim on the other criteria, as a definition of and measure of success for actions, then becomes itself a strong argument for internalism, the thesis that all our practical reasons derive from our concerns or motivations. For reasons indicate ways or means of succeeding in our beliefs or actions. That is why they count in favor of beliefs or actions.

If successful action satisfies the agent's rationalized motivational set, and reasons indicate ways or means of succeeding, then reasons derive from those motivations. And once again it is impossible to act without motivation and without aiming at its satisfaction, just as it is impossible to believe without aiming at truth. One can rationally fail to act on a motive, just as one can rationally fail to believe on some evidence, since the motive or evidence can be overridden. One can fail to act on one's prioritized motives, just as one can fail to believe on the conclusive balance of evidence, but in both cases this defines irrationality or self-defeat. Given the plausibility of these premises and parallels, we have here a powerful argument for internalism of practical reasons.

Another argument appeals to the unified account of theoretical and practical reasoning and reasons that results from taking the internalist demand for coherence as the central rational requirement in both realms. Irrationality on this view is *self*-defeat, defeat of one's own motivations, and ultimately defeat of the constitutive aims of belief or action. Coherence in the belief system is required by the aim of having only true beliefs; and practical coherence is required by the aim of satisfying one's informed and prioritized motivations. Reasons in both cases indicate ways to avoid self-defeat or to succeed in one's deepest first- and second-order aims. A rational person acts on reasons because doing so is the way to achieve coherence with one's aims or avoid self-defeat. Incoherence is practical self-defeat even when it comes to belief as opposed to action. Logical irrationality defeats the aim of belief, so logical rationality is part of practical rationality. The opposite might be claimed, that practical irrationality reduces to irrationality or falsity in belief, as Hume sometimes suggested. The irrationality of not desiring effective means to one's ends might be seen to be based on false beliefs about their effectiveness. But first, an agent may have no false beliefs and still fail to adopt means to her ends because of weakness of will. And second, means are effective or not depending on whether they succeed in achieving their end, a practical criterion.

It might be objected to my account and to my appeal to the analogy between belief and action as supporting it that the aim of truth applies locally: in believing a proposition p, a subject aims to believe truly only that p. Likewise, it might be claimed, in desiring p an agent aims to satisfy only that desire, not her deepest desires at the time, as I claim rationality requires. But the aim of truth also generates a requirement of coherence for beliefs, as I have argued. It defeats that aim to believe inconsistent propositions. Likewise, the aim of maximal desire satisfaction requires practical coherence. Rational agents aim first to satisfy their deepest desires occurrent at the time, since it is self-defeating to satisfy a weaker or shallower desire at the expense of a stronger or deeper one. The natural aims of belief and desire, as any aims, generate a need to avoid self-defeat, and in this respect the aims are analogous.

It is often said that we cannot have reasons to be logically rational or consistent, but in fact we do have prudential reasons to be so. (Of course, if presented with an argument based on prudence in the form of *modus ponens*, the logically incoherent person may not accept it.) What we cannot have are reasons to be rational *tout court*. Avoidance of incoherence or self-defeat is not a reason to be rational: it *is* what it is to be rational. In one sense, as indicated, we can sensibly ask why we should seek truth (some misguided deconstructionists seemed to think we need not, but they also seem to have been selected for extinction). We nevertheless need not add, "If a subject is truth-minded," to the definition of logical reasons, in contrast to our general need to include, "If a subject if F-minded," in the definition of F (moral, prudential, aesthetic . . .) reasons. This is because, as noted, to believe is to be truth-minded, and we are all wired to unavoidably acquire beliefs. By contrast, we have different first-order practical concerns, although we are all concerned to satisfy whichever ones we have.

The sense or openness as opposed to lack of sense or openness of such questions generates yet another argument for internalism as the proper account of practical rationality. It makes no sense, we said, to ask for reasons to be rational, to ask why we should be rational. To accept reasons to be rational we would already have to be rational. We would already have to be motivated to accept the reasons, and so they could not have their usual function of motivating us. We are already motivated to believe what strikes us as true and to act to satisfy our deepest concerns, and so we need only reasons that indicate how to do these things, not whether to do them. Sometimes it is claimed that we can have a reason to be irrational, if, for example, someone offers us a huge reward for being so or if we can escape punishment by acting so. But if the reward or escape satisfies our prioritized concerns at the time, then it is not irrational to act so as to achieve it—one would only appear to be acting irrationally in trying to do so.

Similarly, I claim, it makes no sense to ask why we should try to satisfy our deepest informed and specified concerns. To be concerned or to desire is to be concerned or to desire to satisfy that concern or desire. We can certainly question whether we have reason to satisfy a particular desire, and if that desire is for something harmful, blocks the satisfaction of some more central concern, or is an isolated whim, we may well not have a reason to do so. But we cannot ask whether we have reason to act so as to satisfy desires or motivations in general. All action is to satisfy the motivations that prompt them. (This truism is not equivalent to egoism if there are altruistic desires whose satisfaction amounts to altruism.) To ask whether there is reason to act in order to satisfy desires is like asking whether there is reason to believe what we recognize to be true. To recognize as true is to believe; to aim at satisfying desires is to act. These are once more constitutive aims.

We can question desires only from the perspective of other values or concerns, and therefore we cannot call all our values or concerns into question at once. I can question someone else's deepest values from the perspective of my own, from which his may seem totally without point or merit. Coherent value systems, like particular desires, can be challenged from the perspective of other coherent value systems, with which they are inconsistent or incoherent. But there is no perspective beyond all persons' value systems from which they can be challenged. This would be the perspective of objective value from which external reasons would derive, but there is no such value perspective. (More on this in Chapter 5.)

That we must rationally avoid self-defeat is even more obvious than that we must rationally believe what strikes us as true, since the former constitutive demand of rationality is the ground of the latter. It then makes no sense to ask, if x satisfies my coherent and informed concerns, whether I have a reason to seek x. By contrast, if there are objective values providing purported external reasons that connect with none of our concerns, it makes perfectly good sense to ask why we must be concerned about them. The question may be unanswerable, but it makes perfectly good sense. The demand for practical coherence is self-explanatory; a demand to have totally other concerns than we have, which might be required by objective values, is at best mysterious. Internalism about reasons reflects which questions can be sensibly asked and which cannot.

It remains to clarify somewhat more what the demand for coherence rules out, what forms irrationality or self-defeat take. We can get a better sense of the scope of irrationality by noting first what is not irrational but might appear to be so. Despite what Hume says, it is not irrational to act on a false belief, unless the belief is itself irrational or is a false belief about what it is like to satisfy the desire that prompts the action. We said earlier that if a false belief is justified, then whatever justifies the belief can be the reason rationalizing the agent's action based on it. Although rational agents must be motivated by reasons they have of which they are aware, they need not be motivated by reasons they falsely believe they have. A daughter might believe that she has a reason to do everything her father recommends, but she may be reasonably unmotivated by some of his more outlandish recommendations. Huckleberry Finn believes he has a moral reason to turn in his friend Jim, but he is not irrational for failing to be motivated by this false belief.

It is not irrational to have conflicting desires, desires that cannot all be satisfied because the satisfaction of some blocks that of others. A single fully coherent motivational set for each agent, in which the fulfilment of any desires facilitates that of others instead of blocking their satisfaction, is an unrealizable ideal. In fact, it may not even be an ideal, since agents always have relatively independent sets of motivations to which they give priority at different times. Some of these that cannot be satisfied simultaneously can be satisfied over time, and others cannot be mutually satisfied over time. Conflicting desires generate conflicting reasons, and deliberation aims to prioritize and choose among conflicting reasons. In choosing between a career in philosophy and one in business, I must choose between interesting work and all the nice things that wealth can buy. It is not irrational to desire both, even to wish I had the one after choosing the other.

What is irrational is to intend to have both despite having conclusive evidence that they are incompatible. In general, it is irrational to intend that for the impossibility of which one has conclusive evidence, since such intentions must end in self-defeat. It is irrational to intend ends for which one knows no means are available. More common is to intend what is extremely difficult and unlikely to be achieved at only small gain over what might be much more likely achieved, which again may be irrational, depending on one's general attitude toward risk.

Intransitivity among desires or preferences (prioritized desires) over time is not necessarily irrational, since one may desire variety or change one's mind. But intransitive preferences translated into intentions at a time may well lead to irrationality, since acting on any two will defeat a third judged more valuable than one of the two acted on, absent other reasons that affect the priorities. If I prefer apples to oranges, oranges to bananas, and bananas to apples, then, if I eat apples and oranges, I sacrifice bananas to apples despite preferring bananas. More generally, the most common form of irrationality is acting so as to satisfy a desire that defeats a concern judged more important, and the most common form of this malady is weakness of will.

When I order a piece of cheesecake for dessert despite my recent vow to maintain a diet, what is going on? Clearly I am acting "against my better judgment," and that in some way makes my action irrational. But it is not simply a detached judgment that I act against. In contrast to this cheesecake case, when I judge that I morally ought not to eat meat but order a steak anyway, I do not feel torn between my judgment and my action. As admitted earlier, I am simply unmotivated by the plight of the cows. But when I order the cheesecake, I do feel torn and angry with myself despite at the same time feeling the urge for that sweet lump of animal fat that I cannot resist. Here there is a real conflict within my motivation itself, and not simply a conflict between a desire and a judgment that is not part of the motivation. Nor are there here simply desires for different objects that conflict only in that they cannot be mutually satisfied. In one sense I do desire different things: to be thin and heart-healthy but also to eat that cheesecake. But I also have a conflicted attitude toward the dessert itself: I want both to eat and not to eat it. There is a conflict within my motivational attitude toward the same object. This points to a complexity within the motivational state or desire itself: different aspects of the same motivational state are in conflict.

My evaluative judgment here, implicit and automatically activated by the writing on the menu, is an aspect of my desire closely linked to the affective aspect of feeling torn and angry with myself. At the same time there is the felt urge to indulge, pulling me inexorably in the opposite direction. Because the evaluative aspect, the implicit judgment that it would be bad for me to eat the cheesecake, reflects my more stable and central concerns, which generate my stronger reasons, my allowing it to be overwhelmed by the felt urge is irrational. As noted earlier, desires that generate the strongest reasons are not those most strongly felt, but those most central. The evaluative judgment expresses a more stable preference because I prefer to follow it before and after I act, and when I am in a cooler frame of mind. It reflects more central concerns because these concerns for my health and appearance connect to many others. It therefore reflects the stronger reasons deriving from these concerns. I am irrational in acting against my strongest reasons reflecting deep concerns in giving in to a superficial but seemingly urgent desire.

But since the motivational state is complex, there is no set answer to the question whether I am doing what I desire to do in eating the cheesecake. We can say either that I am knowingly desiring something bad, identifying the desire with the purely affective component or felt urge, or we can say that I do not really desire to do what I am doing, identifying the desire with the judgmental component, which, we have seen, is also motivational, more weakly so although linked to the stronger reason. If desires were merely bare urges or dispositions to behavior, this sort of conflict and irrational outcome would be impossible. We would have to say that I simply prefer the cheesecake over the diet on this occasion. We would always act on the most strongly felt desire at any time. But sometimes I actually do summon the will power to pass up the delicious calories, without feeling an urge to pass them up that in turn overwhelms my urge to devour them. It is the implicit evaluative judgment that does the motivational work here.

Likewise, if preferences or orderings among desires and the reasons they generate were established only by particular choices or actions, we could not detect this form of irrationality. Again, we could note only my preference for the cheesecake. But weakness of will is not only introspectively evidenced, but can be apparent from discrepancies between verbally expressed value judgments and actions, or from patterns of actions and choices themselves. The would-be dieter who alternates between starvation and eating binges is an obvious example. There is a fine line here, however, that the observer must draw between weakness of will and another form of irrationality, self-deception. Self-deception is a form of irrationality in belief, often about one's own or another's motives, failure to base belief on conclusive evidence one has, ignoring or hiding the evidence from oneself. The rich old husband who believes his beautiful young wife married him for his charm deceives himself about her motives. Weakness of will, by contrast, is irrationality in action, not belief, but the evidence for the one or the other can be only subtly different. Occasional or intermittent discrepancy between verbally expressed and behaviorally indicated preferences or between usual behavior patterns and aberrations evidences weak will, while a more consistent discrepancy evidences self-deception. The husband who sincerely insists that he prefers spending time with his wife to playing golf but plays every time the opportunity presents itself is deceiving himself about his preference or motive. But there is also a kind of chronic weakness of will, as when a reluctant workaholic really does want to spend more time with his family but cannot resist remaining in the office whenever the apparent need arises. Here there is indeed a fine line to be drawn between weakness of will and self-deception.

In the next chapter I will spell out the full analysis of desire at which I hinted in describing weakness of will. I will clarify there which evaluative judgments are motivational, aspects of desires, and which are not, as well as which desires create reasons and which do not. Besides weakness of will, both occasional and chronic, and self-deception, there is a form of practical irrationality that we can call lack of will. Lack of will occurs when one is too lazy, distracted, fearful, or depressed to translate one's concerns and reasons into intentions and actions. The perennial graduate student very much wants to complete her dissertation (unless she is self-deceptive about this desire), but is unable to summon the energy to do it. Often temptations to more pleasant activities stand in her way, but equally often she simply lacks the will to meet the struggle to produce her thoughts on paper or on her hard drive. Yet another related form of irrationality occurs in people in the grip of emotions such as anger, which again can cause actions against their cooler and more stable judgments. Once more the nature and role of emotions in bypassing rational processes will be spelled out in the next chapter with some help from our friends in cognitive psychology.

To summarize, an irrational agent acts or fails to act in such a way as to defeat the satisfaction of her most important or central concerns. Such self-defeat can occur because of ignorance of what it is like to satisfy certain desires, or because of conflicts within motivations, or between motivations, intentions, and actions. Irrational action is that in pursuit of ill-conceived or clearly unobtainable ends or that which blocks the satisfaction of more central concerns in pursuit of more trivial but seemingly urgent ones. Irrational inaction fails to translate general concerns into more specific desires, those desires into intentions, or intentions into actions. A rational person acts so as to optimize the satisfaction of her concerns over time. We can also say that a rational person acts in response to her strongest subjective reasons, while an irrational person acts in opposition to those reasons or fails to act in response to them. But since we defined reasons in terms of rationality, it was crucial to spell out the nature of rationality as well as incoherence or irrationality without appealing to reasons.

In saying that a rational person optimizes satisfaction of his central or most important concerns, it is important to keep in mind what was said earlier about coordinating over time. This avoids the implication that we must always be doing something momentous from our own point of view if we are rational. If I need not do anything right now to preserve my health, my job, or personal relationships, then my most pressing concern might be to walk my dog, have some ice cream, nap, or relax in front of the TV. These activities also relate to more central concerns for my dog's health and for my own peace of mind or pleasant experiences. What I should do now is partly a function of what I have done earlier and what I plan to do later. Context will also constrain reasons at a time: dinner time is not the time for serious work. It is important to remember as well that normally we need not deliberate or calculate weights of reasons in order to determine which concerns or reasons reflecting them are strongest at a time. Normally my acting in one way rather than another is itself an indication of my priorities. Practical irrationality is the rare exception.

Sometimes it seems there is nothing I ought to do, so that I can choose which reasons, if any, to act on. But once more the choice will reflect my preference at the time. At the same time, I need not always act on reasons: acting on a whim or without reason is not irrational unless it opposes reasons one has at the time. I can sometimes without fault act on a desire that does not generate a reason. I can go back to sleep when the alarm rings without being irrational if I have nothing more pressing to do.

We said that a rational person acts on her strongest subjective reasons, so as to optimize satisfaction of her concerns over time. In determining one's strongest reasons, an agent in some sense weighs his reasons against each other in deliberation, but not by assigning them individual numerical weights. They get weighted only in the sense that some combinations override others. The strength of a set of reasons pointing in the same direction is determined not by the strength of the felt urge to act on them, but by the centrality of the concerns they jointly reflect, by how much one cares about satisfying those concerns at the time, reflected in choices and judgments of what one is willing to sacrifice in order to satisfy them, and finally by how well actions in light of the reasons will promote their satisfaction. Even if I want more than anything to achieve a certain end, and the only possible way to achieve it is by certain means, I still might not have a strong reason to attempt to employ those means if there is very little chance of success.

In comparing competing considerations, reasons can be not only over-ridden, but defeated or nullified by counter-reasons. And some reasons can arise only in combination with others. The fact that the nearest chess club is in a distant city is no reason for me to move there, even if I love to play chess and lack opportunities to play where I live, if I would have no means of employment in that city. But if I am offered a job there, the fact of the chess club's being there might become a reason. If we say, as we have, that rational agents must be motivated by reasons they know they have, then we must allow that reasons can be cancelled, and not simply overridden, by opposing reasons. I am not irrational not to be motivated at all to move to a city with a chess club, if there is no employment for me there.

The picture of rationality as relevantly informed coherence, such as to allow for self-fulfilment instead of self-defeat, is now as precise as I can make the subject out to be. Externalists have a very different picture. They can allow that certain desires can require others on grounds of coherence, for example that desires for ends can require desires for means, but they will not allow that the demand for coherence, even together with relevant information, exhausts practical rationality. Just as for realists, coherence among beliefs only makes the belief set rational if certain of its members are known to be true, so externalists about reasons will claim that coherence within a set of desires does not make it rational to act on any of them unless at least some of them respond to objective reasons or values. Coherence in either domain is insufficient for rationality, they will claim. Purely fictional stories and beliefs of schizophrenics can cohere, but that does not make them worthy of belief. Likewise, objectivists maintain that coherent desires, even those informed about their objects, are not worthy of action, create no reasons to act, unless reflective of objective value.

In reply, the difference is that, while beliefs must be true of the real world, must match or correspond to their referents and their properties, desires need not match the way the world is (in fact, they do not), but only must be capable of satisfaction in the world through actions in order to rationalize those actions. While a set of beliefs might be anchored to the world through a subset of self-justified beliefs known to be true independently of other beliefs, a set of desires is anchored by those deepest concerns that require no reasons or justification. As mentioned earlier and to be defended more thoroughly in the fourth chapter, I need no reason to care about my welfare, to want an interesting and rewarding career, to love my family. In the last case, giving a reason would be, in the immortal words of Bernard Williams, "one thought too many".

These concerns, and others equally deep and broad, while needing no reasons, provide reasons for many others. I do not choose to have these concerns or even to act in light of them. My motivations in general are not under my control, although I can affect their development and influence on my actions by indirect means. Belief in objective values and external reasons is typically linked to the Kantian myth that we can simply rise above our desires and choose independently of them which ones to seek to satisfy. This is perhaps the simplest story of how objective values can be practically relevant even when unconnected to any of our current concerns. Its plausibility derives from the fact that I can sometimes resist an urge. But this ability can be given a different interpretation.

How, if I simply act on my strongest motive at the time, as it seems I must if I cannot escape my own desires? And how do I deliberate if I am not freely choosing which desire to act on? The answers to these two questions are similar. By calling vividly to mind the negative consequences of acting against my better judgment or deeper evaluation, I can strengthen the motivational aspect it expresses. And deliberation, as described earlier, is calling to mind all those factors that will determine or express what it will be like to act in various ways, reflecting on all one's reasons so as to act in light of all one's motives of which one may or may not initially be aware. Will power is not the power of a Kantian will to cause actions independently of desires or natural influences, but mainly the ability to direct attention toward those reasons that reflect our more stable and central concerns. The way to avoid self-deception is to focus on all of one's reasons for belief; the way to avoid weakness of will is to focus on all of one's practical reasons.

But, to continue to echo Kant, is not the rational person autonomous, and is not the autonomous person precisely the one who is not pushed around by her own desires, the one who can rise above them and act not only on reasons, but on Reason in recognition of true value? Does not the autonomous person do what she does because she recognizes that it is the rational thing to do? And is not the person who lacks autonomy the one in the grip of pathological inclinations? The truth here is that an autonomous agent is not controlled by immediately felt urges, but acts in accordance with those motivations that reflect her deeper concerns. But to do something because it is recognized as the rational thing to do is normally once again to have one thought too many (this thought, however, can sometimes reinforce resistance to an unwelcome urge). Instead, it will be the rational thing to do if it reflects and results from an informed and coherent set of motivations.

3

Emotions, Desires, and Reasons

I. Emotions and Desires

"Why be jealous over things you don't have?"
"If people don't want to come out to the park, nobody's going
to stop them."

This chapter will make good on some promissory notes issued in the
previous one. In clarifying the nature of a common form of irrationality,
weakness of will, I began to suggest an analysis of desire. If weak-willed
people feel torn because of conflicts within their motivational states or
desires, if they allow their felt urges to overwhelm their implicit evaluative
judgments of the desired objects, this implies that desires are complex
motivational states. As we will see, they include other aspects as well as
sensations and implicit judgments.

We will need the full analysis of desire in order to make clear which
desires create reasons and which do not, as we also said earlier that certain
desires in themselves fail to do so. Similarly, we said that certain evaluative
judgments are motivating, themselves aspects of motivational states, and
others are not, and again we will have to make clear the distinction and its
source. The analysis of desire will also help us to solve an interesting puzzle
for the internalist relating to the emotional disorder of depression. To solve
that puzzle we will need in addition an analysis of emotion to parallel that
of desire.

In fact, we will begin with the analysis of the structure of emotions,
since that analysis is more familiar in the literature of psychology than is the
account of desire. And instead of attempting armchair conceptual analysis
of these psychological states, I will borrow freely from the literature of

cognitive and experimental psychology. But I will borrow accounts of what we commonly refer to as emotions and desires, not their neurophysiological bases, since the reasons we recognize, deliberate about, and react to indicate ways of satisfying those desires and concerns.

It is common among cognitive psychologists to conceive of emotions in terms of paradigms or prototypes that have all of a cluster of different types of properties. This sort of analysis has made its way from journal articles to standard textbooks. According to this account, membership in the category of emotion is a matter of degree, a matter of closeness to such prototypes as anger, fear, and sadness, which virtually all subjects classify as emotions in a variety of tests.[1] Other states, such as pride and jealousy, are less universally recognized as emotions. The prototypical emotions involve cognitive or judgmental-evaluative, physiological, motivational or dispositional-behavioral, and affective or sensational aspects. A standard text on cognitive psychology and emotional disorders states: "emotion is a multi-faceted phenomenon and it has been widely accepted that comprehensive theories of emotion must include its different facets."[2] These facets are those mentioned above, and no one of them is considered primary.

Paradigmatic instances of fear, for example, represent an object as danger-ous or threatening (cognitive component), involve a disposition to flee or avoid the object, produce increased heart rate and other bodily changes and facial expressions, as well as sensations that may be interpreted as perceptions of those physiological changes. The behavior that typically results is imme-diate and automatic, bypassing ordinary rational processes that might involve balancing opposing reasons. If I am out in the woods and hear a rattlesnake rattling away in my vicinity, that is not the time for deliberation or even rea-soning of a less conscious sort. Fortunately, I do not have to await the feeling of fear and resultant behavior. I will be gone before you can whistle Dixie. Other prototypical emotions are similar in structure. Anger in its fullest manifestations represents a person as having wronged, slighted, or opposed one's interests, involves a disposition to strike back at that person, and pro-duces muscle tension and related bodily and facial changes and sensations.

---

[1] Early proponents of this sort of analysis were Beverly Fehr and James Russell, "Concept of Emotion Viewed from a Prototype Perceptive," *Journal of Experimental Psychology: General*, 113 (1984): 464–86.

[2] J. M. G. Williams, *Cognitive Psychology and Emotional Disorders* (Chichester, UK: John Wiley, 1997), pp. 5–6.

Less prototypical instances of even these paradigmatic emotions can lack any one or even two of these elements. Sadness can lack specific objects: I can feel sad without feeling sad about anything in particular. Fear in the form of phobias can lack or oppose beliefs about danger: I can fear snakes that I know to be harmless. Fear at a horror movie can lack the disposition to flee. Anger at oneself or at the weather can lack the usual dispositions: I am rarely disposed to hit myself and never disposed to hit the weather. Longer-term anger at my boss or rival can lack the bodily changes and sensations of anger as an immediate reaction, and jealousy as a more specific kind of anger and less prototypical emotion can lack any typical bodily changes or sensations, while being more elaborate in its cognitive aspects or representations: I can be jealous only of what I do not have.

Psychologists who think of these prototypical emotions as basic note that they and some of their physical symptoms are universal across cultures. Each of these paradigms generates subsets of more specific emotional states that differ according to cognitive elaboration, intensity, or duration.[3] We noted those differences in regard to anger and jealousy, and fear and sadness also have their derivative less prototypical offshoots. Fear can take the form of free floating anxiety and sadness can take the form of depression, both longer-term states without representations of specific objects. As also noted, none of these facets of emotions listed above is necessary to their instantiation, and, we can add, none is sufficient either. Any of these facets may be absent in less than paradigmatic instances, as we saw above, and any may be present in the absence of emotion.

There are many examples in the latter class. If I were braver than I am, I could recognize danger without fear, and if I were more even-tempered than I am, I could recognize slight without anger. I do experience muscle tension and increased heart rate without anger or fear when I am winning a tennis match. If I were an actor, I could simulate the facial changes and behavioral dispositions of any emotion without actually feeling it. Given that paradigm emotions involve a cluster of properties, none of which is necessary or sufficient in itself for ascribing the emotion in question, and given that other emotions are judged as such by their closeness to these paradigms, we can properly characterize the concepts of these states

[3] See e.g. P. N. Johnson-Laird and K. Oatley, "Basic Emotions, Rationality, and Folk Theory," in N. L. Stein and K. Oatley (eds.), *Basic Emotions* (Hove, UK: Laurence Erlbaum, 1992), p. 219.

as family resemblance or cluster concepts. We ascribe these states when enough of the symptomatic properties are present in appropriate contexts.

If the ordinary concept of emotion is complex in this way, this only encourages some philosophers and psychologists to emphasize one or another facet as essential, for example seeing emotion as essentially judgment[4] or as a set of bodily responses.[5] Others advocate the elimination or reformation of such concepts of folk psychology when these concepts do not map neatly onto their neurophysiological or computational bases. Paul Griffiths, for example, argues that a proper concept of emotion must refer to a common causal mechanism in the nervous system that underlies the functional roles of these states, the ways that they respond to various stimuli. But, he maintains, there is no single causal mechanism here behind the various states that we naively classify as emotions. The higher cognitive emotions such as jealousy are simply different in their underlying states from such emotions as fear or anger, immediate affects that provide rapid reactions to crisis situations. Both the functions and the underlying neural mechanisms are different. Thus, he concludes, from the viewpoint of explanatory theory, which is the viewpoint that ought to govern our psychological concepts, we do not have a single type of psychological state properly characterized as emotion.[6]

In defending the cluster concept, the first point to be emphasized is that concepts of prototypical emotions such as anger are not theoretical concepts referring to unobservables, but mostly observational concepts. Such observational concepts of folk psychology are not replaceable without loss, including loss of explanatory power, by the theoretical terms of neurophysiology.[7] In a nutshell, we cannot replace the observational concepts by the neurological concepts without losing the reasons why we describe the latter in the functional terms we do. We cannot identify the physical causes of anger without first identifying anger in terms of its observable manifestations. The phenomenological feel, typical behavioral reactions, and implicit evaluative judgments combined in such states as

    [4] Robert Solomon, *The Passions* (Garden City, NY: Anchor, 1977).
    [5] S. S. Tomkins, "Affect as Amplification," in R. Plutchik and H. Kellerman (eds.), *Emotion: Theory Research and Experience* (New York: Academic Press, 1980), pp. 141–64.
    [6] Paul Griffiths, *What Emotions Really Are* (Chicago: University of Chicago Press, 1997).
    [7] For extended defense of this point, see Alan Goldman, "Epistemic Foundationalism and the Replaceability of Observation Language," *Journal of Philosophy*, 79 (1982): 437–53.

anger and fear cannot be in doubt. Saying that there is no such emotion as anger is like saying there is no such state as hunger or thirst, although there can be weak or borderline cases of all these states. We might be mistaken about some of the ultimate causes of an instance of anger (although the offending object is usually immediately apparent), and we certainly might be ignorant of the physiological causes of the resultant behavior and bodily symptoms, but we will not be mistaken in identifying prototypically angry people and the ways they tend to react.[8]

Of course, Griffiths and others do not deny that there are states of anger and fear. What they do claim is that these states have different types of physical causes and functional roles from those of other states such as jealousy. They conclude that the more general concept of emotion is not explanatorily unified, and hence it is not scientifically proper and ought to be replaced. This lack of uniformity on the functional and underlying physical levels, however, defeats neither the cluster concept of emotion nor the explanatory role of concepts of prototypical or basic emotions such as anger and fear. We simply need to add to the cluster of criterial properties mentioned above the typical functional role of these paradigmatic emotions. We have already noted that states less frequently but still identified as emotions will lack some of the relevant cluster of properties.

If the functional role of beliefs, what we called their natural aim, is to represent the world accurately, and the role of a coherent and informed set of desires is to prompt actions based on reasons that indicate how to satisfy those desires, the function of paradigmatic or basic emotions is to displace (temporarily) ordinary rational calculation based on such reasons for and against actions. Paradigm emotions are irruptive motivational states.[9] Their adaptive value lies in their being reactions to events for which rational calculation, even of the more automatic sort, is too slow. On the basis of very rapid and coarse cognitive evaluations, they prompt a limited repertoire of behavior that has been successful in the evolutionary past.[10] It should be emphasized, however, that this functional role is again only one of a cluster of properties defining paradigmatic emotions. Other

[8] Compare Johnson-Laird and Oatley, "Basic Emotions, Rationality, and Folk Theory," pp. 206–9.
[9] Griffiths recognizes that this characterization underlies the ordinary concept of an emotion, but he does not allow that this is a legitimate explanatory category. *What Emotions Really Are*, pp. 243–7.
[10] Johnson-Laird and Oatley, "Basic Emotions, Rationality, and Folk Theory," pp. 206–9.

states classified as emotions, although less universally so, may be more cognitively elaborated and can function otherwise, for example underlying some standing evaluative judgments.

In regard to the paradigm emotions, fear, for example, bypasses ordinary rational calculation to prompt immediate reactions to perceived dangers. Its adaptive value lies in its immediacy. It prompts sudden movements away from more objects than there is good reason to flee, but from an adaptive point of view this is a good play-it-safe strategy. Better safe than sorry. The adaptive value of many other emotions is less obvious. They can cause agents to act not only arationally, as does fear, but irrationally, against their ordinary self-interest as defined by stable concerns or values. This is often true of behavior prompted by anger or loyalty. Even when an immediate reaction prompted by anger is suppressed, the emotion can give rise to urges and dispositions to actions in the face of good reasons. Nevertheless, as Robert Frank and others point out, the communication of such emotions can have adaptive value in social contexts, for example by making others wary of opposing one's interests, or prone to offer one benefits or enter into agreements. I am more anxious to avoid your irrational attacks and insults when you are angry than I am anxious to avoid your well-reasoned reactions to my behavior. And I want more to earn your loyalty than your reasonable impartial regard.

But while emotions may have adaptive value, they do not give rise directly to reasons as desires do, and actions based on them do not typically arise in response to or reflect reasons despite being often in accord with them, as when one flees a dangerous object out of fear. Nor do emotions alter in response to reasons as readily as beliefs do. They can sometimes be cognitively suppressed or controlled, but one may well continue to feel fearful, angry, or envious after deliberately concluding that one ought not to. Finally, emotions do not typically cohere with each other or with the stable motivational set that generates one's practical reasons. When an emotion does provide the unifying force behind one's long-term motivations, when one's life is consumed by anger, jealousy, or fear, this condition is normally pathological, not rational. Nevertheless, if an emotion is itself a fitting response to one's situation, what makes it fitting might provide reasons. That a snake is dangerous is a reason to flee from it, although one may flee out of fear whether it is dangerous or not. When it is dangerous, the judgment or cognitive component in the emotion can be taken to implicitly reflect or recognize the reason for fleeing.

We may summarize the main points of this brief account. First, paradigm emotions as ordinarily conceived enter into genuine explanatory generalizations that are not replaceable by others for at least the reason that those others are not ordinarily accessible. We explain and predict the actions of subjects in the grip of various emotions, with some or most of their criterial properties, differently from the way we explain and predict the actions of unemotional calculators. If I know that you fear snakes, then I can predict that you will avoid them whether they are dangerous or not. These explanations and predictions are as reliable and sound as those based on ascriptions of more stable attitudes, beliefs, and desires, and unrivaled by anything we can appeal to on the neurophysiological level.

Second, the function of prototypical emotions is to interrupt the usual course of rational calculation, even of a subconscious variety, so as to cause more immediate responses. This function may be blocked in particular instances if the emotions are controlled by some prior motivational set, but it remains one of a cluster of criterial properties of paradigm emotions. If I know I am prone to anger and to irrational outbursts because of it, I can set myself to control my anger when it predictably occurs. But my anger will retain other of the criterial properties: the felt tension, the reddening of my face, and even the disposition to behave in the ways I struggle to control.

Third, and most relevant to our broader topic here, paradigm emotions as so conceived are complex states involving cognitive, conative, affective, and functional elements, some of which may be absent in less than prototypical instances or forms of the emotions. This structure will repeat itself in the case of desires, as they may be affected by interaction with emotions (as we will see in the next section), and as they may in turn affect the reasons we have for acting. That there are other states such as jealousy, still classified as emotions but less universally and confidently so, strongly related to paradigm or basic emotions in their elements, but more cognitively elaborated and shading into attitudes or longer-term evaluative states (to be described below), and having different neurological bases, is less relevant to our discussion.

We can proceed to the full analysis of desire. We have seen that weakness of will suggests that desires include both felt urges and implicit evaluative judgments, and that emotions, as related and resembling psychological states, contain both these and other elements. We can add further support for the analysis to be offered by beginning again with some ordinary examples. I desire to have a good time on my next vacation and to avoid serious conflict with my colleagues. My desire to have an enjoyable vacation disposes me to arrange for one, directs my attention to and produces pleasure at the thought of one, involves the evaluative judgment that the vacation would be good for me, and, especially when at my desk with a stack of ungraded student tests, produces a certain yearning sensation. Likewise, especially if I have been fighting with my colleagues over our next hire and therefore desire in the fullest sense not to, this desire seems to include all the same types of components. I am disposed to avoid discussing the open position, find the thought of returning to cordial relations pleasant, feel a certain yearning for such good old days (although not as strong as for my next vacation), and think it would be good to reconcile with them.

In ascribing desires to other people, I identify their desires by how they say they feel about various objects, how they evaluate various states of affairs, what they seem to pay attention to and take pleasure in, and above all by how they act, which behaviors tend to repeat themselves in pursuit of various goals. Thus, we can say that a desire for x prototypically disposes one to bring about x through action or to choose x, produces pleasure at the thought or realization of x, constitutes the realization of x as a reward (a reinforcement of the behavior that brought x about), involves a positive evaluative judgment of x, a yearning sensation in the absence of x, and a direction of attention to the thought of x. None of these components seems especially privileged in the examples mentioned. Instead prototypical desires seem to include all of these dispositional, attentional, sensational, representational, and evaluative components.

While all of these facets are present in the paradigm cases, once more none seems either sufficient or necessary in itself. We may refuse to ascribe desires in the presence of any of these, and we may continue to ascribe particular desires in the absence of any. In regard to the latter, the lack of necessary conditions, instrumental desires to do various things only as means to other things do not typically involve pleasure at the thought of their objects or sensations of yearning for them. I do not feel such pleasure or yearning at the thought of a trip to the dentist even when I want to go for a checkup. Fulfiling this desire does not in itself result in reinforcement or reward. In such cases, as in the case of being motivated to do one's duty, evaluative judgments seem to supply most of the motivation. Standing, as opposed to occurrent, desires do not always direct one's attention. I want to remain in my current position at my college, but I do not often think about doing so. Wishes can count as desires without one's having the ability, hence the disposition, to act on them. I wish for or want good weather tomorrow for my golf date, but I am not disposed to do anything about it. Although the primary function of desires is to prompt actions, mere wishes can count as desires because of the presence of other elements of the paradigm cases. I do have pleasant thoughts of a fine day tomorrow and a yearning that it will stop raining. Finally, I can want something I know to be bad, hence without evaluating it positively, especially if what I want is the object of an addiction, such as my next cigar. Here my motivation consists in an urge without a congruent evaluative judgment. Hence, any of these usual components of desire may be absent in particular cases. But the fact that none of these facets is necessary to the ascription of a desire does not imply that all are not present in paradigm cases.

In regard to lack of sufficiency, I can be disposed to act in certain ways out of habit, not desire. If I always choose the top shirt in my drawer to wear, that implies a disposition to do so, but it does not imply that I want to wear that shirt. One can take pleasure in events that one did not desire beforehand, and rewards can come unexpected, hence undesired, as well. A totally unanticipated and pleasant surprise can give more pleasure than the fulfilment of a relatively weak desire. I can certainly constantly turn my attention to things I do not desire. I can also grant a positive evaluation to things I do not desire. I know that *LuLu* is a good opera, but I do not desire to attend a performance of it. Felt urges are perhaps the best candidates for sufficient conditions for ascribing desires, but even in their case there is certainly a sense in which one might feel an urge, say a sexual urge for one's colleague or student, or a murderous urge toward one's boss, without a desire to fulfil it, without being disposed or motivated to do so. In each of these cases, we can refuse to ascribe a desire in the presence of some element when others are missing; whereas in the cases showing lack of necessary conditions, we continue to ascribe a desire when some typical element is missing but others are present. Although none of these features is necessary for desire, the absence of any renders a desire, if it exists, less than paradigmatic. That makes each feature part of our concept of typical desires.

In light of all these different components, none of which is always primary, talk of strength of desires is ambiguous. The felt sensations, evaluations, and dispositions can all vary in strength. They can vary either together or inversely, and any or all of these can be taken as a measure of strength. Often we measure strength in terms of choice or dispositions to act: a behaviorally revealed preference implies that the desire for its object was stronger than the opposing desires. But actions and dispositions to act are not always the measure of strength of desires. Often we are less disposed to try to obtain things that we have very little chance of obtaining, but we may not desire them less. Here we measure strength of desire not by inclination to act or choose, but by other elements, primarily felt yearnings and pleasant thoughts. Other philosophers' definitions of desires and their components in terms of each other can also run in either direction, depending on the philosopher and the explanatory context. A reward, for example, is anything desired when the desire is fulfiled, or desire is what constitutes certain states of affairs as rewards;[11] desire is what, when satisfied, brings pleasure, or pleasure is the feeling that results from the satisfaction of desire, or a judgment of what is desirable.[12]

As we found in the case of emotions, philosophers have once more been prone to divide the concept of desire into distinct senses or to emphasize one of the above mentioned components as alone essential. The usual divisions are between affective or felt desires, considered desires proper, and mere "pro-attitudes," dispositional and evaluative components implicit in any voluntary actions;[13] or between evaluative judgments and desires, taken to include only affective and dispositional components.[14]

---

[11] This definition is that of Timothy Schroeder, *Three Faces of Desire* (Oxford: Oxford University Press, 2004).

[12] This definition of pleasure is that of Elijah Millgram, "Pleasure in Practical Reasoning," in E. Millgram (ed.), *Varieties of Practical Reasoning* (Cambridge, MA: MIT Press, 2001), pp. 331–53.

[13] This contrast is drawn by Melinda Vadas, "Affective and Non-affective Desire," *Philosophy and Phenomenological Research*, 45 (1984): 273–9.

[14] Alfred Mele, *Motivation and Agency* (Oxford: Oxford University Press, 2003), p. 191. A more recent and idiosyncratic move is to distinguish felt urges from desires proper on the ground that felt urges are perceived anticipatory muscle tensions and, as perceptions, have the wrong direction of fit (the mind must fit the world instead of the world having to fit desires). This argument fails because, as we have seen, desires as ordinarily conceived have cognitive as well as conative elements, that is, both directions of fit. See D. Hulse, C. Read, and T. Schroeder, "The Impossibility of Felt Desire," *American Philosophical Quarterly*, 41 (2004): 73–80.

But if paradigm desires include all of these facets, there is no reason to make these divisions. It is yet more common for philosophers to focus on one aspect, producing a broad diversity of accounts in the literature. Thus Raz and Scanlon emphasize the cognitive aspect, what they see as the recognition of value or reasons; Chang, Blackburn, and Schueler focus on the affective aspect; Mele and Millgram on the dispositional or behavioral.[15]

To me, this diversity only counts in favor of the cluster concept analysis. None of these philosophers simply invents the feature held to be essential: all point to an aspect present in the prototypical cases of desire and point to the absence of other aspects in properly ascribed but not prototypical desires. The moral I draw from the plausibility of accounts that focus on these different elements is that all these features have roughly equal status as indications of desire in the acceptable ordinary sense or use of the concept. Focusing on only some of these aspects to the neglect of others can lead to unsound arguments against internalism. If one views desires only in terms of the affective component, for example, one will easily conclude that we often act on reasons in opposition to our desires, as when we control some urge out of a sense of duty. On the broader view defended here, evaluative judgments expressing that sense can be components of desires that compete with such urges.

As in the case of emotions, there are also scientifically minded philosophers who seek to eliminate or revise the ordinary concept of desire by reducing it to only elements that map neatly onto neurophysiological kinds or physical bases. Thus Timothy Schroeder wants to reduce the referent of the concept to what constitutes various states of affairs as rewards, to what, when satisfied, results in a certain type of learning or reinforced behavior. He appears to have two reasons for this proposed reduction: first, the neatness of fit with neurophysiological findings, and second, because elements eliminated from the constitution of desires can then be explained as consequences of desires or their satisfaction. Such explanations, he maintains, are intuitive and informative but ruled out by the more robust

[15] Joseph Raz, *Engaging Reason* (Oxford: Oxford University Press, 1999); Thomas Scanlon, *What We Owe to Each Other* (Cambridge, MA: Harvard University Press, 1998); Ruth Chang, "Can Desires Provide Reasons for Actions?" in R. J. Wallace (ed.), *Reason and Value* (Oxford: Clarendon, 2004); Simon Blackburn, *Ruling Passions* (Oxford: Oxford University Press, 1998); G. F. Schueler, *Desire* (Cambridge, MA: MIT Press, 1995); Mele, *Motivation and Agency*; Elijah Millgram, *Practical Induction* (Cambridge, MA: Harvard University Press, 1997).

concept.[16] If, for example, we hold pleasure at the fulfilment of desire to be partly constitutive of it, then, according to Schroeder, we cannot explain a subject's pleasure by saying she got what she desired. If we take desire to be a disposition to action, then we cannot explain a person's action by pointing out that he desired to do what he did. But these explanations are in order, if not very profound.

I do not wish to deny that desires turn their objects into rewards when satisfied or that this is part of our cluster concept, one way in which we identify what people desire. In fact, if we combine Schroeder's claim that desire constitutes its objects as rewards with the idea that what is valuable is what is rewarding when achieved or acquired, we conclude that desire is what makes objects valuable, a version of the internalist's thesis. What I deny is that the other elements of the cluster concept do not equally determine or reflect its use. A two-part reply to Schroeder's dismissal of them can be offered. First, exactly the same argument as he offers could be applied to the explanation of why something was a reward for someone. That something can be used as or considered a reward for someone because she desires it seems a perfectly good explanation, showing that Schroeder's argument proves too much. Second, just as we can conceptualize x as the cause of y without thereby nullifying a causal explanation of y in terms of x (although for the explanation to be informative, we must also conceive of x in other ways), so here we can explain parts by appeal to the whole even though the parts constitute the whole. "Why does that bird have a bill of that shape and webbed feet? Because it is a duck." "Why did that morsel of pie contain a piece of apple? Because it is an apple pie." Perfectly good explanations, as far as they go. So, then, is "She derived pleasure from his demise because that is what she desired," even though taking pleasure at the outcome is partly constitutive of desiring it. A deeper point responds to Schroeder's main reason for wanting to revise the ordinary concept of desire: the fit with brain research. The response is the same we made to Griffiths on emotions. Appeal to particular desires can be explanatory even if the bases for desires make up an irreducible disjunction of physical or neurological kinds.

You may have noticed that some of the components of desires are shared with emotions. This prompts some analysts to hold that emotions include

---

[16] Timothy Schroeder, *Three Faces of Desire*, p. 177.

desires as well as beliefs, and some others to classify desires themselves as emotions.[17] The two sorts of states are differentiated not by their kinds of components—affective, cognitive, and behavioral—but by their paradigmatic functional roles. As argued earlier, normal rational motivation is the central functional role of desire, prompting action to fulfil it. Desires are functional paradigms of motivational states, while emotions, as described above, are paradigmatically irruptive motivational states. This is not to say that both types of states cannot lack motivational or dispositional components. Emotional attitudes toward the past, such as pride, may not dispose one toward future behavior, and mere hopes and wishes can count as desires. Nevertheless, the primary function of both states is to prompt action, albeit with different relations to reasons.

A final clarification. Desires, I have maintained, are motivational states. Reasons are states of affairs that motivate rational agents and that are constituted as such by coherent and informed sets of desires. But there appears to be a complication in that the various components of desires other than the bare disposition to act seem to be sometimes motivating factors in themselves and not simply states of being motivated. One can be motivated by the prospect of pleasure or by the fact that one evaluates a certain object positively. These can be reasons, states of affairs such as that one will feel pleasure or that an object has received a positive evaluation, which can motivate a rational agent. "He wanted the massage not for therapeutic reasons, but for the sheer pleasure of it." But can one be in a motivational state such that what motivates one is itself part of one's motivational state?

The answer is yes, but only for reflective beings such as we, and only because reflection introduces a difference in levels. A reflective being can desire to have its desires satisfied and so can desire, for example, to feel pleasure or to act on the reasons it has or on the evaluative judgments it has made. If one can be motivated on a second level by the fact that one desires something, then it is not surprising that one can be motivated by the fact that one will experience pleasure, even though feeling pleasure at its realization is part of what defines a motivational state of desire. What motivates when one is motivated by one's desires is not the bare dispositional component, but the other elements of desire (or the fact of their existence). Partly

[17] Johnson-Laird and Oatley, "Basic Emotions, Rationality, and Folk Theory," p. 209.

for that reason, these other components can appropriately be considered the psychological grounds of the disposition. As such grounds, they make causal explanations of actions in terms of desires informative, as they would not be if desires were bare dispositions to actions. "He did it because he desired to" is an informative explanation (especially when contrasted with his having been forced to), but "He did it because he was disposed to" is not. Again we see that desires must be complex states having components other than bare dispositions.

The dispositions nevertheless lie at the heart of the criterial cluster of properties, so that mere hopes or wishes are borderline desires or functional offshoots of desires. Their borderline status is indicated by differences in language use. We can wish counterfactually for what we know to be false, but it is odd to say we desire something to be true if we cannot do anything to make it true. I wish the Dolphins had won a few more games this year, but I would not say "I desire that the Dolphins had won a few more games," or even "I want the Dolphins to have won a few more games." Among the equally criterial cluster of properties, dispositions to act may be a bit more equal than the others. This is reflected in the fact that desires are directed at the future: they are prospective.[18] We desire what we do not yet have, so that desires prompt actions to remedy that lack. While dispositions to act are functionally central, the crucial component for the remainder of our discussion is the evaluative judgment implicit in prototypical desires. Such judgments are of most concern to us because they are usually more reflective of deeper concerns and so of reasons than are the other components of desires.

These implicit evaluative judgments are themselves motivating, proper parts of prototypical desires or motivational states. As such they are distinct from explicit evaluative judgments that may not be motivating or motivational, that motivate only those who care about them or their objects. As noted earlier, I may judge that *LuLu* is a good opera but be unmotivated to go see it; I may judge that it is wrong to eat meat but have no desire to desist. I do not feel conflicted when biting into a juicy steak. But when I give in to the urge for a rich dessert, I do feel torn, and my anger at myself reflects the motivating force of my implicit judgment that what I am doing is bad, bad for my health and appearance. I do not

---

[18] Compare L. W. Sumner, *Welfare, Happiness, and Ethics* (Oxford: Clarendon Press, 1996), p. 129.

make this judgment explicitly. I am not conscious of making it, but it is an implicit part of my desire not to eat the dessert, overwhelmed by the opposing desire that results in my regretted action. We need to think of the implicit evaluative judgment as a component of a desire in order to explain its immediately motivating force and the resultant feelings.

To turn to another example mentioned earlier, if desires were merely felt urges, then the student faced with a test tomorrow would desire only to party, not to study. But in fact the student may be torn, and her "better self" may in the end win the conflict, despite the fact that she never feels an urge to study. If we are philosophers, we can use Kantian language here to describe her as rising above her desire in order to fulfil her duty to herself. But we are forced to use such bloated terms only if we accept an overly narrow conception of desire that fails in any case to explain why the student feels torn before making her decision. There must be motivational factors on both sides, and the best candidate for opposing the urge is her implicit judgment that it would be bad for her not to study. Of course, to support the motivational force of this judgment she may very well bring to mind vividly what it would be like to fail the exam and let this unpleasant thought further motivate her.

One might question whether desires include a genuinely judgmental aspect on the ground that, as Hume pointed out, we do not say that desires are true or false, as it might seem we should if they are truly judgmental. But truth and falsity, when applicable to psychological states, apply only to beliefs or assumptions as they are satisfied or not by their referents. Desires are had only when unsatisfied—we can desire to keep what we have but only because we have not yet kept it. It would not be useful to think of all desires as thereby false. We do speak of desires as appropriate or not, and as rational or irrational, depending in part on whether they are coherent and whether the beliefs or judgments expressed in them are responsive to evidence. We could call desires false, as opposed to irrational, when they are based simply on false information about their seeming objects, but then it is equally apt and far more common to say that we do not really desire the objects that we think we desire since we do not really desire the outcomes of obtaining them.

In any case, it is most relevant here that in viewing desires as partly judgmental as well as affective and dispositional, I am agreeing with the view of desires held by externalists about reasons, as we will see in the third section of this chapter. I grant that they are right that we need to recognize this aspect of desire in order to explain the relations of desires to reasons, although I will interpret both the nature of the evaluative component and its role in creating reasons differently than they do. Before proceeding to that discussion, the crux of this chapter, I will argue in the next section that recognition of this component also helps us to solve an interesting puzzle regarding the relation of desire and reasons to emotions, specifically the emotional disorder of depression.

II. Desires, Depression, and Rationality

"Slump? I ain't in no slump—I just ain't hitting."

The puzzle to be addressed in this section has to do with a conflict between the internalist theory of reasons, our concept of irrationality, and a prominent feature of the emotional disorder of depression. Solving the puzzle will call upon our account of both emotions and desires and so will help us to further clarify the nature of both and their relation to reasons.

We noted in the previous section that emotions can make one act irrationally or arationally, although they also serve an adaptive function. They interrupt the ordinary train of rational calculation and action, intruding so as to sometimes cause actions inconsistent with one's stable prioritized set of values and desires. Anger and fear, for example, can cause one to act against one's broad self-interest so defined, or to fail to act in accord with it. They prompt immediate reactions that can have adaptive value but that, even when the serve self-interest, bypass ordinary attention to reasons. Anger involves the disposition to strike out and fear the disposition to flee, both of which may contradict one's standing reasons or more stable motivations to do otherwise. Depression seems to resemble fear in this regard, often inhibiting actions that its victim has overriding reasons to perform. Often in milder forms it may have adaptive value in prompting one to come to terms with loss or with the need to revise plans and failed goals.[19] But instead of introducing new motivation, as anger typically does, depression seems to remove or inhibit motivations one had.

[19] J. M. G. Williams, *Cognitive Psychology and Emotional Disorders*, p. 315.

And there's the rub for the reason internalist. For if depression causes irrational inaction, then the reasons for the actions in question must remain intact. Irrationality must ignore or defeat reasons. Irrational agents fail to act on the strongest reasons they have. According to the reason internalist, such reasons must reflect motivations or desires in the agent. Clearly, if lack of motivation implies lack of reasons, then reasons imply the presence of motivations. But depression seems to eliminate the motivation to act. A depressed person is lethargic and lacks the will to engage in normal activities. If motivation is completely eliminated, then, according to the internalist, failure to act is not irrational, since, as noted, irrational action or inaction is acting against one's overriding reasons or failing to act in accord with them, and the reasons one has derive from one's motivations. But depression often makes its victims irrational in failing to act in accord with their reasons, just as other emotions such as anger and fear sometimes do. There seems to be no difference in this regard between depression and other emotions. This is the problem for the internalist that will be resolved here.

We can once again put the problem in the form of an apparently inconsistent triad of propositions: (1) Depression often results in irrationality in that it leads one to ignore overriding reasons one has. (2) One's reasons derive from desires broadly construed or one's set of motivational states. (3) Depression eliminates or suppresses an agent's motivational states. I shall argue in this section that our understanding of the nature of desire and emotion developed in the previous section, together with a preliminary understanding of how an agent's motivational set generates reasons, will resolve this seeming conflict. We will first canvas some possible and partial solutions that will show how some milder forms of depression cause some types of irrationality. But a deeper form of depression will require us to see certain components of desires, those more closely connected to reasons, remaining while others are eliminated. In reflecting and generating reasons, these remaining components allow us to judge the failure to produce actions to be irrational.

One milder form of depression might leave certain deep concerns intact but block their translation into more specific desires and intentions, thus failing to result in actions. We noted earlier that one form of irrationality consists in such incoherence among one's set of desires or motivational states. If one has a deep concern about one's health and appearance, and thus a concern about one's weight, and thus a resultant concern to exercise, but never translates or specifies that concern into a desire or intention to jog, play tennis, and so on (or if one forms the intention but never translates it into action), then one is guilty of this form of incoherence or irrationality. Depression can then cause this type of irrationality. The deeper concerns that remain intact retain motivational force, but they are never specified or translated into action. This account does seem to capture some forms of depression and the irrationality it causes. If I am depressed, I may lack the energy or enthusiasm to go out and play tennis but still be concerned about my health and weight. Indeed, I may well be more worried than I usually am about my health when depressed in this way.

Thus, our puzzle receives a partial solution. That recognition of this particular form of irrationality does not provide a full answer to our puzzle seems clear from the fact that taking it to be the only answer generates a minor paradox. The paradoxical implication is that a somewhat more severe form of depression, in which many of one's deeper concerns seem equally pointless as one's former more specific desires, would fail to render one irrational, while the milder form of depression described above would cause irrationality. It is not plausible that becoming somewhat more depressed could restore the rationality that was destroyed by one's milder depression (assuming there is no good reason to be more depressed). Hence there must be a different explanation for the irrationality caused by the somewhat more severe form of depression.

A possibility related to the one just canvassed is that motivation in the form of a disposition to a specific act remains, but the disposition is not actualized, its realization in action being blocked by the depression. The disposition here might be described as a standing desire that does not in this context produce occurrent desires or intentions.[20] Occurrent desires involve conscious representational content, but in the case of depression one will not represent the satisfaction of the desire with pleasure, as in the more typical case. Just as deeper concerns require specification in a rational agent, so standing desires require occurrent desires when suitable occasions arise for their satisfaction. If we say that actions to satisfy desires in the form of dispositions to act can be blocked by stronger desires while the

---

[20] For a description of this distinction, see Alfred Mele, "Motivation: Essentially Motivation-Constituting Attitudes," *Philosophical Review*, 104 (1995): 387–423, pp. 396–7.

dispositions remain, can we not say that such action can also be blocked by depression while the disposition to act remains?

This interpretation can be supported by a comparison with the irrationality involved in weakness of will. In cases of weak will, we say that a stable preference is overwhelmed by a momentary temptation or urge to act otherwise. I prefer not to clog my arteries but cannot resist the piece of cheesecake. The stable preference is held to remain despite not prevailing in the instance because its object is preferred before, after, and when I am in a cooler state of mind. Can we not say similarly that in a state of depression a stable preference is underwhelmed by a temporary lack of occurrent desire. Once more we might say that the dispositional component of the desire remains because it is efficacious before, after, and when the decision maker is in a more normal state of mind.

We can say that in some cases, but the problem here is the same as that which defeated the previous suggestion as a complete solution to our puzzle. Whatever may be true of mild depression, we need only consider a somewhat more severe and longer-term variety to make it plausible that not only is the actualization of the disposition to act blocked, but the disposition itself disappears. Once more we could not then explain the irrationality involved in the failure to act in this case. The milder kind of depression appears to have an effect similar to that of being too tired to do what we desire to do. In that case the clearly temporary condition allows desires with dispositions to remain without the dispositions being actualized, as in the case of temporary weakness of will. But more severe depression may not be so clearly temporary and may alter dispositions as well as particular actions. When apparent weakness of will repeats itself over and over, we begin to doubt the assumed preference ordering and ascribe self-deception instead. The formerly ascribed disposition to choose can no longer be ascribed; the agent is simply deceiving herself about what she prefers. Similarly, when depression results in prolonged failure to act, we can no longer plausibly hold that the disposition to act remains. Again we must seek a different explanation for the irrationality involved in failing to act, if there are such cases of deeper depression.

But the explanations so far offered suggest our further path in seeing parts of motivational states being removed by depression while other parts remain. Some such explanation must be correct for other cases as well, and that sort of explanation is available to us because we have offered analyses of both emotions and desires as complex states involving different aspects. We need only get the roles and relations among these various parts right to explain the additional cases. It remains, therefore, to specify which are tied most closely to reasons, which are plausibly eliminated by deep depression, and which remain. If a component most closely determinative of or correlated with the generation of reasons remains when depression appears to eliminate the dispositional component of desire, then we have a full solution.

A comparison to the now familiar case of weakness of will is again helpful here. Earlier I described this form of irrationality as the overwhelming of a stable preference by a more immediate and temporary urge. The more stable preference will remain implicit but could be expressed in a comparative evaluative judgment. Thus we can explain the irrationality involved also in terms of incoherence within the motivational state itself, the coming apart of the evaluative judgmental component from the felt urge. When this happens, we noted that questions about the strength of desire become ambiguous, and there is no set answer to the question whether the agent is doing what he really wants to do. Do I really want to eat that cheesecake? We can say either that I do want to eat it, identifying the desire with the affective component or felt urge, or, if I give in to the urge, as I too often do, we can say that I do not really desire to do what I do, identifying my deeper desire with its evaluative judgmental component. The latter identification makes sense because the evaluative judgment can itself motivate or count as motivational. Not being a total food degenerate, I do not always give in to the urge, but sometimes summon my judgment to resist it. Evaluative judgments do not always motivate, but they count as motivational when part of a desire the normal dispositional component of which is challenged.

When we are motivated without any urge or prospect of pleasure, as when we go to the dentist, it must be the evaluative judgmental or cognitive component that is motivationally operative. But we also noted in the *LuLu* example that evaluative judgments are not always motivational, do not always express or comprise parts of motivational states. There is ample evidence in the psychological literature on attitudes that we can use to more clearly distinguish directly motivational evaluations from those that are motivational only when conjoined with other independent desires or deeper concerns. Attitudes, like emotions and desires, are another kind of evaluative state (some psychologists use the term "evaluation" interchangeably with the term "attitude"), once more having affective, cognitive, and behavioral or dispositional aspects. They are distinguished from desires in being directed at objects, not outcomes, and in therefore being disposed to expressions, not realizations. They are distinguished from emotions, which are temporary, in being longer-term and stored in memory.

Attitudes can be explicit or implicit, again involving explicit or implicit evaluative judgments, and the two types can coexist in the same subjects without being strongly correlated. One can be implicitly prejudiced and explicitly fair. Implicit attitudes are formed and activated automatically, without awareness or control, change more slowly than explicit attitudes, and are more directly linked to spontaneous, uncontrolled behavior. Explicit attitudes are deliberately formed, involve awareness of judgmental processes, change with new information, and do not correlate well with spontaneous or non-instrumental behavior, as opposed to judgments. They can override the more direct behavioral influence of implicit attitudes, but only when they are consciously activated and tied to independent motivations to override the implicit attitudes, motivations to be fair and unprejudiced in one's decisions, for example. The simultaneous existence of such opposed attitudes in subjects is common in the case of attitudes toward minorities. Newly developed conscious egalitarian attitudes can leave prejudicial implicit attitudes intact. The latter predict spontaneous avoidance behaviors of which the subject is unaware, such as in choices of seats. Individuals stereotype others automatically, can correct for these prejudicial stereotypes with cognitive effort, but only in their judgments and deliberately controlled behavior.[21]

Those implicit attitudes that directly and automatically influence behavior without conscious awareness include cognitive components closely tied to affect in states that are both evaluative and motivational. These may be

---

[21] For a sampling of the literature on attitudes from which this paragraph was culled, see I. Ajzen and M. Fishbein, "The Influence of Attitudes on Behavior," and J. N. Bassili and R. D. Brown, "Implicit and Explicit Attitudes," both in D. Albarracin, B. T. Johnson, and M.P. Zanna (eds.), *The Handbook of Attitudes* (Mahwah, NJ: Lawrence Erlbaum, 2005); A. Tesser and L. Martin, "The Psychology of Evaluation," in E. T. Higgins and A. W. Kruglauski (eds.), *Social Psychology: Handbook of Basic Principles* (New York: Guilford, 1996); R. J. Rydell and A. R. McConnell, "Understanding Implicit and Explicit Attitude Change," *Journal of Personality and Social Psychology*, 91 (2006): 995–1008; T. D. Wilson, S. Lindsey, and T. Y. Schooler, "A Model of Dual Attitudes," *Psychological Review*, 107 (2000): 101–26.

contrasted with conscious evaluative judgments or explicit attitudes that are not directly motivational, but become so only when supplemented by independently existing desires to act on them. Some, but not all, evaluations activate automatically and influence spontaneous behavior, mixing cognitive and affective components, and these are clearly motivational. The same should be more obviously true of the cognitive, evaluative aspects of desires. In fact, in the case of standing desires, the judgmental evaluative component will likely be an implicit attitude. This is what makes it proper to say in cases of weak will that agents do not do what they desire to do. They fail to act on those evaluative judgments that are normally motivational and that reflect their overriding reasons.

The next point is that these implicit judgments do normally reflect an agent's reasons. If we are rational, we form intentions more often on the basis of such judgments than from the other components of desire, although the other components may be enlisted in carrying out the intentions. Evaluative judgments are typically more closely tied to more stable and deeper concerns than are the other components of particular desires, although we have seen in the case of prejudice that they can also be formed emotionally or irrationally, from stereotyping in opposition to more complete evidence. Despite these cases, rationality is ordinarily retained in cases of conflict or temptation when the agent acts on the evaluation and resists the urge, when she exercises will power, which may call to its aid thoughts of the consequences of violating the judgment, as well as a second-order desire to act on her strongest reasons. These thoughts and desires may then reintroduce pleasure at the thought of acting on the judgment and resisting the urge.

We noted also that when implicit evaluative judgments or attitudes are formed irrationally, they can be partially overridden by conscious, explicit judgments. Just as implicit evaluative judgments as components of desires are normally more reliable indicators of reasons than are temporary urges, so sincere explicit judgments that can serve to override prejudicial attitudes are normally more rational, more responsive to evidence, than are the automatically activated evaluations. But on neither level is this always the case. The cognitive components or explicit judgments may themselves derive from misleading or biased evidence or from pernicious social programming: sometimes it is better to trust to one's immediate feelings or gut reactions.

But not usually. While it is possible that an evaluative judgment is itself false, irrational, or incoherent with one's deeper concerns, for the most part one's automatically activated evaluations reflect and are part of one's coherent motivational set.[22] Since reasons derive from such motivations, if positive evaluative judgments remain when other elements of desire are absent or eliminated, then reasons typically remain as well. This is our first concluding point in the solution to our puzzle about depression. The second point here is that depression does seem to alter the affective and dispositional components of desires for certain outcomes without affecting the judgmental components. This holds for both surface or specific desires as well as for deeper concerns.

Again there is broad support in the psychological literature for this interpretation. Depression is not only compatible with the capacity for evaluation, but certain sorts of evaluations lie at its core, namely negative evaluations of the self and of the possibility of success in endeavors judged to be highly important and reflective of the self. Automatic negative self-appraisals linked to desires for outcomes judged to be good but unattainable contribute to depression. Negative triggering events or disappointments in achievements or social relations create expectations that highly desired outcomes will not occur and that highly aversive outcomes will.[23] Both expected negative outcomes and earlier life events are evaluated as important and as revealing important defects in the self. While optimists like Yogi Berra never think they are in a slump, depressives will interpret any setbacks as indicative of goals unattainable because of personal shortcomings.

The resulting symptoms include retarded initiation of voluntary responses, apathy, and impairment of the capacity to experience pleasure.[24] One prominent diagnostic system (DSM-IV) lists among the symptoms of a "major depressive episode" diminished pleasure, psychomotor retardation, feelings of worthlessness, and indecisiveness. Behavioral frameworks

[22] Nomy Arpaly, "On Acting Rationally Against One's Best Judgment," *Ethics*, 110 (2000): 488–513, denies the rationally privileged status of evaluative judgment, but only by emphasizing the occasions that I take to be in the minority.

[23] See L. Y. Abramson, L. B. Alloy, and M. E. Hogan, "Cognitive/Personality Subtypes of Depression," *Cognitive Therapy and Research*, 21 (1997): 247–65; Tesser and Martin, "The Psychology of Evaluation"; J. A. Bargh, "Automaticity in Social Psychology," in Higgins and Kruglauski (eds.), *Social Psychology: Handbook of Basic Principles*, p. 170.

[24] Abramson et al., "Cognitive/Personality Subtypes of Depression," pp. 250–1.

emphasize reduced frequency of overall activity as the "primary defining characteristic" of depression.[25] The Hopelessness Depression Symptom Questionnaire asks whether the patient has given up trying to accomplish what is important to him.[26] Cognitive therapy often begins by making the patient aware of automatically activated self-evaluative judgments that cause negative emotions.[27] On the one hand, such negative self-evaluations or attitudes toward oneself lie at the core of clinical depression. On the other hand, goals are still evaluated positively but thought to be out of reach.

To summarize, depressed subjects typically lack the energy to act and the pleasurable thought that doing so will bring further pleasure, but they generally continue to recognize that certain states of affairs are importantly better or worse than others. They dwell on their worst prospects, but only because they judge them to be worse than other possibilities. In such depression the motivation to do what they judge they ought to do is greatly weakened and seemingly absent not because the affective components normally involved in translating desire into intention and intention into action are overwhelmed by other urges, but because they are eliminated or overwhelmed by negative feelings. The evaluative component remains in both akrasia and depression, failing to generate action in itself, as it sometimes can, because overwhelmed in the one case by urges and in the other by negative feelings.

It might be objected in light of the cited psychological sources on depression that, if the depression leads to judgments that desired outcomes are not attainable, then it is not irrational not to try to attain them. But in depression these judgments themselves are affectively, not rationally, formed and activated. Their irrationality extends to their behavioral influences. Thus, in both milder and more severe depression resultant irrationality consists in the incoherence introduced within one's beliefs and motivations: between evaluations and the evidential bases for them, or between motivations and intentions and actions. Part of the irrationality involved in depression consists in irrationally formed beliefs that one cannot succeed in what

[25] A. M. Nezu, *Practitioner's Guide to Empirically Based Measures of Depression* (New York: Kluwer, 2002), p. 12.
[26] Ibid. 299.
[27] J. A. Bargh and M. E. Tota, "Context-Dependent Automatic Processing in Depression," *Cognitive Therapy and Research*, 54 (1988): 925–39.

one considers important. But the deeper problem is the division within one's motivations that makes these beliefs self-fulfilling. These divisions take different forms. Milder depression leaves dispositions to act intact while blocking their realization. More severe depression eliminates the dispositions as well, but leaves normally motivational evaluative judgments, judgments of better and worse states of affairs, intact. This implicit evaluational component of desire that typically governs the rationality of actions by reflecting those concerns that generate reasons allows there to be reasons which the agent has but to which she fails to respond. Hence the irrationality caused by depression.

The key to our solution to this puzzle about this form of irrationality, like our explanation of weak will, involved the claim that implicit evaluative judgments are proper elements of prototypical desires. Opponents of this claim point out that we can desire the bad, and desire it without judging it to be good. This point is correct but once more shows only that desires that are not typical can lack elements in the cluster of components all of which are present in the paradigm cases. A misguided Humean might object on another ground. Implicit evaluative judgments reflect or count as beliefs, and Humeans often claim that beliefs are inert in the practical sphere, not motivational in themselves. Hume himself, however, opposed only the claim that beliefs in objective facts could motivate in themselves. He opposed the idea of objective value demanding a rational response in the form of a positive evaluation and subsequent motivation, and this book follows him in opposition to this idea. But for him evaluative judgments do not express recognitions of objective values or external reasons, but instead express a subject's attitudes or motivational states. Moral judgments in particular are intrinsically motivating according to Hume.

I reject this claim about moral judgments and will argue the point in the next chapter. Earlier in this section I distinguished, following the psychological literature on attitudes, between evaluative states that are automatically activated and normally result in spontaneous behavior, and judgments that are deliberately formed and must be tied to independent motivations in order to influence behavior. The cognitive, evaluative components of desires fall into the former class. As aspects of desires they are motivational or immediately motivating. Moral judgments, by contrast, will be motivating only for the morally-minded. I will argue that they are no different in this respect from aesthetic judgments, or the demands of etiquette, law, or religion.

With our analysis of desires as complex states and our account of rationality as coherence and of various forms of irrationality as incoherence within these states, we are now prepared to address the central topic of this chapter, the relation of desires to reasons.

III. Desires and Reasons

"Why buy good luggage? You only use it when you travel."

I have been defending the view that all practical reasons derive from our motivations or concerns. A separate question is whether all desires or motivations generate reasons. I have suggested a negative answer to that question. *Just* feeling like it is not a reason to do something, but reflects the lack of a reason. It then becomes pressing to clarify when and which desires create reasons and which do not. The two initially salient positions at the extremes are that desires taken singly create reasons or that only an agent's entire set of desires generate his reasons. I will advocate neither of these views. The first suggests once more that just feeling like it can generate a reason, while the second might negate the possibility of conflicting reasons, which we have seen to underlie the need to deliberate. The right view, I shall argue, is that multiple coherent but sometimes conflicting sets of desires anchored by deeper concerns constitute as practical reasons various states of affairs that indicate how to satisfy those concerns. A related final question is whether the rationalizing force of those desires that do create reasons derives from their affective, dispositional, or cognitive components. I will agree with externalists that it is the cognitive component that indicates the presence of a reason, but I will interpret its nature and relevance differently than they do.

We may begin, as is now our custom, with some intuition pumping examples, desires that do and those that do not appear to create reasons.[28] We can then determine what is present in the former class and absent in the latter. After isolating this component, we can return to the examples to

[28] Some of my examples are taken from Ruth Chang, "Can Desires Provide Reasons for Actions?" in R. J. Wallace *et al.* (eds.), *Reason and Value* (Oxford: Clarendon, 2004).

confirm our explanation of how desires relate to reasons. In doing so, we will see that some of our initial intuitions become plausibly modified by the proposed account. The examples will involve both trivial and non-trivial decision contexts.

(1) My desire to eat chocolate ice cream gives me a reason to go to Ben and Jerry's, but my desires to turn on radios, to count blades of grass, or to go back to sleep when the alarm rings create no reasons. (2) My aversion to having a biopsy is no reason to avoid one that I need, likewise for my desire to avoid getting wet when a child is drowning in a pond in front of me; but my desire to marry Mary seemingly can be decisive even if there are reasons to marry others that do not obtain in Mary's case, likewise for my desire to pursue a certain career when there might be reasons, such as easier success, to pursue a different one. (3) Japanese food may be healthier than Italian, but it seems I can have an overriding reason to eat Italian based only on my desire to do so, on my feeling like eating it.

Some preliminary comments on these examples. I have claimed that just feeling like it is not a reason for doing anything, but I include example 3 to acknowledge intuitions to the contrary. But in this case of eating Italian instead of Japanese food that I have health reasons to prefer, we need not say that just feeling like it in the sense of a bare urge provides the reason that saves me from irrationality. What does so instead is my preference for better taste or variety over the negligible difference in health effect of one meal. My preference here connects with a more general desire for gustatory pleasure, which specifies a yet more general concern for sensory pleasure, not a trivial value, although perhaps not suitable to be at the core of a life plan. On the other hand, if I constantly eat unhealthy food because I prefer its taste, despite having a strong concern for my health, then I am irrational.

In regard to the lack of reasons in the last three cases of example 1, philosophers who believe that feeling like it or having an isolated desire does in itself provide a reason to do what one desires[29] would hold that the reasons in these case are weak, but still present. They might hold that only prejudice prevents us from recognizing a desire to turn on radios or count blades of grass as providing a reason to do so. We cannot imagine having

---

[29] Ruth Chang is one such philosopher in the article cited. Mark Schroeder in his book *Slaves of the Passions* is another.

such desires ourselves and so cannot imagine having such reasons. A person who had such desires would be highly abnormal. Mental abnormality is linked in our minds with mental illness, and mental illness with irrationality. Since we believe that irrational people fail to act on reasons, we believe that feeling like it in these cases fails to generate a reason. But, these philosophers would point out, abnormality, certainly in the sense of being unusual, is not to be equated with irrationality, and so our inclination to deny the presence of reasons in these cases is misguided. Feeling like counting blades of grass is on a par with feeling like having chocolate ice cream, they would say, and both create reasons, albeit not strong ones.

As noted, I share instead the intuition of the philosophers who cite these examples (usually externalists) that the weird and isolated desires in themselves create no reasons. Evidence in support of this intuition is not only the common locution, "No reason, I just felt like it," admitting a lack of reasons, but the cases in example 2 in which desires in themselves again seem to provide no reasons. In these cases of the biopsy and drowning child, defenders of isolated desires as reasons would hold again that the reasons created are simply overwhelmed by those much stronger ones on the other side. But once more the response, "That is no reason at all," to an expressed desire to avoid the discomfort of a biopsy or of getting wet would be expected and in my view should be taken literally. Just not feeling like getting wet at the particular time when a child is drowning, if not reflective of a deeper aversion to the water, is indeed no reason at all not to save the child. A defender of the view that mere affective or dispositional states in themselves provide reasons could reply a final time that in these cases the strong reasons on the other side cancel the reasons created by these states instead of simply outweighing them. This reply would allow that the desires normally create reasons but admit that such reasons do not always persist.

But there remain, I believe, conclusive considerations on the other side. Reasons, remember, are what justify our actions and what we deliberate about. A bare urge or whim does not justify acting on the basis of it and does not normally enter into deliberations about states of affairs that count for and against actions. This allows that acting on a whim is not irrational unless opposed by reasons, that one might have a reason to want to relieve a felt urge if the feeling is unpleasant, and that we might inductively take a feeling in itself as an indication of a reason if we know that in the past such feelings connected with reasons of which we were unaware at the time. In this last case the feeling would directly create an epistemic reason for believing we have a practical reason. But it remains the case that *just* feeling like it does not create a reason.

Those who agree that such isolated desires create no reasons go on to argue from such cases that desires as a whole fail to create reasons. These externalists often approvingly cite Warren Quinn's example of the weird desire to turn on radios as showing more generally that desires cannot create reasons.[30] The example is that of a person with a strange urge and resultant disposition to turn on radios without any other reason for doing so, that is, without wanting to hear music or news or any other content. The bare desire in itself does not seem to create any reason to engage in the bizarre behavior. As noted, I agree with this verdict. But to generalize so fully from this strange case is to conclude that informed and coherent sets of desires create no reasons. If not, then objective value in the world must create our reasons, and this implies once more that the world can require all our concerns to be other than they are. I have argued that this cannot be the case and will expand on this argument in Chapter 5. There is no perspective from which we could appreciate such a demand.

Quinn himself argues that what is missing from his strange desire is the normal evaluation of its object as good.[31] I have emphasized that this component is indeed a part of prototypical desires. Thomas Scanlon agrees with Quinn that the lack of a reason here relates to the lack of this cognitive evaluative component. He explicitly adds the stronger externalist claim that this component of desire itself does not create a reason, but is instead the purported recognition of a reason. For Scanlon, to evaluate an object positively is simply to take it to provide a practical reason. If I judge that a certain activity or object is good, I am simply judging that there is a reason for me to pursue or protect it.

Once more for objectivists generally reasons that seem to derive from desires derive instead from the value of what is desired, which value amounts to an objective reason both for the desire and for the action to fulfil it. Given these objective reasons that the evaluative component of desires recognizes, to count the desires themselves as creating reasons would

---

[30] e.g. Scanlon, *What We Owe to Each Other*, p. 43.

[31] Warren Quinn, "Putting Rationality in its Place," in *Morality and Action* (Cambridge: Cambridge University Press, 1993), p. 247.

be to count the relevant reasons twice. If I desire to play tennis, and part of this desire is an implicit judgment that playing is good, according to the objectivist account in which values reduce to reasons, I am judging that I have a reason to play and have the same reason to desire to play. The latter might sound circular since the judgment is part of the desire, but the idea seems to be that desires are reflexive in this way: to desire something in the full sense is to consider it desirable, to judge that it provides a reason to desire it.

Quinn too takes evaluative judgment, a component in prototypical desires, to be the purported recognition of value in their objects; and he holds that it is because the bare dispositional component of desire, which is alone present in his example of the desire to turn on radios, does not indicate such value that it cannot create a reason.[32] Our being positively disposed toward some state of affairs cannot in itself make it rational to pursue that state of affairs as an end. If being so disposed in itself provided a reason, then virtually any bizarre behavior would count as rational. While it is true that we rarely ascribe irrationality to agents, this suggested criterion of rationality would be too lenient.

I agree with these externalists that recognition of the role of the evaluative component of full or paradigmatic desires is crucial to understanding which desires create reasons and which do not. But we need not interpret the role of this component as they do. Indeed if we did, given our analysis of reasons as what motivates or gives rise to desires in a rational agent, we would be guilty of a vicious circularity. To be rationally motivated would be to recognize value; to recognize value would be to recognize a reason; a reason is what motivates a rational agent. What we would get out of this is that to desire rationally is to desire as a rational agent desires, not a great piece of philosophical enlightenment. But we need not interpret the evaluative component of desire in this way. It does consist in judging the object to be good in some sense, but this need not be seen as taking the object to provide an objective reason for action, for pursuing or protecting it. That this evaluative component as an integral part of desire does not amount to taking its object to provide a reason is clear from the fact that children can have desires, full-fledged or paradigmatic desires, viewing their objects as good or attractive, before they have the concept of

---

[32] Ibid. 252, 236.

a reason. They can desire things and consider them good before being able to provide what they would recognize as reasons.

What is rational for agents to do is what will satisfy their informed and coherent desires, and reasons are those states of affairs that indicate how to do this. It may be good for agents to be rational or to act on their reasons, but we need not conclude that this is what "good" means, that reasons enter into the definition of "good" or "value". Intuitively, "good" or "valuable" does not mean "provides practical reasons," although it is true that what is good or valuable ought in some sense to be pursued and protected. Nor is the implicit judgment that the object of a desire is good a judgment that the desire is rational, that it is part of an informed and coherent set of desires. That judgment is too sophisticated even as an implicit part of an educated adult's desires. We can leave it that "good" is a primitive concept in such evaluative judgments, expressive of a "pro-attitude" but not subject to definition. To judge something good in this primitive way as part of desiring it is simply to evaluate it positively.

If this cognitive component or evaluative judgment in desire is not taking the object to provide a reason to pursue it, the judgment nevertheless is more indicative of the presence of a reason than are the other aspects of desire. This is not because it reflects recognition of some objective value, but instead, according to the internalist conception, because it is more likely than a bare urge or disposition to reflect the subject's coherent and informed sets of motivations. More specifically, it is more likely to reflect the subject's deeper or higher-order concerns at the time, concerns that anchor these sets of motivations. According to this view, it is not a single desire in itself that creates a subject's reason for acting, but her informed and coherent motivational sets at a time that create her sets of reasons at that time. A single desire enters into the creation of these reasons when it meshes with and is part of these larger and deeper motivational sets.

As described earlier, such sets of motivations have an hierarchical structure. Deeper and broader concerns underlie and support more specific desires. They do so not only when the specific desires are for the means to satisfy them, but also when the shallower desires are specifications of the deeper and broader concerns. If one cares about having pleasant sensations or eating good-tasting foods, the desire for ice cream, along with many other desires to taste different foods, are specifications of that concern. If such sets of motivations create reasons, we can think of the broader and deeper concerns as their ultimate, even if indirect, source. Reasons, we have noted, come in various degrees or strengths. If our strongest reasons derive from our deepest concerns, it is not surprising that the most peripheral and isolated desires fail to generate any rational force at all.

It was said above that an evaluative judgment as a component of desire is to the effect that the desired outcome or object is good for the agent or good for him to pursue in some way. According to the internalist, what is good for agents to pursue is what satisfies their informed and coherent (prioritized) motivational sets, although, as also noted, this is not true by definition. Thus, the evaluative judgments tend to reflect those sets of motivations, even though this is not their intended meaning. They are intended as evaluations of the objects or activities at which they aim, but what they actually evaluate are the outcomes of actions taken to fulfil the desires. That fulfilment will be good for the agent if it satisfies the informed and coherent sets of motivations that prompt the actions. Hence this component of a desire reflects its relations to other desires of the agent, and that is why it is a crucial aspect of those desires that create reasons.

Quinn's weird desire to turn on radios, in lacking this component according to his description, is a completely isolated desire in probable conflict with other activities that the agent has reason to do. It is that isolation and probable conflict, and not simply the desire's abnormality or the strangeness of the activity itself, that makes acting on the desire not only lacking in reasons, but probably irrational. Turning on a radio, unlike counting blades of grass, is not in itself a strange or unusual activity, unless doing so connects to no other motivations. Hitting a ball over a net or shooting one through a hoop is in itself a stranger activity, except that, given the present social framework and institutions into which these activities fit, they connect to many other desires for competition, social interaction, exercise, physical skill, or wealth and fame. It is these connections that render the desire to do these things with a ball suitable even as the centerpiece of a rational life plan.

Compare again catching a ball from someone throwing it from sixty feet away with throwing it high in the air oneself and then catching it. Intrinsically, there is no greater merit in the one activity than in the other. But Yogi Berra was perfectly rational in preferring, as he said, to be a catcher to being the president, even if he had an equal chance at both (and knowing all the candidates, who is to say he did not, especially if use of the English language is a criterion?). It is not the objective value of the goal or activity that provides the reasons, but the way it relates to a coherent set of desires and concerns. By contrast, buying good luggage makes perfect sense for a constant traveler who is concerned to avoid having to do so often, but is not rational on the basis of a bare urge or whim of someone who almost never travels and for whom the purchase would therefore serve no other ends.

Several reminders of points made previously before returning to our initial examples. First, arguing that desires create reasons only when they mesh with other desires and with deeper concerns is not meant to imply that one must always be doing something momentous, of great life importance, or something aimed at directly satisfying one's deepest and longest-term concerns. What is uppermost among one's concerns is constantly shifting with time and one's previous activities. Thus, my greatest concern now may be to walk my dog instead of working on my next book, if he has not been out for many hours. Or it may be to relax or sleep. These activities are certainly not momentous in themselves, although we can take them to reflect broader and deeper concerns for my dog's welfare and for periods of relaxation and rest. Normally I need not deliberate in order to determine which motivations or reasons reflecting them are strongest at a time. Normally my acting in one way rather than another is itself an indication of my priorities and therefore of my reasons.

Second, and related to the first point, in referring to the motivational sets of an agent, I have been careful to use the plural. At any given time, agents may be motivated in different directions instead of having a single fully prioritized or coherent set of motivations. Even if one does achieve a fully coherent set at some point in time, new opportunities will present themselves that create new conflicts within the set. Thus, if a grant becomes available, I am immediately motivated to apply but also to avoid bothering outside recommenders again. Such conflicting motivations create conflicting reasons. Each meshes with different deeper concerns, such as my concerns for support for my research and for not being a pest. Once more deliberation aims to resolve such conflicts by prioritizing the reasons and implicitly the motivations that underlie them, returning the agent to greater motivational coherence. At the point at which intentions must be formed and actions initiated, such conflicts must be resolved, although the priorities established at that time may be later reversed. At some point one must simply stop being a pest.

Third, implicit evaluative judgments as components of desires have been emphasized here, as they are by cognitivist externalists about values and reasons. Subjects also make explicit, conscious evaluative judgments. Normally these implicit and explicit judgments coincide. But they can also come apart, in which case irrationality threatens. A subject can desire something, implicitly evaluating it as good for her in some sense, while at the same time explicitly or consciously judging it to be bad overall. In this case in which the implicit and explicit judgments diverge, the latter usually corrects the former partial view, but that is not always the case. While the implicit judgment is usually only partial, viewing the object as good in some limited sense, the explicit judgment may be a product of self-deception or distorting social pressure. Sometimes one should trust to one's feelings.

This situation of diverging judgments differs from a third case mentioned earlier in contrast to paradigm desires, the case in which one can desire or have an urge for something without judging it positively in any sense, as in a hated addiction. Can a subject, call him Iago, take the fact that something is bad as his reason for doing it? If what we mean here is morally bad, then the answer is unproblematically affirmative. Iago implicitly judges it good for him to be morally bad. One can implicitly judge it to be good to rebel against morality, even to self-destruct, and one can have reasons for doing so. In the contrasting case mentioned above in which one has an isolated urge to do something one judges to be bad *tout court*, that urge fails to create a reason.

Fourth, I have spoken of motivations that create reasons being not only coherent or mutually supporting, but also informed. I argued that the relevant information is mainly what it will be like to satisfy the desire in question. Quinn asks why information matters to rationality if it is not information about what is of true, objective, value.[33] The first answer is that a desire based only on false information about its object is likely, if acted on, to lead to disappointment. If an agent desires an object because of the way she conceives of its properties and those properties are other than she conceives them to be, then she is likely to be disappointed when

---

[33] Ibid. 252, 236.

acting to secure the object. The object as it is, is not what she desires, and so it provides no reason for acting. Another answer is that acting on a desire based on false information is likely to defeat some of the agent's more central desires. This is because the object or outcome is again the opposite of what he thinks, and the opposite of what coheres with his other desires is likely to conflict with them and lead to self-defeat, our paradigm of irrationality.

We may now return to our examples in order to see where the account meshes with our initial intuitions and where it might plausibly modify them. I earlier argued that just feeling like it, considered in isolation from other desires, never provides in itself a reason. If it did, then it would be impossible to see why I would not have a reason to count blades of grass, to go back to sleep when the alarm rings, or to turn on radios, if I felt like it.[34] In the examples of avoiding a biopsy or getting wet, in arguing that my reluctance creates no reasons I have assumed that this reluctance amounts to just not feeling like it. If instead my reluctance to get wet is tied to a deeper concern about my health, and if the chill would pose a threat to my health, then I do have a reason not to get wet, albeit one that is overridden, indeed overwhelmed, by my reason to save the drowning child, assuming that I am normally morally-minded. Likewise, if my reluctance to avoid a biopsy is an instance of a more general heightened sensitivity to pain, and if the biopsy would indeed be quite painful, then I have a reason to avoid it, one that is nevertheless overridden or overwhelmed by my concern for my health or for survival, assuming that I am normally concerned for my physical well-being.

In the seemingly opposed cases of desiring to marry Mary or to pursue the desired career, we need to reassess the initial intuitions in light of the account offered. My considered view is that one would not in fact be acting rationally if he allowed his bare feeling like marrying Mary to override genuine reasons against doing so. To be rational in choosing to marry her, he would have to think that they are compatible over the long term, that they share interests and central beliefs, that they will continue to find each other stimulating for the indefinite future, and so on. It seems probable that one reason so many marriages end shortly and badly is that they are entered

---

[34] Compare Donald Hubin, "Desires, Whims, and Values," *Journal of Ethics*, 7 (2003): 315–35. He defends the view that all desires, including isolated whims, create reasons unless opposed by deeper concerns or values.

into simply on the basis of the partners' desiring to marry without taking into account these less immediately felt but more substantial concerns. It is not always the case that one should trust to one's feelings.

Likewise, in the case of choosing a career, just feeling like pursuing a particular one will in fact not provide a reason unless the feeling reflects one's deeper concerns. A person rationally choosing a career must consider what will continue to challenge and interest her in the long run, what will be sufficiently lucrative to provide for the satisfaction of her other desires, what will serve other people, if she is so oriented, what will allow her to live in a place she finds suitable, and so on. Once more just feeling like it does not begin the scratch the surface of the reasons that a rational choice would take into account. If the account of the relation of desires to reasons offered above had led to more defensible intuitions than those initially suggested, this constitutes strong support for the account. Provoking such reflection that leads to plausible revisions of initial intuitions is one of the less controversial uses of philosophical theory.

That leaves the most difficult, just because most trivial, case of desiring or feeling like having some ice cream. (Read on before the trip to your freezer.) Why, finally, does that desire give me a reason to go to the store where it is available, while feeling like counting blades of grass or turning on radios gives me no reason to travel to fields or rooms with radios? Again Quinn appears to be right that it is the lack of a positive judgmental component in the latter cases, but again unlike him we may interpret this lack as indicating not a difference in objective value, but an isolated whim or urge. Acting on a whim, although it is normally acting without a reason, is not thereby necessarily acting irrationally. Such action is irrational only if it conflicts with other reasons one has for not acting that way. One might even have a higher-order reason for acting on a whim deriving from motivation to be or to appear spontaneous. But Quinn's example of turning on radios would almost certainly count as irrational action. As mentioned earlier, the abnormality of the desire and action does not directly imply irrationality, but it is indirectly relevant. If, for example, the agent is normally concerned to be well perceived by others or to share norms and projects with them, then he will have reasons not to give in to bizarre urges. If, by contrast, he desires to be perceived as uniquely different, then he might begin to have a reason to turn on radios should he feel like it. Reasons come in various strengths, depending on how fully the motivations behind them mesh with other concerns and on how deep those concerns are.

In regard to my desire for ice cream, I typically do judge that it would be good for me to have such very pleasant sensations and to seek them out if I have nothing more pressing to do at the time. I am typically motivated more generally to take advantage of opportunities to have very pleasant sensations. The desire to have some ice cream does then mesh with such broader concerns and thus gives me a reason to go to the store where ice cream is sold. If this reason conflicts with other reasons for doing something else or with a concern for my health or weight, it can, of course, be overridden; or, if these other reasons are strong enough, it can apparently be cancelled, so that the response, "That is no reason at all," to my expression of feeling like having some ice cream becomes appropriate. Desiring to have some ice cream is like desiring not to get wet. When cohering with general desires to have pleasant sensations or to avoid unpleasant ones, both these desires create reasons, but not ones that will hold up in the face of strong conflicting reasons. If I have to make a tenure decision meeting, I cannot begin to justify taking the time to eat some ice cream (I am not talking about ordinary department meetings). But the desire to have some ice cream still differs from Quinn's desire to turn on radios, since his desire connects to no more general or deeper ones and therefore never creates a reason.

Most contemporary Humeans view reasons as combinations of beliefs and desires. Hume himself argued only that beliefs in themselves do not motivate unless connected to desires.[35] His argument is compatible with, although it obviously does not imply, the view defended here that reasons are states of affairs constituted as such by coherent and informed sets of motivations, including both specific desires and deeper concerns. It is perhaps anti-Humean to emphasize that prototypical desires include a cognitive evaluative aspect, although we have seen ample support for recognizing this in the contemporary literature of cognitive psychology. This recognition, interpreted internalistically instead of externalistically, allows us to retain Hume's central claim that all reasons and values derive from motivations and concerns, while also recognizing that not all desires

---

[35] David Hume, *A Treatise of Human Nature* (Garden City, NY: Doubleday, 1961), pp. 374–75 (bk II, pt. III, ch. 3).

create reasons. I have shown that intuitions as to which desires create reasons and which do not, intuitions that initially rested on no obvious ground, can be grounded in an account that takes the cognitive element of desires to signal a connection to other and typically deeper concerns of the agent. It is these connections that distinguish desires that create reasons from those that do not.

4

The Externalist's Examples

I. Learning Reasons for Desires

"I'm learning all his experience."

I have claimed that the internalist account of reasons and rationality is simpler and more comprehensible, both epistemologically and metaphysically, than the appeal to objective values as the source of external reasons. While the latter creates deep mysteries as to the nature of objective values or brute normative facts and our access to them, internalism requires only a grasp of the nature of desires and of coherence within motivational states. Given these obvious theoretical advantages, the only remaining question is whether the simpler theory can successfully capture all the data, all of our reflectively endorsed intuitions about the scope of reasons and demands of rationality. Externalists, of course, claim that it cannot.

In this chapter we will canvass their proposed counterexamples to the internalist account. As noted in the first chapter, these examples include reasons for desires themselves, especially reasons to acquire new motivations from coming to appreciate values not encountered before, as well as concerns claimed to be rationally required of all agents—prudential concerns for one's own welfare and moral concerns for others. The externalist notes that we seem to have the latter classes of reasons whether or not we care to have them, and that we seem to acquire new desires from recognizing values unrelated to our prior concerns. We need to consider each type of example in some detail since not all will be answered in the same way. I will claim that some of these examples can be captured by the account of rationality as coherence that was provided in the second chapter, and I will dismiss others by explaining them away, mainly in terms of the distinction between reasons we have and reasons there are.

We may begin with new perceptions of value that give rise to new desires or concerns in the course of experience. These are motivated desires that seem to derive from the recognition of independent values or reasons instead of creating those reasons. They seem to derive from novel perception of what is valuable in itself, instead of reflecting pre-existent concerns of the agent. I try golf for the first time, having been talked into a round by my neighbor, expecting to be bored by the slow pace of the game, but instead find it very pleasurable and acquire the desire to play again. Elijah Millgram, who calls such learning from experience practical induction, interprets the process as revealing what independently has value or matters, hence what one should care about or desire. In this example I am learning about a valuable activity, not about myself.[1] I have reason to play golf because it is enjoyable, or involves exercising athletic skills in a beautiful setting, and this explains my desire to play rather than the other way round.

But surely the fact that golf involves exercising athletic skills in a beautiful setting is a reason for me to play because I find that sort of activity enjoyable. Many others would indeed be bored, frustrated, or fatigued on a golf course. I find it enjoyable, it is the sort of activity that pleases me, because of my broader dispositions, inclinations, or motivations, for example my proclivity for outdoor sports. We noted earlier that desires and priorities or relative strengths among them are typically revealed only by what we find valuable or pleasurable, where valuable features are most often taken to be objective features of the objects that have them. They appear so in experience. Nevertheless, according to the internalist, what we are really learning about when we discover value are relational properties, relations between objects or states of affairs and our motivational dispositions. Millgram in effect acknowledges this when he draws a comparison to the perception of secondary qualities, pointing out that we learn something about an object when we see that it is red, not something about ourselves.[2] But once again, with a bit of scientific and philosophical sophistication, we realize that in perceiving colors we learn about relational properties, relations between

---

[1] Elijah Millgram, *Practical Induction* (Cambridge, MA: Harvard University Press, 1997), pp. 80–1.
[2] Ibid. 81–2.

emitted or reflected light and our visual systems, however objective colors may appear in perceptual experience.

Millgram is, of course, right that only perception directed outward, and not introspection, will tell us the colors of things, and he is similarly right that only practical induction, and not introspection, will tell us what is valuable or worth pursuing. It is not our perceptions that are colored, but their objects; and it is not our desires that we find desirable or valuable, but the objects we desire. Desires are backgrounded in everyday activities even more than in typical deliberation. But just as colors only appear as such to subjects with certain visual systems, so values or reasons may be constituted as such only by subjects with certain concerns or motivations. Whether the properties perceived or desired are objective, independent of particular subjects' perceivings and desirings, or relational, is left open by the fact that the perceptions and desires have external objects and that the properties which appear in such experiences appear to be properties of those objects.

Perceptions and motivations might reveal in experience what is out there independent of them, or they might reveal only ways things appear from particular subjective perspectives. Which metaphysical account is preferable will depend on such theoretical criteria as simplicity and comprehensibility, and on the totality of data to be captured by the account. How the properties in question seem in the experience of naive observers is only a small part of that data. Of greater moment are the subtle and not so subtle differences in the ways these properties appear to different observers, whether the properties admit of independent measurement, and how differences in appearances are to be explained. These differences are less subtle in the case of values than in the case of colors, and while in the latter case some such differences can be explained as the results of color blindness, which itself has a clear physical explanation, appeal to value blindness is more contentious and less clearly explainable. If subjects disagree about what is valuable and none of them are ignorant or value blind, then values are relational properties. The fact that we must learn from experience what is valuable for us (Millgram's main point) actually attests to the personal or subjective nature of values. The testimony of others is unreliable in this domain precisely because people differ in their tastes and values. If we do seek the testimony of others as to what may be of value or worth pursuing, we seek out those who share our tastes and values. This fact is well noted in the domain of aesthetics, but it is true for matters of value generally.

We desire so many things wrongly because we rely on the views of others instead of finding out firsthand what it is like to experience these things.

To return to the golf example, we noted the obvious fact that the game appeals to some people and not to others. Those to whom it appeals have reason to play, and others do not. These reasons then appear to be relative to differing inclinations or motivations despite the fact that they are discovered only in the course of actually trying out the game and experiencing its features. We also noted earlier a response of the defender of objective values that pushes appeal to them back one step in such examples. This reply claims that while different people derive pleasure from different activities, all have reason to pursue pleasure, which is objectively valuable. Pleasure or enjoyment figures centrally in the objectivist's account, almost as centrally as does desire in the internalist's account. For the objectivist, the strongest reasons to fulfil desires derive from the values of the objects desired. But we can also have reasons to fulfil desires because doing so brings pleasure and failing to do so causes frustration and distress.

I will take up the question of the objective value of pleasure in detail in Chapter 5. Here we can point out first that we differ in the activities that we find pleasurable. We react differently because we are differently disposed, and we take pleasure only in what we are disposed to take pleasure in. We may find pleasure in some unforeseen event or in some activity of which we had no clear concept beforehand, but if so, we will still have been the sorts of people who are disposed to enjoy such things. So if there is a reason to pursue pleasure, this reason remains relative to our pre-existing inclinations. I take pleasure in golf because I am disposed to enjoy that kind of outdoor activity. As many philosophers have pointed out, instead of the direct object of every rational person's desire, pleasure is typically a byproduct of fulfilling desires for other objects, desires that may differ from person to person.

The objectivist will respond that even though there are different sources of pleasure for different people, it is still the objective value of the pleasure that gives people reason to pursue those sources. But we can question second whether we have reason to pursue every conceivable pleasure or activity that we might find somewhat pleasurable, even those we do not care about pursuing or having, and even after we have experienced them and find that we do not care to pursue them further. If I try golf for the first time, find the five hours on the course mildly pleasing, but do not desire to take the game up or play again, do I really nevertheless have a reason to do so (assuming no other reason relating to friendship, business deals, or the need to exercise)? Am I irrational for not playing again when I have nothing more pressing to do? I would think not. Thus, while I learn whether I do have a reason to play by playing and seeing whether the game itself is a worthwhile pursuit, I am really finding out whether it is worthwhile for me. The fact that I learn by practical induction, only by experiencing the object or activity, does not show that the reason it affords me is not constituted as such by my pre-existing inclinations or broader motivations.

A more likely source than practical induction for many motivations is social indoctrination. We come to have motivations and reasons to satisfy them when we internalize norms prevalent in society, norms that define acceptable behavior and social success. These models of appropriate behavior are absorbed from authority figures by both the child and young adult, perhaps without prior motivation to mimic them. But once internalized, they guide interpersonal and career oriented behavior, indicating acceptable ways of achieving an agent's socially defined goals. Thus, once more they might be considered external sources of reasons that at least equal in influence the recognition of objective values.

In this case there are two replies available to the internalist. First, a child is typically motivated to obey authority figures, and an adult is motivated to be socially accepted and successful. The acceptance of social norms is dependent on these prior motivations and so, then, are the reasons that follow such acceptance. Second, even if there were no such prior motivations, the socially programmed reasons one acquires click in after the social indoctrination succeeds in creating new motivations to conform to its norms. Hence reasons to conform are relative to these newly acquired motivations and do not exist until their acquisition.

Opponents of the internalist position will claim not only that experiences of new objects reveal objective reasons in the absence of prior desires for those objects, and perhaps that social norms are an additional source of external reasons, but also that all desires must themselves be supported by reasons in order for it to be rational to act on those desires. Reasons for desires are not reasons to choose to have the desires, as reasons for actions are reasons to choose the actions. In contrast to actions, we do not choose which desires to have. We do not reflect on the values of objects, decide that we ought to desire them, and then come to desire them (although this seems to be the picture for which externalists yearn). Our dispositions to be moved by various objects or considerations typically reflect our deeper concerns. But we can nevertheless evaluate desires to decide whether it is good or bad to act on them (this leaves open whether our choices always reflect our motivations or can rise above them). There must be reasons why it is good to act on some but not others, and these will also be reasons to have the desires themselves. Such reasons to desire objects, externalists claim, derive from the values of those objects and not from desires. Just as a belief must correspond to its object in order to be true, so a desire must reflect the value of its object in order to be worth acting on. I ought to desire to read certain books because they are well written, ought to desire to exercise because it is good for me, ought to desire to help those in need because they are in need. These appear to be reasons independent of my present motivations for desiring these objects.

My answer is similar to that just given to the example of practical induction. Reasons for particular desires that may not yet exist can be provided by deeper and broader motivations and concerns. We saw in the second chapter that such reasons express the rational demand for coherence within motivational sets. Thus, even if I do not desire to read a well-written book, I have a reason to read it and to desire to read it, but only if I have a broader interest in good literature, or should have one because I desire to be educated or cultured or desire to broaden my experience, or should desire these things because I care about what others think of me, or desire to be sensitive or well rounded, and so on. I have a reason to exercise if but only if I like the feeling in my muscles that exercise brings, or if I am concerned about my health or weight or appearance, or should be concerned about these things if I am concerned about my own welfare. These objects and activities merit my desires because of my deeper concerns. If I am concerned about my health, then I have reason to exercise and to desire to exercise, whether I do desire to do so or not. But this is still an internal, not an external, reason.

I will consider whether I must rationally be concerned about my own welfare or that of others in the next sections. I want to deal first here with another objection of the objectivist to this coherence account of reasons for desires. I alluded in the previous chapter to this objection to the coherence account of rationality, but we need to deal with it more fully here as a specific objection to the account of reasons for desires. Again there is a comparison here to the domain of beliefs. In both domains it is claimed that coherence is insufficient to generate our full stock of reasons. It is relatively easy to construct a set of propositions that fully cohere with each other but do not connect or correspond to any object in the real world. Coherence in that case does not indicate truth. Nor can reasons for beliefs regress infinitely to prior beliefs and their reasons. Neither a circle nor an infinite regress of reasons for beliefs is acceptable. Coherence or transmission of reasons for belief indicates truth only if some members of the set of beliefs reflect the way the world is independently of their logical or evidential connections to other members of the set. Without such anchoring to the world, it will be possible to have incompatible sets of fully coherent beliefs not all of which can be true. There will be no reason then to think any of them true on grounds of coherence alone.

Externalists regarding practical reasons claim that a similar situation exists there. Bizarre desires may be coherent with each other. Such coherence does not create reasons for desires or actions unless at least some members of the set properly connect to objects in the world by reflecting their independent values. Externalists will admit that some reasons for desires can derive from reasons for other desires. Reasons for desiring means derive from the reasons for desiring the ends to which they are means. But such reasons must bottom out in reasons to desire certain ends or objects for themselves, reasons which cannot derive from or be transmitted from other desires. Even if there can be reasons for non-instrumental desires, reasons to desire ends in themselves, such reasons cannot regress indefinitely to reasons for other desires. The regress must end with some reasons based on the intrinsic properties of the objects desired, their independent value. Just as coherence among beliefs is insufficient for rationality, and just as an infinite regress of reasons is not an acceptable alternative, so neither of these alternatives is acceptable in the domain of practical reasons. In both cases the circle must be anchored or the regress terminated in beliefs or desires that connect directly to the properties of their objects. Or so the externalist will argue.

In reply, there is first of all an important difference between beliefs and desires. Since the aim of belief is truth, and since truth is the same for all believers, the possibility of incompatible (not jointly true) but fully coherent sets of beliefs shows that coherence alone does not render a set of propositions worthy of belief. By contrast, incompatible but coherent sets of desires can be satisfiable by different agents and can be equally worthy of directing their lives. The desires of an investment banker are very different from mine, and the combination of his and mine probably could not be all satisfied, but that does mean that one of us must be wrong to desire as he does. Different agents have different and incompatible desires, but that does not indicate that any of them are wrong to have those desires (as such incompatible sets do imply wrongness in the case of beliefs). The implication might hold for desires only if we already assumed a single objective set of values to which desires must correspond (even then, the values might not be all achievable together).

Second, it is problematic to describe a set of foundational beliefs that we should accept as true independently of their relations to any other beliefs or evidence, and yet such foundational beliefs seem to be required to avoid the problems with coherence and infinite regresses of beliefs providing reasons. The problem is that we seem to need some reason for thinking foundational beliefs true, and yet any reason we give seems to imply that these beliefs are not foundational, seen to be true independently of other beliefs. (This is one problem that keeps the epistemology industry in business.)[3] But since desires need not be true, and since the question here is whether they need to reflect objective values, we need not recognize any similar problem in their case. All we need is a set of motivations or concerns that provide reasons for other desires but require no reasons themselves. And, as noted earlier, we seem to have such concerns. It might seem in the abstract as if desires that have no reasons cannot transmit reasons for having other desires. But in fact concerns that need no reasons do create reasons for many other desires, even desires for ends in themselves.

I need no reason to love my wife or children, to care about my own health or welfare, to want to have a successful career. In some of these cases I could have reasons to have these concerns. I might have a reason to be concerned about my health in order to preserve myself for writing my philosophical masterwork. But I need no reason to be rationally concerned about my health. In other cases reasons seem more strongly out of place.

---

[3] For my solution, see *Empirical Knowledge* (Berkeley, CA: University of California Press, 1988), chs. 7–8.

Citing reasons to love my children would be worse than odd. Yet these concerns create reasons for many others, including desires for ends or objects in themselves. I might initially desire to work hard in order to have a successful career, but ideally, and actually for those of us lucky enough, our work becomes something we are motivated to pursue for itself. Since we work harder when we desire the work for its own sake, and since hard work makes for a successful career, we have a reason to desire an object for its own sake that derives from a deeper or broader desire.

As David Schmidtz has shown, internalists can even provide reasons for such broad and deep concerns as having a career or forming interpersonal relationships, reasons deriving from the desire to have something to live for, for example.[4] But our deepest concerns still need no reasons and, we have seen, for some of them reasons are out of place. These fundamental concerns, such as our love for our children or concerns for their welfare, confer value on states of affairs, such as living in a neighborhood with good schools, instead of being rationalized by the values of their objects. What is valuable for us reflects these concerns instead of being the basis for choosing them.

Other philosophers have contended that, even in the case of love, we do have reasons to love other people, and these reasons are external, independent of our actual feelings. Velleman suggests that we ought to love people for their rational natures.[5] The first problem with this suggestion is that ought implies can. Even if we could choose to love on the basis of reasons, many rational people are not even likeable, let alone loveable. Rational nature does not then seem to be a sufficient reason for love, and it is not necessary either. People love their dogs and babies, and their romantic involvements do not seem based on degrees of rationality (to put it mildly), nor ought they to be. The deeper problem is that love is an emotion, as Tina Turner reminds us, and, as emphasized earlier, emotions arise automatically, not in response to rational appraisals. This is again a good thing for the species, for if we loved only for reasons, reproduction might decline rapidly. Just as analytic philosophers over-intellectualized sex, seeing it primarily as a means to interpersonal communication instead

---

[4] David Schmidtz, *Rational Choice and Moral Agency* (Princeton: Princeton University Press, 1995), ch. 3.

[5] J. David Velleman, "Love as a Moral Emotion," *Ethics*, 109 (1999): 338–74.

of an instinctual physical drive,[6] so they have over-rationalized love. Love, as opposed to sexual desire, is a complex emotion that involves a deep identification with and concern for another's welfare. It would be nice if we were all concerned for everyone's welfare, and if we had some reason to be, but love as an emotion does not arise in response to reasons.

It is true that emotions, like desires, are appropriate or inappropriate. At the extreme, their pathological versions are habitually inappropriate. Phobias are such versions of fear, and love too has its degenerate forms, as when it is fawning, overindulgent, obsequious, or overly possessive. Emotions, as also noted, have their cognitive elements, and when they are appropriate, they seem to respond to reasons. We say, "She is fearful for a good reason: that snake is dangerous." But not only is it a mistake to emphasize the cognitive aspect of emotion to the exclusion of other facets, it is equally a mistake to assimilate emotions to rational processes on the evidence of such locutions. We noted earlier that the adaptive value of emotions lies precisely in their bypassing rational processes as preliminary to responses or actions. On the basis of rough cues, they initiate fixed responses immediately. We do not first find out whether the snake is dangerous in order to decide whether to fear it, although some of us can be trained to control or suppress our initial reactions. Likewise, we do not appraise the rationality of those we love before deciding whether to love them.

Of course, for Velleman all people have a rational nature, and he does not suggest proportioning love to degrees of rationality. But he does imply that we should love everyone, or as many as we can. In response, I would say that respect is the proper response to rational nature, but respect is not an emotion and not to be confused with love. While we should respect all, love seems by its nature more selective. We do not love all children (some are little monsters) as we love our own, nor should we. And we love our own immediately, without appraising their rationality. Jesus, like Velleman, demanded that we love all (or did he intend to refer only to our neighbors, those close to us?), but the demand seems too strong. In fact, we do not love people for any properties they have. When we say "I love the way she laughs," that is shorthand for strong liking, not literal love as

---

[6] See Robert Solomon, "Sex and Perversion," in R. Baker and F. Elliston (eds.), *Philosophy and Sex* (Buffalo: Prometheus, 1975); and my "Plain Sex," *Philosophy & Public Affairs*, 6 (1977): 267–87.

love for the person herself. Not only do we not choose to love others on the basis of assessing their properties as reasons for loving them, properties of persons do not make us love them. Instead, their properties become loveable to us when we love the persons; they are constituted as loveable by our love. Whatever properties of a loved one we list as loveable, those same properties in another would not imply that we rationally ought to love that other person. And finally, rational nature is not among the properties we typically find loveable.

Niko Kolodny avoids this extravagance by claiming that only our unique relationships with other individuals provide our reasons for loving them.[7] In his view, especially long-term personal relationships are reasons to love. But this view seems to get things backward. We can fall in love almost at first sight, and then we will seek to have such relationships with those we fall in love with. And, as noted, we love our babies at once. Our biological relation to them disposes us to love them, but we do not treat this relation as a reason, as something that we deliberate about in order to justify our love to others or to ourselves. Again our love for our children or for others requires no justification and hence needs no reasons.

Kolodny argues that a wife who loves her abusive husband or is coldly indifferent to her child fails to respond properly to the reasons these relationships provide or fail to provide. But the failure here is not one of reason: it is a failure of the heart, not the mind. As an emotion, love, like fear, does not necessarily go away when it is recognized to be inappropriate to its object. Emotions contrast in this respect with beliefs, which do arise and extinguish in response to perceived reasons. Beliefs may be recalcitrant in the face of new evidence, but that is because their subjects will fail to pay attention to new evidence once fixed in their beliefs, whereas subjects in the grip of emotions will remain so even after admitting their inappropriateness. On the other side of the spectrum, an emotionally cold person may be incapable of love, but his problem is not that he fails to appreciate a reason. If relationships were the rational ground for love, then I ought to love all my colleagues equally, but even as colleagues, I love only some of them (at most).

In ending this section, we need only reiterate that our deepest concerns, deriving in some cases from our deepest emotional attachments, need no

---

[7] Niko Kolodny, "Love as Valuing a Relationship," *Philosophical Review*, 112 (2003): 135–89.

reasons but ultimately provide reasons for the many other desires that nest in coherent motivational sets. When anchored by such concerns, these sets, and the demand for coherence within them, provide reasons for desires that have reasons.

II. Prudence

"The future ain't what it used to be."

Externalists claim not only that reasons for our desires, including our deepest concerns, must derive from the objective value of their objects, but also that there are certain concerns that we are all rationally required to have. These include concerns for our own well-being or health, for our own futures, and concern for the welfare of others, or moral concerns. Not to care about these things at all, to completely neglect them, is irrational. These requirements of rationality are once more claimed to be objective, independent of whatever other desires we happen to have. In this section I will respond to the claim about prudence, concern for our own welfare and futures, and in the next I will discuss moral concerns.

Before proceeding to the main question here, however, I want to point out that philosophers who seek to impose these requirements sharply disagree again over which they are. In fact, we find not only a lack of convergence in recent books on whether it is prudential or moral concerns, or both, that we are required to have, but seemingly a random distribution of positions. Thus Joshua Gert claims that we are required to be concerned about our own welfare—to refuse medicine when sick or to cut off one's finger without compensating benefit is irrational—but we are not rationally required to have moral concerns or altruistic desires for the welfare of others.[8] If immorality were irrational, he argues, then we could not hold people responsible or blame them for their immoral patterns of behavior, since we do not blame people who are habitually irrational, but instead seek to treat them medically.

Stephen Darwall, by contrast, holds that while we are not required to be concerned about our own welfare, we are rationally required to

---

[8] Joshua Gert, *Brute Rationality* (Cambridge: Cambridge University Press, 2004).

have moral concerns.[9] In support of the first claim it can be argued that heroes and saints who are completely unconcerned for themselves and therefore perfectly willing to sacrifice their own welfare or lives for the good of others are not condemned as irrational. But Darwall points out that when we blame people for immorality, and especially when we make moral demands on them, we assume that they have reasons to comply with these demands. We address them as equals who are responsive to moral reasons, and we blame them if they are not. Thus we assume that we are all equally required to be responsive to such reasons. Darwall's position is the inverse of Gert's. Roger Crisp completes the recently drawn conceptual map by holding that we all have reasons to promote both our own welfare and that of others, so that as rational agents we must be motivated by both.[10]

When analyzing emotions and desires, I held that the divergence of philosophers' views as to which facets of these states are essential to or definitive of them is evidence that all these views are partially right, that we are dealing with cluster concepts in which none of the features are necessary or sufficient, but all are indicative of the states when occurring together. We find a similar situation here. In this case, it is more plausible that all these philosophers are right in their denials, as opposed to their affirmations. First, the charge of irrationality is a strong and unusual one, so that, in contrast to other norms, rational requirements are relatively weak, in my view demanding only coherence or the avoidance of self-defeat. Second, when there is a dispute over which values are objective or which rational requirements real, it is less plausible to think that some people are value blind than to think that others are seeking to impose their values on them.

For those who like their arguments less broad and speculative, we may turn to the specific examples, beginning with the claim that we are required to be prudent or concerned for our own welfare and future. This claim is initially more plausible than the like claim about moral concerns, both because intuitively it seems more irrational to harm or neglect oneself than to harm or neglect others, and because the requirement of self-concern is often cited as a premise in the argument for a requirement of concern

[9] Stephen Darwall, *Welfare and Rational Care* (Princeton: Princeton University Press, 2002); *The Second-Person Standpoint* (Cambridge, MA: Harvard University Press, 2006).

[10] Roger Crisp, *Reasons and the Good* (Oxford: Clarendon Press, 2006).

for others. In my view the intuition of greater irrationality in self-neglect derives only from the fact that most people care more about themselves than about others, and not from the truth of the claim that this rational requirement of self-concern is real or objective. But let us proceed more slowly.

In fact, the question about self-concern is not one question. It does not admit of a single answer since it masks several relevant distinctions. First and foremost is the distinction between broad and narrow self-interest. Much of the plausibility of the claim that self-concern is rationally required rests on an equivocation between these two concepts. Then there is the double distinction between the future satisfaction of desires I have now, some of which will persist and others of which will not, and the satisfaction of desires that I know I will have in the future but do not now have. Finally, there is the distinction between pleasures and pains that I can have now or at a later time, assuming that I am concerned about these states now and will continue to be so.

A person's broad self-interest can be defined as the satisfaction of her informed and coherent desires, her rational concerns. In this sense of self-interest, what benefits my children contributes to my welfare as well, since I am concerned about their welfare. Their doing well makes my life go better, at least if I know of it, and what makes my life go better contributes to my welfare or broad self-interest. In this sense of self-interest, if an agent has any informed and coherent desires, then he is concerned about his welfare, since he desires the satisfaction of these desires and that satisfaction *is* his welfare. In this sense, if we all have desires and must have them as long as we are agents at all, we must be concerned about our self-interest. As argued earlier, we cannot be unmotivated to act on our own desires, since desiring is just being motivated. But this is a conceptual truth, hence trivial, not a requirement of rationality that one could fail to meet. Thus there is no point in claiming that we are rationally required to be concerned about our welfare in this sense, except to lend plausibility to a more controversial claim by equivocation.

There is, however, an interesting objection to equating personal welfare in the sense of broad self-interest with the satisfaction of rational desires, even when the subject knows of the satisfactions. The equation seems to imply that persons would be better off if they could transform their desires into the most easily satisfiable ones.[11] This would result in more rational desires being satisfied. Yet we do not consider people with shallow, easily satisfied desires better off. The television couch potato who desires nothing but to see the latest soaps may have all his desires satisfied, but he does not rank high on our list of good lives. It does not matter that we could not choose to transform our desires into his. The objection stands that if we could, we would not be better off. Of course, this judgment is made from our point of view with very different desires, so there is some question whether we are fit to judge the quality of life of those whose values are very different from our own. But let us accept the judgment and see what it implies for our notion of personal welfare from our perspective.

What it implies is that personal welfare in the sense of broad self-interest is not a function merely of what percentage of a person's desires are satisfied, but also of how deep those desires are. Deep concerns, we pointed out, connect to many others and provide reasons for them, so that the satisfaction of deep concerns entails the simultaneous satisfaction of many other desires and usually culminates the efforts involved in long-term projects. Such satisfaction is itself deeper. My desire to complete this book, for example, involves desires to fully work out my views on the topic, to advance my career, to meet intellectual challenges, to fulfil my commitment to granting agencies, and so on. It is not surprising that its fulfilment will contribute more to my welfare than would satisfying my desire for some chocolate ice cream. In fact such shallow and momentary satisfactions make vanishingly small contributions to personal welfare. Combined, they make life more pleasant, but that sort of pleasure is not what the vast majority of us are most concerned to achieve. It might be replied again that a person who did seek only such pleasures and succeeded in getting them would have to count as having a good life. But the point remains that such pleasures are repetitive and not cumulative in the way that the gradual satisfaction of a deep concern over time is, and that depth of satisfaction (not to be equated with pleasure) still counts more than percentage of desires satisfied.

So much for broad self-interest, at least until Chapter 5. While we are all concerned about our welfare in this sense, there is, as we have seen,

[11] The objection is raised by Richard Arneson, "Desire Formation and Human Good," in S. Olsaretti (ed.), *Preferences and Well-Being* (Cambridge: Cambridge University Press, 2006).

no objective rational requirement relating directly to it. The possibility of self-sacrifice requires a different notion of self-interest.[12] According to the broad concept, I cannot sacrifice my self-interest for that of my children, whom I care about, since their interest or welfare is part of mine. But there is certainly another narrower concept of self-interest according to which one can sacrifice one's own interest for that of others whom one cares about. In fact, as parents all know, one only learns the meaning of self-sacrifice when one has children.

According to the narrower concept, what is in one's interest makes essential reference to oneself, as one's children's welfare need not. Thus, if I spend part of my income (essential reference to me) on their education (no reference to me), I sacrifice part of my self-interest for their welfare. In this sense of self-interest, however, I may not be concerned about my own welfare, and I am not rationally required to be. The fact that something would seem to serve my narrow interest may give me no reason to pursue it. I may without rational fault have no desires for things that make essential reference to me. I might be content with personal hardships as long as they contribute to the welfare of others. In certain contexts my concern for my children or comrades, or for art or the revolution or God, may loom so large as to eliminate concern for myself without irrationality.

Such complete elimination would be highly unusual and perhaps contrary to biological instinct, but not necessarily irrational. As noted above, moral saints and heroes, if not misguided martyrs, who are perfectly willing to sacrifice themselves for the greater good or higher cause, caring nothing for their own welfare, need not be irrational. If they are not irrational although unconcerned for themselves, then they have no desire-independent reasons for narrow self-concern. Rational agents must be motivated at least somewhat by reasons they are aware of having. It follows that if agents are rational and not motivated by certain considerations of which they are aware, then those considerations are not reasons for them. Even more obviously, if rational agents can be unmotivated by their apparent narrow self-interest, by any seeming goods that make essential reference to them, then there is

[12] See Mark Overvold, "Self-Interest and the Concept of Self-sacrifice," *Canadian Journal of Philosophy*, 10 (1980): 105–18.

no rational requirement to be so motivated, and so no desire-independent reasons to be so motivated.

Considering health more narrowly, it is once more true that health is required for the satisfaction of many desires other than the desire for health itself. A rational agent is therefore required to be concerned about her health if she has any of these other desires, which she very likely will. But concern for one's health can also oppose other concerns in various contexts, and there is no priority required of a rational agent. Concern for a certain achievement that can be accomplished only at high risk to one's health may be so dominant as to eliminate altogether concern for health without loss of rationality. We have seen that opposing reasons can not only override, but cancel, reasons that might otherwise exist for an agent.

Richard Tucker was told by his doctors that continuing to sing opera imposed a very high risk of death by heart attack. Knowing that, he continued to perform and eventually did suffer a fatal heart attack during a performance. In placing his art so far above his health, the great tenor was certainly unusual, but who are we to condemn him as irrational? Opera and his contribution to it were the central values in his life, and we might surmise that something similar is true of most great artists, in fact of most people who make spectacular contributions in any field of human endeavor. A charge of irrationality from us mere mortals would smack only of envy. But perhaps Richard Tucker escapes that charge because he was still partly motivated by considerations of health, although more motivated to continue singing. Perhaps not. Perhaps, having made his decision, he felt no further conflict at all. Of course, we do not know, but this description, in which his concern for his health was cancelled and not simply overridden, is not implausible.

Can it then be rational for a person to cut off his finger without prospective compensating benefit simply because he does not care about having the finger? Would not we consider that person irrational, and does not this show that concern for one's own welfare is rationally required? The vast majority of people are concerned about their own health and comfort and have a strong aversion to pain and disfigurement. Thus the person who would cut off his finger would certainly be highly abnormal as well as self-destructive (in the ordinary sense, which is not the same as self-defeating). Abnormality is often confused with irrationality. But considering his behavior irrational is not a simple confusion of abnormality with irrationality. The odds are enormous that the person would also be acting irrationally in cutting off his finger. This is because it is difficult to imagine that there would not arise some situation in which the satisfaction of some desire or avoidance of some undesired consequence would be facilitated by having the finger. Even if the person does not care about having his finger, coherence or the avoidance of self-defeat requires that he does care about it if there are other such desires or concerns, and so his action would almost surely reveal an incoherence in his motivations amounting to irrationality.

Even accepting the serious risk of frustrating one's other desires without any compensating consideration is irrational for the same reason. Such a risk seems impossible to deny in this case. And, of course, if there is no compensating benefit to the action, as the example posits, then there is no reason in favor of the action, so that it would be at best arational. But in the highly unusual situation in which a person has no concerns that relate to or require his health or physical well-being, the example fails to demonstrate a rational requirement to be so concerned. Our initial reaction to the example is based on our feelings. We may be biologically wired to find the very thought of physical maiming repulsive, but it is not irrational to lack a feeling that it is natural to have. To think that lack of feeling is irrational *is* to confuse abnormality with irrationality. Once more the only clear conception we have of irrationality as a failure of practical reason, the only clear generalization from the paradigm cases, is that of self-defeat or incoherence.

The conclusion stands that we are all concerned about our broad self-interest as long as we have any rational desires, but need not be concerned about our narrow self-interest,[13] although virtually all of us are concerned for that too. What about concern for our own futures? In its most obvious sense, this question is the same as the question about broad self-interest. All desires must be satisfied in the future. As noted earlier, we desire what we do not yet have. Desires reflect a lack. Thus, in so far as we have any desires and hence desire their future satisfaction, we are concerned

---

[13] It is really seeming narrow self-interest to which I am referring here, since if one has no concern for goods that refer to oneself, one has no narrow self-interest.

about our own futures. Having any desires is having a concern for the future in which they could be fulfiled. And having any reasons for having desires is having reasons to be concerned about the future. Once more these are conceptual truths and not rational requirements that we could fail to meet.

Related questions do not admit of such trivial answers. Should I continue to be motivated by desires I now have that cannot be satisfied until the relatively distant future, when I cannot confidently or reliably predict that I will continue to have the desires then? Conversely, must I be concerned about satisfying desires that I do not now have but can predict that I will have in the future? These questions, although perhaps philosophically more interesting, are somewhat arcane. I cannot think of a desire that I currently have that fits in the first category. Perhaps teenagers with desires for future careers should know that these desires are very likely to change before careers will be chosen and begun. But since they do not choose which desires to have, they could not simply choose not to have those they can predict not to persist until they might be fulfiled. If they do have such desires that they know will change, there will not be any reasons to take steps now to facilitate their future satisfaction. If agents are simply uncertain whether present desires will continue to exist, then it seems rational to discount the expected payoff by the degree of uncertainty, and to discount present reasons accordingly. An exception occurs when they can predict that their future lack of desire will be irrational, a lack of will. A student who knows she will not want to study before a future test might reasonably take steps now to make it more probable that she nevertheless will study.

The second question is yet more relevant to people who recognize themselves to be imprudent, to have a devil-may-care live-for-the-moment attitude that they might wish to question in a rare reflective mood. I, like most, am not one of those people. I am presently concerned about my future health and well-being. But suppose I presently had no concern for my health ten years from now, although I do care about my present health, and also know that I will be concerned for my health at that future time. Is my present lack of concern and consequent acting in ways that might jeopardize my future health irrational? Most would agree that it is, and externalists once more claim that its irrationality implies a desire-independent, object-generated reason. It is because health and other objects have the same value whenever we consider them that they provide the same reasons at different times. Because the same objects provide the same values and reasons in the future as they do now, we must be equally concerned about their future instantiations as we are about their present ones. That is why, externalists claim, our concerns must be temporally indifferent or constant if we are rational.

There are two problems with this argument. First, there is data for which it does not account. If objects present the same value through time in which they remain unchanged, and if our concern for them is based on and must reflect such constant value, then we must always value them to the same degree. But there is nothing irrational in valuing the same objects more or less at different times. Our desires change as we mature, and if the previous sentence is true, it indicates again that the values various objects have for us result from and are therefore a function of these changing desires instead of being the rational bases for them. One might claim that as we mature, our values tend to become more in line with objective values, and that is why they can rationally change. But some things I used to value doing, such as playing baseball, I no longer do, although I do not think the value of baseball itself has changed.

Second, the internalist can offer an explanation for the rational require-ment to be concerned about your future health, if you are concerned about your health now. Her explanation will in fact be similar to the externalist's, except focused on the self and not on the object. The externalist claims that we ought to value the same object in the same way in the future as we do now precisely because it is the same object with the same value persisting through time. The internalist can reply that we ought to be concerned about a future object, if we are concerned about that object now and predict that we will continue to be concerned about it, because we will be the same selves in the future with the same concerns that we have now. The defeat of these future concerns will therefore be self-defeat, defeat of ourselves or our values, and therefore irrational. My future pain, for example, will be present pain to me when its time comes. If I am continuously concerned to avoid pain but take no steps now to avoid future pain, then my concern to avoid pain will be defeated. Concerns, like selves, persist through time, and they can be defeated at any time during which they exist. The idea of a present desire is itself an abstraction from desires that always extend in time to some extent.

The future value of an object is relevant according to the externalist because the same object persists into the future. But the same is true of the self and its concerns. This reply requires a liberal notion of personal identity according to which the same self does persist through time, but this is the common sense and, I believe philosophically defensible, notion.[14] Since I will be the same self in the future as I am now, being concerned only for my present self would be like being concerned for my left side but not for my right side without having any reason for distinguishing these spatial parts of myself. In both cases there would result literal self-defeat. Just as my bodily self has two sides, is extended in space, so it is extended in time, as are its concerns. The rational requirement to be concerned for my future self, and hence for my future self's desires that continue my present desires, is part of the demand for coherence with those present and persisting desires.

The case just described is that in which I care for my health now but not for my future health, although I can predict that I will care for it then. A different case is that in which I can predict a future desire although I have no similar desire now. The usual example is the prediction that I will become more conservative in my views as I get older (already proven false in my case). If this is simply a prediction based on typical concerns of older people, then I see no rational demand to prepare now for the satisfaction of the predicted future desire, especially if it is opposed by a present desire. If I am now a liberal, I am certainly not rationally required to act now for the future ascendancy of conservatives. The demand for coherence extends into the future and requires concern for future desires, but it is a demand for coherence with one's present motivational set.

A final and much discussed issue in regard to prudence is the irrationality of choosing a lesser satisfaction now over a greater one later (discounting for the probability of the latter's not occurring), or avoiding a lesser pain now when that will lead to a greater pain later. For the externalist, the fact of irrationality here either is a brute normative fact or is once more based on the objective value of the pleasures and pains. But for us it is either an instantiation of weakness of will or failure to act on one's strongest reasons once they have been prioritized. I have described weakness of will as the overwhelming of an evaluative judgment expressing reasons

---

[14] For my defense of it, see "Reasons and Personal Identity," *Inquiry*, 28 (1985): 373–98.

that reflect deeper concerns by a temporary urge. Its irrationality derives from the rational requirement to do what is overall best (in terms of broad self-interest) at a given time. To prioritize our reasons or values and then sacrifice the higher to the lower is to be incoherent. It is to defeat one's own preference. But once more there is no line to be drawn between the requirement as it applies at a given time and over time. Once more the same self is extended in time, as are temptations and greater satisfactions or the avoidance of greater frustrations. The success of one's ongoing projects or extended concerns is not momentary, and in general, the more extended the project or concern, the greater the satisfaction at its success. The point is again that the rational requirement is one of coherence among existing motivational states, future ones, and actions or choices.

But, the externalist will reply a final time, suppose I simply now prefer to avoid the lesser pain, knowing that this will result in a greater pain later. Can the internalist say that this present preference is irrational? How, if irrationality is always a matter of incoherence with present preferences or motivations? The answer is that acting on the stated preference is irrational in the same way that acting on persisting intransitive preferences is irrational in always leading to the frustration of a stronger desire by satisfying a weaker one. If asked whether I prefer a greater pain or a lesser one *tout court*, we can assume that I will say that I prefer the lesser one. If I do not prefer lesser pains to greater ones, then my action on my initial preference is not clearly irrational (I will have more to say about the disvalue of pain in the next chapter). Furthermore, rational desires must be informed, and if I vividly picture to myself what suffering the greater pain later will be like, I will not prefer to avoid the lesser one. If I do act to avoid the lesser pain now, that action will result only from a non-rational emotional reaction of fear, similar to a temporary urge in typical cases of weak will. It will be inconsistent with my standing preference for lesser pains over greater ones. I will defeat my more stable preference by acting from a temporary non-rational state, demonstrating simply another form of weakness of will, an internal incoherence.

To sum up in three sentences, the demands of prudence as usually stated are either internal demands or bogus. As internal demands, they are all a matter of avoiding self-defeat. None has to be interpreted as either brutely normative or object based.

III. Moral Motivation

"Always go to other people's funerals; otherwise they won't go
to yours."

A major motivation for reason externalism, the view that agents have reasons
independently of their existing motivations, is moral judgment internalism,
the view that agents must be motivated by the moral judgments they make.
According to this sort of view, to judge that an action is right is to hold that
all agents have a moral reason to do it, and to judge that an action is wrong
is to hold that all agents have a moral reason not to do it. Since rational
agents must be motivated by the reasons they have, these judgments must
motivate rational agents whatever their pre-existing desires.

Expressivism is the view that moral judgments do not state facts or
ascribe real properties of rightness and wrongness to acts, but instead
express feelings of approval or disapproval, positive or negative attitudes
toward the acts.[15] This view, although a form of judgment internalism, is
not opposed to reason internalism, since those attitudes themselves involve
motivations to follow the judgments, motivations that exist at the time of
the judgments and are expressed by them. Expressivism is a form of both
reason and judgment internalism, if it holds that there are moral reasons for
actions. This meta-ethical theory is therefore compatible with the theory of
practical reasons defended here. But it seems to be falsified by the obvious
empirical fact that some evil people are unmotivated by their judgments
of moral right and wrong. If they understand and utilize the ordinary
meanings of moral terms in their judgments, then at least the judgments in
question are not expressions of their attitudes. (More on this below.)

The thesis that interests us here is the claim that rational agents must
be motivated by moral considerations or judgments, and that this rational
requirement holds independently of their prior motivations. The second
clause is the thesis of reason externalism, while the first is a form of

---

[15] A more recent and sophisticated version holds that such judgments do not express attitudes directly
toward actions, but express acceptance of norms that permit or prohibit the actions. See Allan Gibbard,
Wise Choices; Apt Feelings (Cambridge, MA: Harvard University Press, 1990). This version is yet more
recently attacked in Jesse Prinz, *The Emotional Construction of Morals* (Oxford: Oxford University Press,
2007) and Shaun Nichols, *Sentimental Rules* (Oxford: Oxford University Press, 2004).

judgment internalism. The entire thesis expresses a view that we would like to be true, at least true of others. Since we want them to accept moral facts as constraints on their behavior toward us, we want these facts to be independent of their existing motivations but to require motivation of them. Philosophers since Plato have spilled seas of ink trying to justify in very different ways this thesis that we would like to be true. According to it, if evil people are unmotivated by their moral judgments, they are irrational, an implication implausible on the face of it. The desire that the thesis nevertheless be true is a main motivation for the more general thesis that there must be desire independent reasons that require motivation from us, that motivate us if we are rational, as we all like to think we are. Hence reason externalism.

Let us more closely consider first the claim that explicit judgments of moral rightness and wrongness are motivating for rational agents. Michael Smith is one who has recently argued for this view.[16] He holds that to believe that some action is right is to believe that there is a normative moral reason to do it. A reason for him is anything that would motivate a fully rational agent. If a reason is a consideration that would motivate one's fully rational self, then one must, if one is rational, be motivated by that consideration. The main problem with this argument from my point of view is that it ignores the distinction emphasized earlier between reasons there are and reasons agents have. Although all reasons there are motivate some agents, particular agents are motivated only by reasons they have. On the reason internalist view, agents are motivated by moral reasons if they are rational and morally-minded. Smith simply omits the last condition without giving us a reason in this argument for its omission. To believe that an action is right is indeed to believe that there is a moral reason to do it, but that gives an agent a reason only if she is morally-minded. Smith needs to give us a further argument why rational agents must be morally-minded. In fact he does.

His further argument as to why rational agents must be motivated by their explicit judgments of rightness and wrongness is that only such intrinsic motivational force explains why a rational and virtuous person's motivations track changes in his moral judgments.[17] Without such force to his judgments, he might continue to care more about properties he

---

[16] Michael Smith, *The Moral Problem* (Oxford: Blackwell, 1994), pp. 180–7.   [17] Ibid. 71–6.

previously thought to be right making even after changing his moral judgments that refer to them. If, for example, he previously thought the Iraq war right but now considers it wrong, he might continue to favor the war if not motivated directly by his moral judgment. Or, without such force, if his motives did track his moral judgments, this could only be because of a fetishistic *de dicto* desire to do what is moral, in Bernard Williams' famous phrase, "one thought too many."

But consider again the more famous fictional example of Huckleberry Finn. As described earlier, Huck sincerely believes that morality strictly requires that all stolen or missing property be returned to its rightful owner. He does not simply believe that what local folks call morality requires this: he believes morality requires this. He also believes that his friend Jim, the runaway slave, is rightfully owned and that he, Huck, therefore has a moral obligation to return Jim to his owner. But having made this sincere moral judgment, Huck decides to wash his hands entirely of moral demands, to defy his own moral judgment in favor of his friendship. Having borrowed his moral judgments from suspect sources, he justifiably fails to be moved by them even though he accepts their status as expressing moral requirements. And having renounced morality, it is not the case that his desire to help Jim escape overrides his motivation to follow his moral judgment: he rightly reports no remaining motivation to do what he believes morality requires.

If Huck is rational, then a rational agent need not be motivated by her explicit moral judgments. But several interpreters, including some philosophers, interpret Huck as being irrational in his attitude, a victim of weak will. Weakness of will, we have seen, is a paradigm form of irrationality. If it consists simply in failure to act on one's judgment of what one ought to do, then it may well appear that Huck is irrational in failing to act on his moral judgment. Jonathan Bennett sees Huck as being irrational in being unable to resist acting on his feeling of sympathy for Jim, feelings themselves being irrational according to Bennett (better to have said "arational").[18] Bennett sees Huck as irrational because a bare feeling propels him to act against his considered judgment and moral principles, however corrupt those principles may be. Huck believes he should act on

[18] Jonathan Bennett, "The Conscience of Huckleberry Finn," *Philosophy*, 49 (1974): 123–134, p. 126.

those principles but finds himself incapable of doing so, and he blames himself for this emotional incapacity. Thus he appears to demonstrate the classic symptoms of irrational weakness of will.[19]

But this verdict rests on simplistic views of emotions and weak will. Weakness of will is not best characterized as failure to do what one explicitly believes one ought to do, but as failure to act on the strongest reasons of which one is in any sense aware. And sympathy is not a bare feeling. I earlier offered a cluster concept analysis of emotions according to which especially complex intentional emotions (directed at objects or persons) contain an implicit cognitive or judgmental aspect. I pointed out that while this implicit judgment does not typically arise from or alter in response to reasons in the way that conscious judgments or beliefs do, it may reflect such reasons when the emotions are fitting or appropriate reactions to their objects. Huck's guiding emotion is sympathy for his friend Jim. Sympathy contains the implicit judgment that a person needs help in light of his situation. In Huck's case this emotion is entirely fitting and reflects the reasons to help Jim escape from slavery. In reflecting such reasons this is a moral emotion, although Huck does not recognize it as such because of his very limited view of what morality requires. Indeed, it is clear that Huck's trip on the river constitutes and in the novel symbolizes a moral transformation, and that this transformation is prompted by his developing emotional attachment to Jim.

The judgment implicit in Huck's sympathy reflects a deeper concern than his concern for morality as he conceives it. Hence Huck's reason for helping Jim is stronger than his reason for turning Jim in and returning him to slavery. Although Huck does not engage in moral deliberation, does not consciously weigh the moral reasons on both sides, he does act on his strongest reasons deriving from his friendship and his implicit sense of justice as reflected in his sympathetic feeling. I have noted several times that an agent can have reasons of which she is not consciously aware and be motivated by or act on such reasons without conceiving of them as such. This is the case with Huck Finn. Because he in fact acts on his strongest reasons, he is not weak willed. (Indeed, it takes strong will to risk his own freedom by continuing to hide Jim.) If he is not weak willed, then he is not

---

[19] Other philosophers who see Huck as weak willed are Nomy Arpaly and Timothy Schroeder, "Praise, Blame and the Whole Self," *Philosophical Studies*, 93 (1999): 161–88.

irrational, since this is the only form of irrationality of which a misguided interpreter would accuse him.

Mark Twain is neither approving of irrationality here nor condemning Huck for being irrational. Huck's motives do not track his judgments of wrongness, even though he is rational and virtuous. Thus a rational agent need not be motivated by his explicit moral judgments. In this sense Huck is not morally motivated. In another sense he is, since his motives do track his more concrete judgments of what is harmful to his friend and what is owed to him as a friend. In this last trait he is not unusual. As I will argue below, most people's motives generally track their judgments of rightness and wrongness only because these judgments themselves generally track their beliefs about less abstract right and wrong making properties. It is these attitudes toward the more concrete properties that are more directly connected to the motives of morally-minded people, somewhat independently, as we see in Huck's case, of their explicit moral judgments.

A moral judgment internalist might respond to the example by claiming that it is relevant that Huck is mistaken in what he takes to be his moral obligation. I argued earlier that a rational person need not be motivated by false beliefs about reasons. Huck may be unmotivated by the moral judgment that he mistakenly believes because, it might be claimed, he implicitly senses the error. This interpretation does not quite fit with Huck's wholesale dismissal of moral obligations based on his false judgment regarding this obligation to respect property. He fully trusts this judgment as representative of morality in general, and so the claim that he implicitly senses an error is *ad hoc* at best. It is true that Huck implicitly recognizes opposing moral reasons to help Jim in his sympathetic emotion, but he does not recognize these as moral reasons. Instead, he fully trusts his judgment that hiding Jim is wrong, fully believes that this is what morality requires. And he is not irrational for being generally unmotivated by his judgments of wrongness, based on his generalization from this judgment. An inference based on a false belief is not thereby irrational.

But error might be claimed to be crucial to the example in a different way that still disqualifies it from refuting the rational requirement of moral motivation. If an agent only falsely believes that she has a reason R to do something, then R is not a reason to do it. And if R is not a reason, then there is no rational requirement to be moved by it. Hence Huck is not rationally required to be moved by his false moral judgment, but this does not show that rational agents can fail to be moved by judgments that reflect genuine moral reasons. It might be claimed along these lines that when Huck seems to make moral judgments, he is really only making inverted commas judgments and for that reason need not be motivated by them. In reply, we might point out first that Huck not only fails to be moved by his judgment of what he ought to do with Jim; he fails to be moved by any explicit judgments of rightness and wrongness *per se*, many of which will be correct. More relevant is that we all believe that our moral judgments are correct (from the moral point of view) when we sincerely make them. We cannot be rationally required to be motivated only by our actually correct judgments, when we do not know that our incorrect judgments are incorrect.

This claim might seem to be incompatible with my earlier claims that rational agents need not be motivated by false beliefs about reasons but must be moved by reasons they have of which they are aware. But the claims are not contradictory if rational agents are motivated not by their judgments or beliefs as such, but by their awareness of genuine reasons that some of these judgments reflect.

Either we must be motivated by all our sincere moral judgments, or there is no such rational requirement at all. A requirement of rationality must be able to be followed, and it must be used to guide rational agents. We cannot be guided by a requirement to obey only our correct moral judgments. Rational agents need not be motivated by false beliefs about reasons (example of the girl who believes that everything her father wants gives her a reason). But neither can agents be required to be motivated only by true beliefs or judgments. Instead, they must be motivated by their reasons of which they are aware, their subjective reasons as defined earlier, although they are rationally permitted to be motivated by false beliefs about reasons as well.

Thus, it does not seem to matter to the connection between rationality and motivation that Huck is mistaken in his initial judgment. But there is one final reply to the example that could be offered by the moral judgment internalist. This is their standard reply to lack of motivation: that agents who are not moved by their moral judgments do not make genuine moral assertions but only judge in an inverted commas sense. Huckleberry Finn's judgments simply mimic those of his corrupt society, they will point out. In simply mouthing his society's moral principles, he is quoting their morality without sincerely adopting it as his own. Hence he is not making genuine moral assertions, and that is why he is not, and need not be, motivated by them.

But this appeal to pseudo-moral judgments is an *ad hoc* invention of the defenders of moral judgment internalism. The only evidence possible for their claim that certain judgments of wrongness are not genuine is the failure to be motivated by them. Citing this as evidence is, of course, circular or question-begging. Huck Finn's explicit moral assertions are borrowed from his society and his religious education, but then so are the moral judgments of most people. That the judgments derive from these sources does not begin to show that they are not ordinary or sincere. These are the only moral beliefs that Huck knows as such, and he is entirely sincere in taking them to be expressions of what morality requires.

That Huck's mistake in moral judgment is irrelevant to his lack of motivation is clear also from another comparison. Consider a person who decides to help a friend, when she correctly judges that morality requires a greater impartiality, a deference to the conflicting interests of others. This person seems no more irrational than Huck for failing to be motivated by the moral requirement. It is by hypothesis wrong in such a case to place friendship over conflicting interests of others, but how can this be seen as a failure of reason? In this second example, however, it will be replied that it is a matter of one motivation overriding another, if the person is rational. It can still be claimed that she will be somewhat motivated by her judgment that what she is doing is wrong. We can believe that moral judgments motivate rational agents even if they do not always override or determine their conduct. Of course, this claim is substantially weaker than the claim that moral requirements always override all other demands for rational agents, and weaker also than the belief that moral judgments are intrinsically motivating for all who sincerely make them.

One might think that if a rational person is morally motivated at all, then this motivation must override considerations of personal or partial interests, since a moral calculation, a determination of what morality requires, will already take into account both self-interest and the interests of all those affected by the person's actions. But it matters how all the competing interests are taken into account, how they are weighed against each other. Moral reasons are a particular class of reasons that emerge from the adoption of an impartial point of view that places the interests of all people on the same scale. Society seeks to impose the constraints on behavior that these reasons reflect in order to reduce or resolve conflict and promote cooperation. If these constraints are to be successful, many people must accept them as providing generally overriding reasons. But, while common morality allows a degree of partiality toward family and friends on the ground that all tend to benefit from such partial relationships, it demands a degree of impartiality that an agent may not be willing to grant fully as a guide to his personal conduct. Thus the demands of morality may be discounted in relation to other concerns in accordance with the importance assigned to them in a person's life.

Not only narrow self-interest, but also concern for particular other people or role-oriented obligations can oppose the demands of impartial morality, as we saw in the case of a person giving her friend more than his moral due. While common morality allows some favoritism of friends, and even requires some forms of partiality toward or selective responsibility for others, it also limits the amount of favoritism allowed, requiring also respect for the moral rights of all. If moral requirements reduce to social conventions for reducing conflict and promoting cooperation, as suggested above, they are unlikely to be at the base of people's life plans. But first, moral demands can be claimed to be more than that: moral reasons, for example, can be claimed to reflect recognition of the equality of all persons, and moral concerns can be seen to be not allegiance to convention, but an outgrowth of natural altruistic motivations. And second, moral considerations can motivate without always overriding. We still must determine whether a rational person must be motivated by moral demands at all.

Let us focus on the weaker claim that moral requirements are somewhat motivating for all rational agents. We may focus the issue further by making explicit what was implied above: that judgments of rightness and wrongness are typically verdicts on the balance of more concrete morally relevant considerations or obligations—not to cause or to alleviate suffering or threats to the autonomy of others—and it is such considerations that typically underlie the motivating force of the more abstract judgments. Abstract or derivative reasons inherit their normative force from the more concrete reasons that ground them, and the former add nothing additional to the latter. Rightness and wrongness are derivative in this way. When an act is wrong because harmful, coercive, deceptive, threatening, or risky, its wrongness reduces entirely to one or more of these other properties. If an act is wrong because harmful, then its being harmful is the reason one ought not to do it. To think that its wrongness counts or should motivate over and above recognition of these other properties is to count the same considerations twice.

If judgments of rightness and wrongness ascribe value properties that are objective or reasons that require motivation of all agents, then other more concrete properties that underlie these judgments must include or comprise objective values as well. Causing undeserved pain, for example, must have objective negative value. We will assess the plausibility of such claims in the next chapter. Here we can equate being morally-minded with having impartial other-regarding concerns. To focus our question, then, we may ask whether rational agents must care about the welfare or suffering or freedom of others, whether it is irrational not to care. Must rational agents be impartially concerned about the welfare and freedom of all others? Moral agents are moved directly by the considerations that underlie their judgments of rightness and wrongness, and we are asking whether rational agents must be moral agents, must have moral concerns, must be sympathetic to the plights of strangers, for example.

In this sense, as noted, Huckleberry Finn appears to be morally motivated, although not by his explicit judgments of rightness and wrongness. He simply fails to see the connection between the more concrete and more abstract judgments. In this he is mistaken but not irrational. His moral motivation is expressed in his emotion of sympathy for Jim. If most moral motivation is expressed in such moral emotions as sympathy, empathy, anger, and disgust (at those who violate moral norms), then, since emotions seem not to be rationally required even when they are appropriate and reflective of reasons, this sort of moral motivation is not rationally required. When fear is appropriate in the face of danger, we nevertheless do not typically blame or hold the person to be irrational who faces the danger fearlessly. We are more likely to praise her unusual courage (although we also sometimes condemn fearless actions as rash or unnecessarily risky). Likewise, when anger at a slight would be fitting, we do not condemn as irrational the person who remains calm or forgiving; and when pride would be warranted, it is not irrational to remain modest or even self-effacing. Thus, in general, emotions seem not to be rationally required even when they would be fitting or appropriate, even when there appear to be reasons to feel fear, anger, or pride.

Huck Finn's sympathy is entirely appropriate and reflects the genuine reasons to help Jim escape his plight. Might there be something about moral emotions, and specifically about the concern for others expressed in this emotion of sympathy, that makes them rationally required when other emotions are not? Put another way, is it irrational to lack this emotion, when it might be not only rationally permitted, but praiseworthy, to lack others? Are all rational people sensitive to the suffering of others? I take it that one cannot be morally motivated and yet be completely indifferent to the suffering of others; or, if one could be so indifferent and yet morally motivated, this would be Williams' and Smith's strange *de dicto* fetishistic motivation. Is sensitivity to suffering then a requirement of reason, or is this claim a confusion, as it seems to be, between two different sorts of capacities, rational and affective?

Clearly we cannot address all or even all recent arguments for a rational requirement to be morally motivated. We can, however, begin with a simple argument that initially supports the claim of a rational requirement to be moved by the welfare or suffering of others. (1) There are moral reasons amounting to obligations not to harm and to alleviate suffering. (2) We cannot escape our moral obligations by being unconcerned to fulfil them. (3) Hence, we cannot escape having these reasons. (4) Rational agents are motivated by the reasons they have of which they are aware. (5) Thus, rational agents must be motivated by moral reasons not to harm and to alleviate suffering.

The focus of this argument is on the non-optional nature of our obligations and the fact that moral obligations reflect strong moral reasons. It seems initially plausible that when we have an obligation to do something, we have a reason to do it. The argument, however, appears to prove too much. For the same could be said of aesthetic, religious, or legal obligations. I have an aesthetic obligation not to wear mauve pants with a chartreuse shirt, a religious obligation not to work on a holy day, and a legal obligation not to drive over twenty-five miles per hour in my neighborhood. In the case of the aesthetic requirement, we can refer interchangeably to an aesthetic obligation or an aesthetic reason. In fact, the latter sounds more natural. But the proper reference is to a reason there is, not necessarily to a reason I have.

It seems clear that if I am completely unconcerned about aesthetic matters, specifically about the colors of my clothes, and also unconcerned about offending aesthetically-minded or color sensitive people by my manner of dress and about the possible effects of such offense, I lack reasons to forgo the clashing combination. I lack these reasons while understanding perfectly well what aesthetics requires, which color combinations clash for example, if I do not care what aesthetics requires. Of course, if I did intentionally avoid wearing that combination, that would show that I was concerned in one of these ways and that I had a reason for not dressing that way. But intuitively, if I do not care at all what I wear, I do not seem irrational for wearing mauve with chartreuse. Ignoring reasons that one has and is aware of, when there are no conflicting overriding reasons, *is* irrational. Therefore, if I am not irrational in ignoring aesthetic requirements or obligations, these obligations give me no reasons to fulfil them (although they reflect reasons there are).

The transition from premise 2 to 3 in the above argument can therefore be dismissed in the domain of aesthetics. It again ignores the distinction between reasons there are and reasons we have. We are irrational only in ignoring the latter. The internalist claim that agents' reasons must connect to their motivations is supported by our intuition that it is not irrational, although contrary to aesthetic requirements, to wear clashing colors. There are reasons whenever some people are motivated by them, but agents have reasons only when they connect to their motivations, at least, so far as we have now established, for some classes of reasons, including aesthetic reasons. Such reasons require motivations only when they connect to an agent's deeper or broader concerns. I have reasons not to dress in certain ways if I care about my appearance. But I can also have such reasons if I care about what others think of me. I would then be irrational not to care about my appearance. But if I have no direct concerns about my appearance and no other concerns that require me on grounds of coherence to care about my appearance, then I have no reasons to restrict my choice of what I wear.

As opposed to dismissing the transition from 2 to 3 in a generalized version of the above argument, we could hold premise 2 to be false by holding that accepting aesthetic obligations is optional. I prefer to attack the move from 2 to 3 in light of the parallel to be drawn to other obligations and reasons. In the case of religious obligations, some adherents would claim that having both obligations and reasons is not optional, as it is in aesthetics. If being born to Jewish parents makes one Jewish, then, as a Jew I have religious obligations not to eat pork or ride on Saturdays. But

I would argue that, since I am not religiously-minded, having no religious concerns, I have no reason not to eat pork or ride to football games. I am not irrational in doing so or in totally lacking the motivation to resist doing so. Again, if I did intentionally resist, then I would have been motivated to resist and I would have had reason to resist, but that does not show that I now have such reason, being unmotivated to do so. Once more the transition from premise 2 to 3 in the religious domain is not sound, although it is somewhat more contentious that premise 2 is false, that I have no obligations in this domain.

The defender of a rational requirement to be morally motivated might accept that a fully generalized version of the above argument cannot license premise 2 or the transition from 2 to 3, specifically in the domains of aesthetics and religion, but might draw the line at legal obligations and reasons, maintaining that these are more analogous to moral obligations and reasons. Here it may seem clearer that legal obligations and the reasons they provide are not optional. Clearly premise 2 as applied to law is true: legal obligations are not optional. Just by being a citizen, which I am by being born in a particular country, the legal requirements of that country, including local laws where I live, apply to me. And I will certainly not be absolved of my legal obligations by declaring sincerely that I am totally unconcerned to fulfil them. I will be held legally responsible and punished for my transgressions if I am caught. I am justifiably held legally responsible for my actions only if I have legal obligations. And I am not excused from responsibility by indicating a lack of concern.

In regard to the transition to premise 2 to 3, if I am obligated to obey the law, do I not therefore have a reason to obey it? Certainly I have prudential reasons, since I am threatened with sanctions or punishment for disobeying, which I am concerned to avoid. But it is not so clear, if I am totally unconcerned about suffering any sanctions, if this lack of concern is not itself irrational for failing to reflect my other concerns (such as for freedom or for keeping my money), and if I have no moral obligation or concern to obey the law, that I still have reason to obey.[20] In fact, no one intuitively would think me irrational for driving over twenty-five miles per hour, even if I have no particular reason to do so and it is against

[20] I have argued elsewhere that we have no moral obligation to obey the law as such. See *The Moral Foundations of Professional Ethics* (Totowa, NJ: Rowman & Littlefield, 1980), ch. 2.

the law in my neighborhood. In this case it seems that I have a legal obligation but no reason to obey, if I have no relevant concerns. If I did have a reason to obey, but disobeyed without any reason to do that, then I would be irrational. But it seems I am not. So it seems I have no reason to obey. The only differences between my country's and my religion's laws in this regard are the sanctions attached to the former, the concern that nearly all of us have to avoid those sanctions, and the fact that people may feel greater allegiance to the one set of laws or to the ideals they embody than to the other set. But my reasons still seem to depend on my allegiances and concerns, even though my obligations do not. Thus, obligations more generally do not always give reasons to the agents to whom they apply.

According to many of those who are aesthetically-, religiously-, or legally-minded, I cannot escape any of these obligations by not caring about them. But we have seen that being unconcerned myself in any of these domains makes it doubtful that I have reasons to fulfil these obligations. I do not appear irrational for failing to do so. The moral rationalist must therefore argue that there is something special about morality that licenses the transition from premise 2 to 3 above. It might seem that we always have moral reasons to do what is right, but then it equally seems that we always have legal reasons to obey the law. I have claimed that while in general there are always F (aesthetic, religious, legal . . .) reasons to do what F requires, we only *have* such reasons if we are F-minded. There may nevertheless seem to be a relevant difference between the legal and moral domains in this respect, in that the legal obligations we have are a matter of institutional or historical fact. To derive normative reasons from such facts alone violates Hume's stricture against "deriving an *ought* from an *is*." But our moral obligations, by contrast, seem to depend in some sense on our endorsements of them. And, it might be claimed, we would not endorse the moral obligations that we do endorse in our moral judgments unless we were somewhat motivated to accept them.

But the collective or plural subject is significant in the last sentence, and it does not automatically translate to the singular or personal. We collectively endorse moral restraints because social living requires that most people accept them. Even if these restraints are not simply conventional, my sincere moral judgments that reflect and seek to impose them need not express my willing acceptance of them as guides to my own behavior. Even if there are objective moral facts to which these judgments refer, they need not refer to reasons that all people must have simply in virtue of making the judgments. As pointed out above, they refer instead to a limited class of reasons that exist from a special impartial perspective that we are not forced to adopt as our own.

When I make a moral judgment, I state what ought to be done from a moral—that is, impartial—perspective. But once more we need a further argument why a rational agent must always adopt this impartial perspective that allows partiality only if all tend to benefit from it. It is true, as will be emphasized in further arguments below, that from an objective point of view I am only one person among all other equals. But it is also true that this is not the natural personal standpoint. From that standpoint, the interests of my family and friends, not to mention myself, are of far greater concern than the interests of strangers, greater than even common morality, not to mention abstract moral theory, allows. In morally judging, I may typically recommend impartial moral reasons to others or endorse them myself, but my judging does not entail such personal endorsement or acceptance. And even if I do endorse them as promoting social ends, I need not accept them as constant guides to my conduct.

John Searle, who is not averse to deriving an occasional *ought* from an *is*, has sought to reinforce an argument like that which began this section by adding to it the notion of commitment and its connection to moral reasons.[21] He argues that we commit ourselves in various ways through our actions and that we then have reasons amounting to moral obligations to fulfil those commitments. Once we have committed ourselves, we have reasons to make good on those commitments whether or not we desire to do so. These reasons, a subclass of moral reasons, are then independent of our pre-existing desires or concerns, but they require motivation of us if we are rational. According to Searle, if I order a beer in a bar, I am committed and so have a reason to pay for it. Once I drink it, it seems clear that I have a reason to pay for it, having implicitly agreed to do so. This reason exists independently of my desire to pay, but it requires that I be moved to do so. Since it amounts to a moral obligation, having acted as I did, I must be motivated by this moral consideration. Thus, at least some moral considerations require motivation of rational agents.

---

[21] John Searle, *Rationality in Action* (Cambridge, MA: MIT Press, 2001), ch. 6.

Do all rational agents, then, have such moral reasons? There is no question that normally morally motivated people who enter into such transactions have both prudential and moral reasons to live up to their implicit contracts or agreements. They are already motivated to fulfil their moral commitments, having both the *de dicto* desire to do what is right and also concerns for honesty, fair dealing, and the rights and welfare of others. They are also concerned for their own reputations and future opportunities and motivated not to jeopardize those by failing to pay. These moral and prudential motivations are virtually unopposed when it comes to such trivial burdens as paying for a beer (written before the stock market crash). Agents concerned in these ways commit themselves to future interactions with others in the same way as agents can commit themselves to rules or patterns of conduct that resist predicted temptations. Not carrying through on such commitments without change in underlying attitude is in both cases weakness of will, not acting on an intention formed and maintained with the weight of reasons behind it. These are again internal reasons and so say nothing about moral requirements demanding motivation.

The question here is whether those who abnormally lack such concerns have these reasons and are thereby irrational for failing to be motivated. To simply assert that they have such reasons is to beg the question. Once more, if they do pay for their beers, then almost certainly they were prudentially or morally motivated to do so and they had reasons to do so. But are they irrational if they simply walk out without paying? Has a person who does that sort of thing really even committed himself to pay? Others will interpret his action of ordering the beer as a commitment, but must he take himself to be committed? For Searle, he commits himself and accepts an obligation simply by uttering the words that order the beer. Searle points out that insincerity is possible only because most who utter these words do thereby accept an obligation, and that deception is possible only because others understand the deceiver as accepting an obligation.[22] But that successful deception depends on such common practices and understandings among the morally-minded does not show that the deceiver really accepts an obligation, endorses a moral norm, or thereby incurs a reason. Immoral people in general are parasites on the moral behavior of others, without whom social interaction of any significant kind would be impossible, but

---

[22] Ibid., p. 197.

parasites are not by definition irrational (I have known some very clever mosquitoes).

The case of the parasitic deceiving beer drinker is similar to that of successful liars. Liars are parasitic on truth-tellers. Unlike typical speakers, they are not committed to the truth of what they state, although others will interpret them as being so (otherwise, they could not be successful). They will not make inferences from their statements, as they would if they were committed to them, and they will not be irrational for failing to do so. In intentionally making false statements, they do not give themselves reasons to draw the usual inferences from such statements, although they appear to have such reasons. Similarly, those who are more generally morally unconcerned only appear to commit themselves or give themselves reasons to fulfil their moral obligations. Like liars, they create the appearance of personal commitment in order to achieve their immoral ends. But they may well remain personally uncommitted. At least Searle does not show us otherwise. And so neither does he show us that we must be morally committed to fulfil our moral obligations. The appearance, as opposed to the reality, of such commitment does not create reasons. And the reality once more creates only internal reasons, those that arise from existing motivations.

To say that moral motivation is rationally required is to say that those who are unconcerned about the welfare or freedom of others are irrational. The charge of irrationality is a strong and unusual one. What it alleges, I claim, is incoherence or, from the practical point of view, self-defeat. This analysis was derived as a generalization from paradigm cases of irrationality. An irrational belief is one that flies in the face of known or available evidence. This amounts to self-defeat because the aim of belief is truth, and evidence indicates truth. To fail to believe that for which one has conclusive evidence is to defeat the aim of belief, to defeat one's own purpose. Hence it is irrational. The aim of actions is the fulfilment of the prioritized motivations that prompt the actions. We act in order to fulfil our concerns or motives in acting. Hence irrational action is that resulting from unfulfillable motives or that which blocks the satisfaction of more central ones. Irrational inaction fails to seek to satisfy central concerns. The paradigms are weakness of will and inaction resulting from states like depression. In these cases one desires an outcome and has the means to achieve it, but fails to adopt those means because in the grip of an urge or emotion that interferes with normal rational processes. In a related kind of weakness of will, one cannot resist a temptation to act in a way that defeats some aim that one judges in cooler moments to be more important, again defeating one's own priorities among values. In all these cases there is some kind of self-defeat, defeat of one's own aims or values.

Moral reasoning also operates under a constraint of coherence: we must not judge cases differently without being able to cite a morally relevant difference between them. Such reasoning aimed at ordering rights in controversial contexts typically proceeds from agreed cases in which those rights are ordered and considers analogies and differences between those cases and the contexts in question. If, for example, we judge that a woman's right to her own body overrides a stranger's right to live in a context in which he can stay alive only by using her body, then we cannot prohibit abortions unless we can state a relevant difference between the stranger and the fetus.[23] The central constraint that we are not to judge cases differently without specifying morally relevant differences between them aims at avoiding incoherence, overriding more central values by others we judge to be less important in the relevant contexts.[24]

To judge one case right and another wrong when they are similar in every morally relevant respect is to promote and defeat the same moral value at stake in the same way, again a form of incoherence. It may therefore seem similar to paradigm cases of irrationality or self-defeat, implying that as rational agents we must be motivated to follow our correct moral judgments. But first, the constraint would require moral motivation only if such concern already existed in other contexts. This could be seen, therefore, as an internal requirement. Second, and more important, violation of this constraint does not amount to self-defeat in the way that paradigm cases of irrationality, as described above, do. It may amount simply to a narrowing of the scope of accepted moral values in an arbitrary way. The moral values in question may have limited motivational force for agents who must balance them against non-moral concerns. These limits may be expressed in ways that are morally arbitrary but that enable agents to better achieve their personal aims.

[23] See Judith Thomson, "A Defense of Abortion," *Philosophy & Public Affairs*, 1 (1971): 47–66.
[24] For expansion on the centrality of this constraint on moral reasoning, see my *Practical Rules* (Cambridge: Cambridge University Press, 2002), ch. 4; also *Moral Knowledge* (London: Routledge, 1988), ch. 5.

The meat eater, for example, who cannot find a difference between dogs and pigs that morally justifies eating the one but prohibits eating the other arbitrarily narrows the prohibition against killing. But while his carnivorous action lacks justification by his own lights, it does not defeat any aim or purpose that he accepts as his own. In fact, it satisfies his desire for gustatory pleasure, although it balances that desire in an arbitrary way against the reasons for not killing, accepting an arbitrary subclass of them as his own. While his division of the edible and inedible is morally arbitrary, he may be quite content to treat others of his own species with kindness and respect. His case is not one of weakness of will: his moral motivation is not simply overwhelmed every time he is confronted with a barbecued rib. Being confronted by a rib feels different to him than being confronted by a sweet dessert that he knows he should resist by his own lights. He is not giving in to an irresistible urge at the expense of a deeper concern he has when he orders his ribs. And it is certainly not the case that his use of moral terms like 'right' is radically ambiguous, being strangely aberrant and uncomprehending when he uses them in gustatory contexts. He understands perfectly well what it is to judge that eating pigs is wrong. He is simply unmotivated by the moral argument that he has no problem understanding. He recognizes that what he does is wrong in this instance, and he understands and uses the concept of wrongness as do others, but that recognition does not move him.

The above description seems perfectly natural. No ordinary form of misunderstanding or irrationality, for example weakness of will or self-deception, seems to explain the philosophically sophisticated meat-eater's lacking concern for pigs or being unmotivated by his admission that eating pigs is wrong. If his admittedly immoral action resembles no paradigm of practical irrationality, then its irrationality must be *sui generis*. But on what basis do we then identify it as such? The classification does not capture any intuition we have that villains are irrational or that we are when we act immorally. The feelings of moral guilt that might arise in us automatically when we do wrong are different from feelings of stupidity or anger at ourselves that we get from recognizing our own irrationality. But is not the meat-eater irrational in the sense earlier defined: his actions fail to cohere with his own evaluation of the reasons? No, because he need not judge that he has overriding reasons not to eat meat, only that there are such reasons for those motivated by them. In his case, unlike Huck Finn's, it would be morally better if he could summon, as people sometimes can, a desire to be moral (not in this instance fetishistic at all) to remedy his lack of direct concern for the pigs. But if irrationality consists in self-defeat, then his failure to respond to moral reasons does not appear to be irrational. His failure is one of lack of empathy or sympathy for the pigs, not a failure of reason.

To be moved by moral reasons requires moral concerns, and to be morally concerned is to be sympathetic to the interests of those affected by one's actions. Sympathy is primarily an affective state, not a cognitive one, a matter of feeling, not reason. Its lack is therefore a failure of affect, not reason. We speak also of reasons for feelings or emotions, as when we say that Mary had every reason to feel angry or offended, having been insulted by Max. But such talk refers only to the fact that feelings can be appropriate or inappropriate, fitting or unfitting. We noted earlier that paradigm emotions do contain cognitive elements or judgments, perhaps better described as proto-judgments since they are not formed deliberately from assessments of epistemic reasons. Emotions, we noted, arise automatically, prompting immediate reactions that bypass deliberative preliminaries. They may sometimes be controlled or suppressed after the fact, but then again they may persist in the face of knowledge that they are misplaced. I may continue to fear a snake after learning that it is harmless. My emotion continues to represent the snake as dangerous after my belief responds to the evidence.

The judgmental or representational aspects of emotions are accurate or inaccurate, and this is what makes emotions appropriate or inappropriate. We speak of reasons for emotions as if these judgments were based on reasons, but we saw earlier that we do not choose our feelings after assessing the reasons for and against them. In fact, we saw that the adaptive value of emotions lies precisely in their bypassing such rational processes. Full-fledged reasons are what we deliberate about; hence emotions do not arise in response to reasons in this full sense. Furthermore, as also noted, even when an emotion would be appropriate, it is not irrational to lack it. If rational people respond to reasons they have, then they would be irrational in not responding to reasons for emotions, if emotions were literally based on reasons. If moral motivation is based on moral concern, and moral concern is fleshed out in such affective reactions as guilt, sympathy, and indignation on behalf of others who have been wronged, then moral motivation does not seem to be a rational requirement. Rational requirements presuppose the capacity to respond to reasons. Morally-minded people are precisely those subject to moral emotions of empathy, sympathy, and guilt, reflecting concerns for others, not those with superior powers of reason. Those who lack moral concerns do not lack such powers, but instead fail to respond affectively to the plights of others as moral people do.

Just as not every epistemically unjustified belief is irrational, so not every morally unjustified action is irrational, even for generally morally-minded people. There is a difference, in that a belief recognized by its subject to be unjustified but still held would be irrational, and I have been arguing that an action recognized to be wrong but still done is not irrational (unless done out of weakness of will). But this difference again reflects the different aims of belief and action and the way these aims determine what counts as self-defeat. Only beliefs and actions that are clearly self-defeating are irrational. This difference between self-defeat and usual cases of moral incoherence indicates that immorality, even among generally morally concerned agents, does not amount to irrationality. And if immoral actions by generally moral people can escape the charge of irrationality, this seems much clearer in the case of actions of those who have no moral concerns. They are not even guilty of narrowing the scope of any moral values they accept in an arbitrary way. Of course, they may be irrational if they have prudential concerns that can be fulfilled only if they are morally concerned. But, as I shall argue below, this need not be the case.

One could nevertheless accept that we are not rationally required to be concerned for the welfare of animals but claim that the case is different when it comes to concern for our rational equals. Whatever we say of the pigs, it can still be argued that rational agents respond to reasons they have, that their reasons reflect their values, that moral reasons, at least those that govern behavior toward other persons, reflect the value of persons, and that as rational persons ourselves we must recognize the value of all persons, that is, adopt a moral point of view and accept moral reasons that reflect their interests as our own. The argument often holds that as rational agents we must first value ourselves, be concerned for our own welfare or interest, and second, if concerned for our own welfare, must be concerned for the welfare of others. Since one's own value or well-being counts objectively no more than anyone else's, and since the satisfaction of our own interests almost always depends on the cooperation of others, if a rational agent must respond to her own value or welfare, she ought to respond to that of others as well. Indeed, we do naturally respond to the welfare and suffering of others, and sociopaths who do not are typically judged not only statistically, but mentally or medically, abnormal.

We saw in the previous section, however, that the premise of this argument is first of all problematic. On the one hand, there is, I argued, no rational requirement for agents to be concerned about their own welfare in the usual sense of narrow self-interest, the sense in which the goods in question make essential reference to the agents. And, to turn the initial argument on its head, if there is no rational requirement to be concerned about one's own welfare, how can there be a requirement to be concerned about the welfare of others? How can their welfare rationally count for more than one's own? This seems to be neither the natural nor the moral point of view.

On the other hand, we noted that agents with any rational desires are concerned for their broad self-interest, which is defined in terms of the satisfaction of those desires. Since we are all concerned for our broad self-interest, must we also, if rational, be concerned for that of others? Need we then be concerned to satisfy or share the interests of all other people? We also noted earlier that, as Graham Oddie has shown, if I am concerned for others and therefore concerned to see that their rational desires are satisfied, our interests will converge or come to be shared. If I care about my wife and therefore care that her interests are satisfied, I will share her interest in satisfying them, and therefore share the interests themselves. Utilitarianism requires that we be concerned equally for the interests of all,[25] that we therefore come to share their interests. But it is a common, and I believe correct, objection to this moral theory that this demand is too strong. Some people might rationally desire to knit or to collect beanie babies, and I cannot see myself sharing those interests. But other moral theories that are more plausible are less demanding, requiring only that we respect the moral rights, representing important or central interests, of others, especially if we demand respect for those same rights ourselves.

---

[25] It requires this at least on the most basic level of justification, although it can allow that some people caring more for certain others might maximize the satisfaction of interests for all.

There is an important difference, however, between my concern for my own broad self-interest, which is implied by my having any rational desires, and my concern for the interests of others, which is not so implied. A separate argument is required to bridge the gap. Traditionally there are two main approaches to the attempt to do so. On the one side, Hobbesian and Humean arguments hold that prudence demands morality, that immoral behavior is not worth the risk to reputation, self-respect, or open cooperative relations with others. Not only do we need to cooperate with others in order to have our own desires maximally satisfied, but we need social interaction itself. We therefore join groups, identify with their members, and internalize their norms as part of our social identities. Violating these norms runs the risk of ostracism from the groups with whom we need to interact, and it results as well in unpleasant guilt feelings once the norms are internalized.

But these claims, while true, ignore the fact that clever or powerful enough scoundrels can minimize their risks of exposure, for example by transgressing only when they are virtually certain that they will not be found out or sanctioned. More importantly, people can have the respect of and open relations with selected others in preferred groups without treating more distant strangers as morality requires. We may be biologically wired to care for certain close relations, and find it socially necessary and natural to care for certain others, but morality requires a broader and more artificial impartiality, and prudential rationality does not bridge the gap left by biology. We are, for example, morally required to be concerned about distant future generations, but we have neither natural feelings for them nor prudential reasons to be so concerned. Is it irrational to lack such feelings and concerns?

A positive answer would probably appeal to Kantian arguments that rely either on the premise that one's own self-interest is objectively of no more value than that of any other person, present or future, or on the claim that we must value the source of all other values in rational, valuing agents. The first premise may be true, but it does not imply the conclusion that we must be concerned for everyone's welfare. We saw above that arbitrarily limiting one's concerns does not amount to the kind of incoherence or self-defeat in which irrationality consists. I have no objective or impartial reason to prefer as strongly as I do myself and my friends and relatives over others, and so I cannot justify to others limiting my concern to myself or to those relatively few people I care about, but I do not necessarily defeat my own aims in doing so. I may in fact promote them. I will promote them in cases in which my interests conflict in the long run with those of others, as well they might. Thus, if irrationality consists in the form of incoherence that amounts to self-defeat, I am not irrational in so limiting my concerns.

The second premise mentioned above is also false. There is no rational requirement to value the sources of all the things we value.[26] I value philosophy. One of its sources was the institution of slavery in ancient Greece, which helped to support the upper-class leisure to devote to intellectual pursuits. I take it that I am not irrational in failing to value slavery at any time in history. To take another example, I can value a sculpture (especially a contemporary sculpture) without valuing the material from which it was made (which may be urine, cow dung, or rusty metal). I may not even value the creativity of the sculptor, if that creativity lay behind many harmful acts. Thus I need not value all the sources of what I do value. And even if I were rationally required to do so, it would not follow that I am rationally required to value all other persons as sources of value. They may be sources of value for themselves, but not necessarily sources of value for me. Again the logical gap between my concern for my own welfare and concern for the welfare of all others, demanded by morality, fails to be bridged.

If these direct arguments for a rational requirement of moral motivation fail, it is useful to compare more closely the morally virtuous person to the immoralist and amoralist. We can then see better whether the properties of the former lacking in the latter might be rationally required. The morally virtuous person is precisely the person who takes moral reasons to be reasons for her, her reasons for acting. She does this because she is concerned about violations of rights, the impediments to freedom and the suffering of all sentient beings. Her good upbringing has made her sensitive to the interests of all others, but it seems doubtful that it has succeeded by developing her powers of reason, her rational capacities that allow her to appreciate arguments, whether practical or theoretical. Not all people are like her. Not all have this universally directed concern, and certainly not all people

---

[26] This premise seems to be presupposed in the argument of Christine Korsgaard for the rational requirement of moral motivation. See her *The Sources of Normativity* (Cambridge: Cambridge University Press, 1996). p. 123.

manifest such concern in all contexts. If all those who do not are irrational, then most people are irrational.

At the opposite extreme is the immoralist, who makes the immorality of an action his reason for doing it. Can it be rational for him to desire the bad and make it his reason for acting? It can certainly be his explanatory reason, the cause of his acting, but can it be his normative, full-fledged, reason; can it justify his action in any sense even in his own eyes? The answer depends on disambiguating the concept of badness. There is moral badness, and then there is badness *tout court*. For the latter to be a reason to pursue it is indeed problematic.

We saw earlier that one can desire what one considers bad *tout court*. While a positive evaluative judgment is a component of paradigm desires—to desire something is ordinarily to judge it desirable in some sense—it is not a necessary component of all desires. I can desire my next cigar without thinking there is anything good about it. It may no longer give me pleasure, for example, but I still desire it. Addictive desires can be like that.[27] But to think that these desires provide reasons is problematic. They typically oppose other deeper desires or concerns, so that giving in to them is typically a pure case of weakness of will, not a matter of acting in response to reasons. One could pursue what is totally bad out of anger, perhaps anger at the state of the world in general. It is hard to imagine pursuit of the bad for its own sake from any motive other than some such negative emotion. Actions that express such emotions are not thereby rational, but, as we saw earlier, the reason why an emotion is fitting or appropriate can be a reason for actions that are expressive of that emotion. Thus, if anger is a fitting response to the world, and bad, harmful, or destructive actions are therefore rational responses to the state of the world, then it seems that their badness could be a reason for doing them.

The problem is that if such actions are fitting responses, then they seem not to be thoroughly bad. If it is good for responses to be fitting, then it is good in some sense to act badly in such a context. And this argument seems to apply in all cases in which the badness of an action or object seems to provide a reason for doing or pursuing it. I am not implying here that a person must desire to perform such actions only because he

---

[27] For other examples, see Michael Stocker, "Desiring the Bad," *Journal of Philosophy*, 76 (1979): 738–53.

thinks they are fitting or in some other way good. He may desire them simply because they are harmful or bad.[28] But it is still the case that any justifying reason must derive from more than simply a desire to harm. To provide a reason, this desire must, as argued earlier, connect with others in a coherent set, and it is hard to see how these connections will not imply some claim that the harmful acts are fitting in some way. If a person's good is equated with his broad self-interest, constituted by the satisfaction of his coherent and informed desires, if all goodness is goodness for some person, and if rational action is also action in pursuit of broad self-interest, then it is indeed hard to see how badness *tout court* could provide reasons, how it could be rational to pursue it. I do not want to insist that badness *tout court* cannot be a reason, however; I only want to point to the problematic nature of the claim that it can be. Our real concern here is only with moral badness, not badness *tout court*.

Considering moral badness or wrongness a reason for action is not problematic in the same way. It appears that desiring the morally bad can be both informed and coherent. Two wrongs cannot make a moral right, but the second might nevertheless be a rational response to the first, or at least have some reason behind it deriving from the first. The paradigm of a character who pursues evil for its own sake is Iago in *Othello*. By all ordinary criteria of rationality, for example clever and efficient pursuit of his aims, he appears to be also a model of (misguided) rationality. Nothing in his complex plots is without single-minded purpose. His ends cohere with his overarching goal of evil, which he takes to be a fitting response to the injustice of his world, and his means are well designed to satisfy those ends. He might be seen to be motivated solely by an all-consuming anger, but under some acceptable interpretations his anger is at least in small part warranted. The actions that flow from it are not products of blind rage or total delusion, but deliberately orchestrated elements of a coherent, albeit malevolent, life plan. The charge of irrationality would again seem to reflect only a desire to condemn such characters as thoroughly as possible.

While focusing on immoral characters and asking whether their actions can be rational, we can ask also a related question: whether a moral action could be for that reason irrational. Here the notorious story of the artist Gauguin comes to mind. He famously abandoned family and friends to

---

[28] Again Stocker makes this point in the article just cited.

pursue his art in the South Pacific. Let us for the sake of argument ignore the benefits to posterity of that move, or assume that such distant consequences are morally irrelevant in the face of immediate moral obligations. It seems certain in his case that his motives in moving were not moral, that in his eyes the moral thing for him to have done would have been to remain with his family. Had he done so, this might have revealed him to be more morally motivated than he in fact was. If so, his action would have been rational. But it might also have been the case that the moral qualms that at the last moment had led him to remain with them would have been cold feet, an instance of weak will and hence irrational for him, given the overall structure of his concerns or motivations.

If I were to fail to write this section of this book out of concern that it would weaken readers' moral motivations (such effects of philosophical books are once more highly fictionalized), the same might be true of me. Thus, it seems both that it can be rational to pursue the morally bad and irrational to pursue the morally good or right. If that is correct, then there is no uniformly right answer to the question whether it is more rational to act morally or in one's narrow self-interest, when these conflict. Either answer might be correct for particular individuals if rationality equates with broad self-interest, which includes satisfaction of self-centered and of altruistic and moral concerns.

The character usually contrasted with the morally virtuous person is not the immoralist who pursues evil for its own sake, but the amoralist who simply lacks moral concerns. It has yet to be shown that we are rationally required to have any concerns except those required for the satisfaction of deeper concerns. Total amoralists are fortunately rare in real life and are, as noted, typically labeled sociopaths by psychologists and laymen alike, looked upon as mentally abnormal if not irrational. (A somewhat inconclusive debate ensues as to whether their mental deficiencies are emotional or cognitive, or both.[29]) But many of us more normally morally concerned people are nevertheless partial amoralists. As indicated earlier, I am only mildly abashed to admit that I am the partial amoralist described above: I am unmoved by the moral requirement not to eat meat, which I see as genuine. I believe I understand the concept of moral wrongness (I have written some other ethics books) and can sincerely describe my eating

---

[29] For a recent summary of this debate, see Nichols, *Sentimental Rules*, ch. 3.

habits as wrong while being unmotivated to change them. I do not think that eating meat is simply labeled wrong by misguided vegetarians: I think it really is wrong but do it without qualms anyway.

Similarly, my students whom I convince of a moral obligation to aid distant people in dire need are nevertheless seldom moved to do so. They seem to be partial amoralists too. Their moral judgments do not begin to prompt the actions required by them, and yet again there is no self-defeat of the kind that constitutes irrationality. The students are not prone to irrational inaction, are not irrational in any way I can detect. They are not defeating aims or reasons they have, only failing to accept certain moral reasons there are, perhaps arbitrarily limiting the scope of their moral concerns. They are not too depressed to act on moral aims they have; nor do they find an urge not to contribute to charity irresistible in overwhelming their concern to do so. It is far more plausible to admit that they do not have such concerns about these distant peoples, although it is not hard to convince them that they morally ought to have these concerns. The failure of their motivations to track their moral judgments is not a good thing, as it is in Huckleberry Finn's case, but a moral failing. But it is not a fault of rationality.

Once more, as in so many cases, what is missing here is not a failure of reason, practical or otherwise, but sufficient sensitivity or sympathy, which is, if anything, more difficult to impart. Concern for others is not imparted through reasoning or argument, but through exposure and example. Through such means, if at all, we gradually expand the small group of people with whom we are naturally concerned. Broader experience with others usually means broader concern, but not always. If morality were ultimately a matter of reason, then since my students are rational people, all I would need to do to get them to feed the starving in Africa is to cite the moral reasons there are to do so. But my citing the obvious moral reasons does not have this effect.

That is the bad news. The good news is that it is natural to be concerned about the welfare of others, at least of others with whom we come into contact, and most of us have been brought up in the right way, the way that does expand our natural concerns for others. And for most of us who are not clever or ruthless enough to exploit others without fear of retaliation, who care about our reputations and our self-images tied to those reputations, and for whom the fulfilment of other-regarding concerns is a source of satisfaction, prudential reasons require recognition of moral reasons, acceptance of them as our own and consequent motivation.

But again, for most of us non-saints, the expansion of our natural sympathies and empathies through social programming is only partly successful. These feelings are expanded from their narrow origins, but not all the way to all those we might affect positively or negatively. And prudential concerns for our reputations and the good feelings we get from virtuous actions also take us only so far, sometimes not as far as morality requires. Our reputations and feelings of pride and shame depend upon our actions toward those with whom we come into contact, not on our concerns for more distant strangers. It is quite easy to be amoral when it comes to them, quite common and natural too, as irrationality is not.

Most of us are morally-minded, although the scope of our concerns is not as broad as it morally ought to be. To the morally-minded person, moral judgments when made have a motivating force, and they may seem to be intrinsically motivating. Moral deliberation, judgment, and argument are intended to be action guiding. If I deliberate about what I morally ought to do, it is normally because I know that I will be motivated by the outcome of my deliberation, that it will result in intention and action. Likewise, if I express a moral judgment to another, I normally intend to motivate that person. Ordinarily, once I convince him that a moral requirement applies to his situation, I do not also have to convince him that he has a reason to do what morality requires. "You morally ought to do A, but you may have no reason to do it," is certainly odd and hard to imagine ever uttering. Typically, I would not tell you what you morally ought to do if I were not trying to influence your action. And my aim in offering such advice is to influence you by appeal to reasons.

When we address not only advice but moral demands to others, we again assume that they can accept these demands as reasons. This claim is central to the argument of Stephen Darwall in his recent book.[30] He points out that to assert a right against someone is distinct from merely threatening or attempting to coerce that person, even if the assertion is backed by a threat of sanctions for non-compliance. It is to address the person as a rational agent as opposed to the object of a brute threat. To address the person as a rational agent is to assert that the person has a moral reason to honor

---

[30] Darwall, *The Second Person Standpoint*, esp. pp. 269–76.

the right or accede to the demand. To sincerely assert such a right is to think it reasonable to do so, which implies that one would accept a similar claim against oneself as a reason to honor it. Since we all do make moral demands and assert rights and address these as reasons for others to act or forbear acting in various ways, and since we believe the reasonableness of these demands gives us the authority to make them, we must accept that we have reasons to accede to the same demands made by others against us. And these reasons once more exist independently of our desires to conform to them.

Whether or not these moral demands we address to others are backed by threats of sanctions, we hold people accountable for failing to respond to or be motivated by them. We blame them for failing to honor the rights we assert. And when we hold people accountable or blame them, we again presuppose that they had reasons to act in the ways we blame them for not acting. It would be odd at best to blame people for not doing what we admit they had no reason to do. If persons can show us they had every reason to do what they did and no reason not to, we must stop blaming them for acting as they did. In blaming them, we think they are blameworthy, that they should accept the blame, acknowledge that they had overriding reason to act otherwise and should have been aware of and motivated by that reason. Thus, these central moral practices we all engage in of making demands of each other and holding each other accountable rest on the assumptions that we are free and rational beings who address each other as such, that we can and should respond to the reasons embodied in these demands, and that we must accept such reasons ourselves if we justifiably hold others accountable for acting on them.

This extended argument, if sound, again establishes a rational requirement to be morally motivated, to accept moral reasons as one's own. But what it mainly asserts is what we assume when we make moral demands of others and hold them accountable for meeting those demands. The fact that our moral practices rest on certain assumptions does not show that these assumptions are true. Even if we cannot help making certain assumptions, this still does not establish their truth. Our religious practices rest on certain fundamental assumptions too, such as the existence of God, but that does not refute atheism. In the ethical sphere, what we mainly assume is moral motivation on the part of ourselves and others with whom we engage in moral dialogue. This assumption is correct most of the time. When it is correct, agents have moral reasons, but these are internal reasons deriving in part from existing motivation or concern.

When we engage in moral dialogue with others, it is because we are concerned to justify our behavior to each other. This concern expresses both respect for each other as moral agents and those moral emotions of sympathy, empathy, guilt, and resentment for bad behavior that such agency involves. If I accept another's authority to make moral demands of me, it is because I share her moral concerns, and if I make moral demands of her, it is because I assume she shares my recognition of these as reasons. Just as I grant epistemic authority to another, trust him to provide me with information under the assumption that he has knowledge of the facts in question, so I grant moral authority to another to accept my assertions of rights and make similar demands of me under the assumption that we share moral outlooks and concerns.

But do we not make such demands of all rational people, and do we not blame them for not meeting these moral requirements? Yes, but the assumptions that underlie the practice of blaming wrongdoers are not trustworthy indicators of the reasons they have. The emotions and attitudes expressed in blame are automatically activated as a response to perceived wrongdoing, not based initially on a rational assessment of responsibility. In one study it was shown that, while subjects do not blame in the abstract if told that actions result from a neurological condition, when presented with concrete cases, they do not withhold blame for this reason.[31] Their condemnations seem to depend only on their own moods and on how harmful or bad the actions described are. They do not depend on their beliefs that the agents committing the actions were themselves responding to reasons. This study is in keeping with much contemporary psychological research, some of it surveyed here earlier, which shows that automatic processes are more widespread and deliberative decision procedures more epiphenomenal than naively thought.

If blaming reflects emotional responses and automatically activated attitudes, then it does not depend on and hence does not attest to the rational justification of the assumptions that underlie it in the abstract. Indeed, the practice admits of a different explanation that does not appeal to its

---

[31] F. De Brigard, E. Mandelbaum, and D. Ripley, "Responsibility and the Brain Sciences," paper read at Conference on Ethical Theory and Moral Practice, Amsterdam, 2008.

rationality. Holding people accountable for their harmful or antisocial acts has survival value, evolutionary advantage, and so can be given an evolutionary explanation. The automatic reactions underlying blame evolved not on the basis of rational assessments of the responsibility of agents for responding to moral reasons they have, but on the basis of the survival of groups that held their members accountable and punished them for transgressions of the groups' ethical norms. Thus, even if we now assume that blame is rationally justifiable only if wrongdoers ignore moral reasons they have, this does not imply that they have these reasons and hence are rationally required to be motivated by them. Many of our moral practices rely on assumptions, of free will or the ability to rise above our desires for example, that can be called into question by scientific evidence.

But if we make moral demands on others, must we not accept similar demands they make on us? And since we all do make such demands or sometimes assert our moral rights, must we not accept that we have moral reasons to accede to similar assertions by others? Certainly we are morally required to accept such reciprocal relations (to go to other people's funerals if they go to ours). But our question once more is whether we are rationally required to do so. Immoral wrongdoers are once more parasitic on the moral behavior of others without whom society could not survive. But being a parasite has not been shown to be irrational. Asserting a right myself when not honoring the same right in others is certainly objectionable on moral grounds, but no more irrational than lying while relying on the truth-telling of others. Just as the liar does not commit himself to the truth of what he says, so the scoundrel who asserts his rights is not committed to the proposition that all such assertions provide reasons, although he hopes that others more morally-minded than he is will accept his assertions as reasons.

Treating people as if they are morally-minded encourages them to be so; assuming they have moral reasons encourages them to accept such reasons. But none of this refutes the claim that they have moral reasons only if they are morally-minded. In fact, we do need to train, socially condition, or educate people to be morally motivated, and the training is not primarily through argument. If it were simply a matter of replacing ignorance with knowledge, the social problem of immorality would be far more tractable, similar to that of illiteracy. And if it were only a matter of showing people how to avoid defeating the aims they really desire, it would again be a more tractable problem. But our deepest social problems result from the fact that moral indoctrination is only partly successful. The defect that must be remedied is not a defect in intellect or rationality, or a matter of ignorance. Acting morally only on the basis of accepting an argument instead of out of concern for others is once more having one or several thoughts too many. Those who lack such concerns need not be fools or even philosophically unsophisticated. Nor do they have to struggle to overcome their rationally required moral motivations. Moral motivations are no more rationally required than prudential concerns. In both cases externalists fail to provide examples of reasons we have independently of our existing motivations.

A final complication will end this long section. I have been speaking so far as if there is a single set of moral concerns that agents might or might not have. But much earlier I pointed out that being morally-minded must be specified in a more fine-grained way. The egalitarian has concerns that the libertarian does not have; the collectivist is motivated in a way that the individualist is not; likewise for the consequentialist and deontic pluralist. If moral relativism is true, then there is no value neutral way to choose between these competing moral frameworks. I have argued elsewhere that it is true, but this is not the place to rehearse all those arguments.[32] It suffices to point out here that its truth would greatly complicate the externalist's position. If even morally-minded people do not have the same moral reasons, then certainly not everyone does. Which moral requirements would the externalist then endorse as rational requirements? By which framework or set of reasons must we be motivated? It could not be all moral requirements that must motivate us, since the requirements of different frameworks contradict one another. Which subset then, and on what grounds? We need not wrestle with these questions, because our simple answer is "none".

IV. A Different Approach and a Last Ditch Reply

"It's déjà vu all over again."

Joshua Gert has argued that externalism is true not only because some reasons require motivation and action independently of pre-existing

---

[32] A. Goldman, *Moral Knowledge* (London: Routledge, 1988), pp. 174–214.

motivations (a claim answered in the previous section), but also because other reasons of a different type do not require motivation at all.[33] Agents have these reasons, he claims, but since they do not require or imply motivation, they are external reasons. His central distinction is that between requiring and justifying reasons, the latter being the bone of contention here.

Requiring reasons require that a rational agent be somewhat motivated by them and act on them when they are unopposed by equally strong or stronger reasons. Justifying reasons can justify actions, indeed can override or be stronger than opposing requiring reasons, but they never themselves require an agent to be motivated by or to act on them. Gert's main examples of the latter kind of reasons are altruistic reasons, those relating to the welfare or interests of others. These reasons can justify large sacrifices, hence override even strong self-regarding reasons, without ever requiring agents to act on them. It can be rational to risk one's life in order to save several children, but it is not irrational to fail to donate even small amounts of money to charity in order to prevent several children from starving. We are not rationally required to do so, even if we are morally required to do so; but if we are morally required to do so, then we are rationally justified in doing so. He agrees with the claim of the previous section that we are not rationally required to be morally motivated, but disagrees that it can ever be irrational to act morally. Since altruistic actions are morally but not rationally required, and since they are always rationally justified, the distinction between requiring and justifying reasons is implied by the existence of altruistic reasons, according to his account of them.

What is most important here is the claim that justifying reasons need not motivate rational agents, while remaining genuine reasons for them. It seems that if there are such reasons, then reason internalism of any kind, which requires that rational agents be motivated by reasons they have, must be wrong. Gert defends the existence of justifying reasons not only by appealing to our intuitions about altruistic or moral reasons, but also by arguing that there is no single measure of strength for reasons that requires us to act on the strongest reasons we have. Simplifying somewhat from his discussion, consider the following three propositions: (1) it is rational to risk one's life in order to save several children; (2) it is not rational to risk one's life in order to save two hundred dollars; (3) it is rational to save

---

[33] Gert, *Brute Rationality*.

two hundred dollars instead of donating that amount to charity in order to save several children. Together these intuitive propositions seem to show that the reason to save several children is as strong or stronger than the reason not to risk one's life, that the reason not to risk one's life is stronger than the reason to save two hundred dollars, and that the reason to save two hundred dollars is as strong or stronger than the reason to save several children. In other words, they seem to reflect an intransitivity in strength of reasons, which could lead to an irrational sequence of actions that defeats a stronger motive in order to satisfy a weaker one.

Such incoherence can be avoided by means of Gert's distinction between types of reasons. Since saving several children provides a strong justifying but not a requiring reason, it can justify risking one's life while not requiring sacrificing two hundred dollars. To the question "Which reason is strongest?" there is no answer *tout court*. There is no single measure of strength, since justifying reasons do not become requiring when strong enough, although they can excuse us from what would otherwise be requirements. If there is no single measure of strength, we can accept all three of the intuitive propositions without creating an intransitive sequence of reasons ranked by strength. That Gert's distinction between justifying and requiring reasons resolves such apparent inconsistency provides further support for it. But accepting it once more defeats internalism in regard to reasons. If justifying reasons do not require actions, they do not require rational agents to be motivated by them. Internalism is false if rational agents need not be motivated by reasons they have.

You might think that Gert's justifying reasons are simply my reasons there are, while his requiring reasons equate with my reasons agents have. But such is not the case. Our distinctions are not mere terminological variants of each other. For him, certain reasons are intrinsically requiring. We are required to be concerned about our own welfare, whatever our actual motivations are. I denied that in the previous section: no states of affairs in themselves require motivation from us. And for him, merely justifying reasons never require motivation or action, although they always justify them, and moral reasons are always of this sort. In my view, any reason an agent has requires some (minimal) motivation, and agents have F reasons, for example moral reasons, only if they are F-minded, for example morally concerned. An agent has a reason if she is rational and motivated by it or ought to be, given her other concerns or desires.

I argued in the previous section that an agent could be irrational in acting morally, which Gert denies in holding that moral reasons always justify actions. I argued that moral qualms could amount to cold feet or weak will, when agents forgo actions in pursuit of their deepest personal commitments at the last minute. Of course, such qualms could reveal that the agent was more morally-minded than he appeared to be, but either interpretation could be correct for different agents, situations, and actions. The issue in this section is whether my distinction can provide a different accommodation of the three intuitive propositions that seem to support Gert's position. If so, the internalist interpretation of reasons can stand. In fact, I will claim that it provides a better account of these three propositions than does Gert's distinction between requiring and justifying reasons.

The internalist would interpret our apparently inconsistent triad as follows. On the one hand, if an agent is more strongly motivated by his concern for the threatened children than by the threat to his own life in trying to save them, then it is certainly rational for him to risk his life trying to save them. Not to accept the risk would be irrational for that agent with motivations as defined, an instance of weakness of will. This is true even though a failure to take the risk would most likely indicate that the agent's motivations were not as defined above. If he verbally asserted such a motivational ranking while neglecting to act, we would have to choose between an interpretation in terms of self-deception and one in terms of weakness of will.

On the other hand, if an agent abnormally lacks altruistic concerns or moral motives, then she will not have a reason that opposes her keeping her two hundred dollars. There will certainly be moral reasons amounting to moral obligations, but if the agent is a true amoralist, or coherently amoral in regard to distant children, as we are imagining her to be, then these obligations will not give her reasons, will not be *her* reasons, any more than religious demands give reasons to those who are not religious. If she is mildly concerned about distant children, but this concern is weaker than her purely self-regarding concerns, then it will still not be irrational of her to refuse help.

So far we have noted that different agents can be rational in risking their lives to save children or in saving two hundred dollars that could save the children. This point does not require appeal to purely justifying reasons. The more crucial question is whether it could be rational of the same agent to be willing to risk his life to save the children but not to spend two hundred dollars to do so, assuming he values his life more than two hundred dollars. Gert's argument implies a positive answer, since altruistic reasons are justifying but not requiring. According to him, a person could be rationally justified in risking his life to save the children but not rationally required at the same time to spend two hundred dollars to save them, even when he would not risk his life for two hundred dollars. But this again strikes us as incoherent. The correct answer to our crucial question clearly seems to be "no". A person who values his life could not be rational in risking it for what he would not spend two hundred dollars, if he would not risk his life for two hundred dollars. The internalist gives the right answer here, and Gert's distinction implies the wrong answer. The internalist account is superior.

In Gert's terminology, we could say that all reasons one has are requiring reasons. Reasons motivate rational agents, and we sometimes say that they require motivation when it is absent. But in ordinary contexts using those terms might be misleading. Normally one will perform that action that one is most motivated to perform, so there is no sense of requirement. Normally one's motivations, including dispositions, felt urges, implicit evaluative judgments, thoughts pleasant and unpleasant, and ensuing intentions will cohere and result smoothly in chosen actions. If talk of requiring reasons is normally out of place, there is less, in fact no need to talk of merely justifying reasons. Whatever use this notion might have is better served by appeal to reasons there are, although, as noted, these concepts are not the same. All normative reasons rationally justify actions to some degree when acted on, since all indicate ways to satisfy informed and coherent motivations. (Of course, we are speaking here of rational, not moral, justification.)

It is then another advantage of my account that it is simpler, in that Gert splits practical reasons into two different kinds, which division requires two different accounts of why and how they are reasons. By contrast, the distinction between reasons there are and reasons that agents have is not a distinction between different kinds of reasons. There is only one kind of (full-fledged) practical reason, although particular reasons may or may not be the reasons of particular agents. There is one account of what reasons are: they are states of affairs that motivate rational agents. And there is one account of how and why they are reasons, of what constitutes these states of affairs as reasons: their relation to coherent and informed motivational systems of subjects, their being the objects of those motivations or indications of how to fulfil them.

Second, his distinction splits practical reason from theoretical reason more sharply than does mine. In the case of reasons one has for belief, if one knows that one's reasons sufficiently justify a belief, then one is rationally required to believe. Once more one normally automatically does so believe on the basis of reasons of which one is aware without feeling any requirement, but the requirement is there whether felt or not. Since the natural aim of belief is truth, since what constitutes a psychological state as belief is its aim or function of tracking the truth, and since the justifying reasons one has for believing indicate the truth of the belief, it would be self-defeating of that aim not to believe on the basis of such reasons. Once more here incoherence in the form of practical self-defeat, defeat of the natural constitutive aim of belief, underlies the requirement of rationality. Theoretical rationality can be seen from this point of view as simply a part of practical rationality.

The demand for coherence and the avoidance of self-defeat defines rationality, I have suggested, in the case of practical reasons for action as well. And, as argued earlier, in this realm too we can speak of a natural aim that constitutes intentional actions as such. Here the natural aim of action is to fulfil the motivations that normally prompt the actions. Reasons on the internalist's view are indications of how to satisfy those informed and coherent or prioritized motivations. Hence it is self-defeating in the practical realm too not to act on the strongest reasons one has. There is a close parallel between practical and theoretical reason, reasons in both areas playing parallel functional roles. In both realms reasons are facts or states of affairs that indicate how to satisfy the natural aims of the states—beliefs or actions—for which they are reasons. Not so on Gert's account. He admits that justifying reasons for belief may at the same time be requiring reasons,[34] but he draws a sharp distinction between the two in the practical realm. The appeal to the simplicity, unity, and intelligibility of the internalist account has been a major argument in its favor throughout this discussion.

This takes us to the last ditch reply of the externalist, who argues for the irreducibility or non-natural nature of the normative, of what we ought to

---

[34] Ibid. 22.

believe or do. For the internalist, what we ought to believe and do derives ultimately from the aims of beliefs and actions. There are no external reasons, purely objective values, or normative facts that do not derive from natural aims or psychological states of sentient beings. The externalist at this point can grant that an informed and coherent motivational set can confer values on various states of affairs, can constitute them as reasons for actions and therefore rationalize the actions that flow from the motivations and that pursue and maintain the states of affairs. But he will now take the argument to a deeper level. If there is such a demand for coherence and relevant information, and if an informed and coherent motivational set creates reasons, then, he will claim, these are irreducible normative facts. Whatever reasons are, and whatever it is that creates them, that these are reasons and are so created will be irreducible normative facts.[35] Normative facts not reducible to psychological states or relations imply categorical or objective demands or values. There must therefore be categorical or objective value to basing actions on coherent motivations and true beliefs. Such values are not perceived through the five senses or felt as desires and emotions are; nor do they enter scientific explanations. They are therefore non-natural properties.

According to this argument, on the view of reasons defended above, it must be a normative fact that motivations create reasons for action, and another irreducible normative fact that evidence of truth is reason for belief. But, as Derek Parfit argues, these normative facts are in the same philosophical boat as the normative fact that certain states of affairs are objectively good and provide reasons for action, the objectivist's and externalist's claims.[36] Thus, the internalist has no rational motive for denying objective value or external reasons. Her metaphysics must include irreducible normative facts anyway. So there is no theoretical advantage to refusing to allow such additional facts as that we all have agent-neutral moral reasons or ought to recognize such reasons.

Once such normative facts or states of affairs are granted, the externalist will extend the argument to claim that whatever motivational set or set of psychological states we consider, it remains an open question how we

---

[35] Thomas Scanlon, *What We Owe to Each Other* (Cambridge, MA: Harvard University Press, 1998), p. 57.
[36] Derek Parfit, "Rationality and Reasons," in D. Edonsson, J. Josefsson, and T. Ronnow-Rasmussen (eds.), *Exploring Practical Philosophy* (Aldershot: Ashgate, 2001), p. 37.

should act.[37] Whatever concern I have, I can still intelligibly ask whether I ought to act to fulfil it. How I should act is determined not simply by my motivations, but by normative facts about how these motivations count. If I am concerned about my children, this alone does not tell me that I ought to provide for their education; instead, it is this concern plus the normative fact that such concerns generate reasons to fulfill them that determines what I ought to do.

The general point, emphasized by Thomas Nagel, is that the normative is not reducible to the descriptive, whether in regard to belief or action.[38] The argument is a contemporary version of Moore's open question argument, endorsed by Nagel, Parfit, and Scanlon. If we can sensibly ask of any set of concerns whether we ought to act to fulfil them, and if the answer depends on additional normative facts, then, since what we ought to do does reduce to what we have most reason to do, our reasons do not reduce to indications of how to fulfil our motivations or to what motivates us. There must be the additional normative fact that we ought to do what motivates us. It follows from this argument, as Scanlon notes, that "neither claims about what count as evidence nor claims about what count as reasons for action can be plausibly understood as claims about natural facts."[39] There simply are no natural facts to fill the bill if informed and coherent motivations do not do so. And the upshot for Nagel and Parfit is once more that once we admit irreducible, non-natural normative facts, there is no further philosophical liability in endorsing objective values and external reasons.

Perhaps it is true that once we have tasted the philosophically forbidden fruit of non-naturalism, there is no further shame in going all the way metaphysically. But need we really go that far in regard to reasons and their origins? This last ditch argument, like Darwall's previously considered argument that we must accept norms in order to be motivated to draw logical inferences or adopt practical means to ends, again contains too many thoughts, or in this case too many metaphysical kinds. In place of such mysterious non-natural facts, I have appealed to natural aims. The constitutive aims of beliefs and actions take the place of these irreducibly mysterious facts as the ultimate source of reasons or normativity.

---

[37] Thomas Nagel, *The Last Word* (Oxford: Oxford University Press, 1997), pp. 103, 121–5.
[38] Ibid. 105–6, 117.   [39] Scanlon, *What We Owe to Each Other*, p. 60.

Proponents of the argument accept that reasons for belief are in the same ontological boat as reasons for action. We may then review first the internalist account of reasons for belief. Is it really an irreducible, therefore non-natural fact that evidence, as indicative of truth, provides a reason to believe? Belief, it is universally acknowledged, aims at truth. Beliefs aim to exist only when true. This natural aim is part of what defines belief to be the type of psychological state it is. There is nothing non-natural about this. Belief is as natural a psychological state as any we have, and truth is its natural aim, representing the world as it is its natural function. Presumably beliefs as psychological states (or brains that produce them) were naturally selected because they regularly succeeded in this task in the distant past.[40] As noted earlier, if we did not aim at true beliefs, we could not communicate or distinguish environmental threats from sources of nourishment. We could not have survived without this natural wired in aim. Such natural functions are the beginning of normativity.

What else is required is first, the possibility of failure in such aims, and second, the possibility of controlling at least some of the means to their success. In the case of belief these amount to the possibility of basing one's beliefs on the evidence and maintaining coherence among beliefs, and the possibility of failing to do so. It is true, as noted earlier, that we do not choose what to believe. We cannot help believing what appears to us to be true, and, despite H. L. Mencken's insightful crack about religious faith,[41] we cannot believe what strikes us as false. But we can direct attention toward or away from evidence, even hiding it from ourselves in cases of self-deception. Thus we have partial control over the means to belief, and therefore it makes sense to say what we ought to believe or to recognize normative requirements on belief. The demands for coherence and to base one's beliefs on the evidence follow from the aim of truth, since incoherent beliefs cannot all be true and beliefs without evidence are unlikely to be so. These demands are normative—they determine what we ought to believe—but not irreducibly or non-naturally so, since they follow from the natural function or constitutive aim of the psychological state.

---

[40] See Ruth Millikan, *White Queen Psychology and other Essays for Alice* (Cambridge, MA: MIT Press, 1993), ch. 11.

[41] "Faith is believing what you know ain't true."

Reasons for action were provided a similar account. Action too can plausibly be claimed to have a constitutive aim, an aim that an agent can succeed in or fail to pursue, which generates reasons and irrationality in the failure to heed them once recognized. The constitutive aim of action is fulfilment of the rational, prioritized motivational set at the time of the action. We can fail in this aim through weakness of will or other recognizably irrational frames of mind, or through failing to achieve this coherence among our motivations in the first place. Reasons, internalists maintain, exist relative to these motivational sets. Rationality makes the normative demand that we follow them, but again there is no non-naturalness here. Desires, like beliefs, aim at their own satisfaction, and their natural function is to prompt actions in accord with the reasons that indicate how to satisfy them.

All is natural here since all follows from the type of creatures we are, creatures who believe and desire and act to fulfil our desires. We would not survive without true beliefs about our environments and actions that are guided by them, that are prompted by desires, and that satisfy our needs. Beliefs and desires are the kind of states that aim to be satisfied. Thus we need not ask why we ought to aim to satisfy them. That question is superfluous: we can no more ask why we should be motivated to satisfy our desires than we can ask why we should believe what is true. Some desires should be resisted when they conflict with others, just as some conflicting beliefs should be rejected, but the general aims are fixed. These aims, constitutive of the psychological states, can plausibly be construed as naturally selected biological functions. Normative naturalism is possible precisely because certain psychological states have natural aims, aims that derive from the type of biological beings we are, beings that believe, act, and are capable of reflecting on their reasons for believing and acting. Given aims and the possibility of succeeding or failing in them, we have normativity; given natural aims, we have natural normativity. What determines what counts as a reason is a basic normative fact, but natural and of internal derivation, not irreducible and external. The account requires no ultimate, non-natural normative facts as the source of reasons, and this is another argument in its favor. Metaphysical economy serves both simplicity and unity, primary theoretical virtues.

As Darwall has pointed out, Hobbes was a model for philosophers to think in terms of naturally imposed ends as the source of normative requirements.[42] For him, self-preservation was our natural end, and the desire for it was the source of other psychological states, such as the desire for power, which nevertheless could frustrate this aim in the wrong circumstances. This natural end and the threat to its fulfillment impose certain rational demands on us, Hobbes' "laws of nature," for example the demand to seek peace. These laws of nature give ultimate authority to other more conventional norms, as means to maintain peace for example. Thus, for Hobbes there is a natural, biologically imposed source of normativity. It must be admitted in opposition to Hobbes that even as basic an aim as self-preservation fails to always have overriding priority over all other ends, as he thought. But nature does impose this goal of surviving on us, as well as those aims necessary to survival. We are all creatures who believe and act, and these universal states do impose natural ends, their constitutive aims, on us. These aims require coherence among motivational states and beliefs in order to avoid self-defeat; hence the demand for coherence and information, which according to the internalist are all that rationality requires, follows from the natural aims themselves.

As for what remains of the open question argument, the standard answer to it now suffices. The question seems open only to those who do not know or accept the correct account of the origin of reasons. To me it is not an open question whether I have reason to do what will fulfil my coherent, informed, prioritized sets of motivations, containing my deepest concerns and specifications of ways of satisfying them. To say that I ought to so act is simply to say that I have most reason to do so. Normally, as pointed out, I am aware of the structure of my motivational set only through encounters with reasons of apparently different strengths that shift over time. This phenomenology, the fact that the normative presents itself to us primarily in the form of valuable or disvaluable states of affairs, is another and more respectable reason why there seems to be an open question regarding reasons for action even when all the motivations are known or stipulated to be informed and coherent. Despite this apparent space between motivations and reasons, the question is no more open than is the question

---

[42] Stephen Darwall, "Internalism and Agency," *Philosophical Perspectives*, 6 (1992): 155–174, pp. 162–4.

what to believe once all the evidence is in. Our deepest motivations might be unsatisfiable in the end, but then our ultimate evidence might be misleading also. But, as will be argued in the next chapter, we lack a vantage point from which we can sensibly question either as the ground of belief and action.

5

The Case Against Objective Value

I. Objective Value and Motivation

"If the world were perfect, it wouldn't be."

I have now provided an account of rationality in terms of relevant information and coherence, or the avoidance of self-defeat. I have offered an analysis of reasons as facts that motivate rational agents by indicating how to satisfy their deeper concerns. I have provided an account of motivations or desires themselves and of which desires generate reasons, namely those coherent sets of desires anchored by deeper concerns. In the previous chapter I argued that we are not forced to recognize other sources of reasons. If we are not forced to do so, if there is no data for which the internalist theory cannot account, then we ought to prefer that theory for its intelligibility and metaphysical economy. In this chapter I want to attack the opposing theory more directly, by attacking the notion of objective value on which that of external reasons is based.

Despite much discussion of the nature of reasons in recent philosophy, the debate over the objectivity of values, certainly one of the discipline's central topics, currently stands pretty much where it did after John Mackie's attack on the notion and Thomas Nagel's answer to Mackie.[1] Mackie had famously argued that objective values would be "queer" properties, in that prescriptivity, a strange "to-be-doneness," would have to be intrinsic to them. Objective values, which would exist or be instantiated independently of human faculties or ways of apprehending them, would nevertheless have to be intrinsically motivating and action guiding. No natural properties of

---

[1] John L. Mackie, *Ethics: Inventing Right and Wrong* (New York: Penguin, 1977), esp. pp. 38–42; Thomas Nagel, *The View from Nowhere* (Oxford: Oxford University Press, 1986), pp. 138–63.

objects, it seems, could be both independent in that way and yet necessarily motivating.

Nagel answered this argument in two steps. First, objective values need not actually motivate us, but instead give us reasons to act: they determine what we ought to do, what ought to motivate us, whether or not we are actually so motivated. Second, objective values are not strange new properties of objects suddenly revealed when we adopt an impersonal point of view or abstract from our self-centered motives. Objectivists require no strange new properties in a non-natural realm. Instead, objective values reduce to reasons independent of our actual motives, reasons that do emerge from an impartial or impersonal viewpoint. By abstracting from our personal perspectives, we can often discover what we ought to do and want, and these discoveries can correct our self-centered motivations, which may be mistaken and give us a distorted view of our real or objective reasons for action. On this view, to be good is to have other properties that give reasons for positive responses.

Thus, objective value need not always motivate, but it ought to motivate; it merits desire; it provides reasons or motivates a purely rational agent. Such value is not relative to particular subjects' valuings; instead, it is what we ought to value, what ought to be loved, pursued, and protected. Furthermore, if one thing is objectively better or more valuable than another, then it ought to be preferred, and if preferred, chosen over the other (perhaps discounted by the probability of acquiring it). This is not an argument for consequentialism, prudential or moral, as ordinarily narrowly construed. We are not to aim only at the best consequences, measured by the aggregate happiness or well-being of those affected by our actions. If there is objective value to equality in distributions or in keeping promises, for example, then this value will count in determining which states of affairs are better and therefore to be preferred or pursued. If it is not better that promises be kept, then why keep them? If it is not better to do one's moral duty, then one should do what is better instead. Similarly, if it matters not only that good is produced, but also for whom it is produced, then the additional value of doing good for those who deserve or need it can be included in the calculus.[2]

---

[2] Richard Kraut, by contrast, takes the point that it matters to whom good accrues as an argument against a maximizing view. *What is Good and Why* (Cambridge, MA: Harvard University Press, 2007), p. 39.

Value, even if objective, must still be of practical relevance: there can be value that is not valued by anyone, but it would still demand to be valued. For the objectivist, how much an object demands to be valued depends on how valuable it is. As noted also, objective value would be identified from an impartial, or, more precisely, an impersonal perspective. From this perspective we are supposed to intuit what is truly valuable. But how do we do this? One answer is that such value is identified through a proper response to it—an emotional response such as love or conative response such as desire. These responses once more contain implicit evaluative judgments, and rational agents are motivated by their evaluative judgments, by their immediate estimates of objective value for believers in such.

This link between objective value and motivation must be maintained if appeal to objective value is to have any philosophical or practical point. While avoiding appeal to Mackie's strange property advances the position of the objectivist, a property with no link to motivation would be metaphysically as well as practically superfluous. The question is whether a property that exists independently of all our concerns but nevertheless demands that we be concerned about it by providing reasons for such concern is any less strange than an objective property that intrinsically does motivate us. It can be asked why certain properties merit positive responses, and if the answer is simply "because they are valuable," the circle is very tight and unilluminating. Remember that meriting anything, if irreducible, is not itself a natural property.

The subjectivist, as pointed out earlier, has an obvious explanation for why recognition of value, reflected in implicit evaluative judgments, should motivate us: these judgments express existing motivations. Our values reflect what we are concerned about. There can be no question why we should desire to pursue or protect what we care about. For the objectivist, the reduction of objective value to external reasons grasped from an impersonal perspective links value to rationally required or merited motivation. We must still be capable of recognizing reasons for us from this perspective. This link between value and motivation is central not only in Nagel's account, but is standard in later versions as well. Thus Noah Lemos defines what is intrinsically more valuable, which he takes to imply objectively more valuable, as what is fitting to prefer;[3] Michael

---

[3] Noah Lemos, *Intrinsic Value* (Cambridge: Cambridge University Press, 1994), p. 67.

Zimmerman defines the intrinsically good as what, when contemplated, requires that one favor it;[4] Joel Kupperman defines objective value as what is better brought about or preserved;[5] and John Broome writes that the normal meaning of 'good' must be connected in an appropriate way to how one ought to act.[6]

The practical relevance of grasping objective value is supposed to be that such recognition can correct for subjective valuings that are out of line with it. A person who spends her life pursuing what is objectively worthless is, according to this view, wasting her life. And pursuing less rather than more value is acting less well than one could. To the charge that most of us seem rational most of the time doing things that do not aim to maximize objective value, it might be answered that, while objective value provides reasons to pursue it, these are not our only reasons. Perhaps other things we care about give us stronger reasons. But again, grasping what is objectively so corrects for distortions in subjective appearances. According to believers, what is objectively valuable is truly valuable, as opposed to worthless things we might misguidedly care about. It cannot be better to aim at or produce what is truly of less value.

If objective value comes in degrees or amounts, and if it provides or indeed equates with practical reasons, then the strength of these reasons will vary with the amount of value. Rational agents will therefore be attracted to objective value in proportion to its amount or degree. And all rational agents should be attracted to the same amounts of value to the same degrees. The impersonal point of view from which objective value is to be identified corrects for personal differences in valuings, just as the perspective from which any objective properties are to be identified must correct for the distortions of partial personal perspectives. Objective value is what we should all equally want if we grasp the nature of the objects that are valuable. And if pursuing objects of little or no value is bad, then pursuing objects of more value is better, and better to precisely the degree to which the objects are more valuable.

It follows that if objective value exists, then we all ought to aim to maximize it. If the more valuable is better than the less valuable, then we

[4] Michael Zimmerman, *The Nature of Intrinsic Value* (Landau, MD: Rowman and Littlefield, 2001), p. 86.
[5] Joel Kupperman, *Value . . . and What Follows* (Oxford: Oxford University Press, 1999), p. 89.
[6] John Broome, *Weighing Lives* (Oxford: Oxford University Press, 2004), p. 74.

ought to prefer it. If we ought to prefer it, then we ought to choose to produce and protect it. If we ought to choose to produce and protect it, then we ought to produce and protect it. If we always ought to produce and protect more rather than less objective value, then we ought to maximize objective value in the world. For any particular things of value, more of them might not be of greater value. The trees in my back yard have aesthetic value, but there are just enough of them so that more would not add to that value. But for value itself, more of it must always be better. Conversely, if something is better, it must be of greater value. And we should always choose to do what is known to be better over what is worse. That we should aim to produce the most value, however, again does not imply that we should always aim to produce the best consequences as measured by aggregate well-being.

Since objective value is not relative to subjective valuings, but corrects for them in providing external reasons, its existence would imply that we all have this same overriding aim. If particular things in themselves are objectively valuable, and yet people disagree about their value, then one side of each dispute must be wrong. This implication is, however, already highly problematic. If the side that fails to see value where others do is always seen to suffer from some kind of value blindness, we will get a very bloated class of real or objective values. Counting blades of grass might have to enter the ranks of the truly worthwhile. The denial that such activities are worthwhile is as central to the values and hence characters of individuals as is the affirmation of other worthwhile pursuits. On the other hand, we cannot count only universally or even widely shared values as objective, since mavericks might discover new things of value. How then are we to adjudicate such disputes? Is not the suspicion overwhelming that the referees as well as the disputants will simply be affirming what they value, what is of value to or for them, what is subjectively valuable?

To be fair, the call to maximize objective value does not imply that we all ought to aim at the same values with the same degree of effort. We need not all aim to produce the most valuable objects we possibly could produce. We may have different abilities to produce value in different domains, so that value will be maximized by a division of labor. The goal of maximizing value would have to discount the value of each object by the probability of actually producing it. According to the objectivist, we must aim not at the highest value, but at the highest expected value. There may be enough value to go around so that we should be motivated to produce what we are best able to produce. It might be better, for example, other things equal, if each parent prefers her own children, being better able to care for them, even if objectively one child is of no more value than another. Then too, the pleasure we get from pursuing what interests us is itself of value. The degree of preference would still need to be constrained by the overarching aim of maximizing objective value, if more expected value generates stronger reasons and rational agents act on their strongest reasons. Furthermore, there should be little difference in this regard between proper prudential and moral reasoning. If recognition of objective value corrects for desires to pursue what is less worthwhile, these two types of reasoning should mesh quite neatly together.[7]

Theories of practical reason that do not require that one choose the better of two available options are conceivable—two such theories have been proposed—but they are not coherent. The first of this kind of theory is one that allows satisficing on a global scale, that allows one to choose what is "good enough" over what is known to be available and better overall in the long run. I and others have argued at length that, while local satisficing can be an effective strategy for global optimization in the face of uncertainty, global satisficing makes no sense, given the meaning of "better".[8]

Local satisficing makes sense because it may not be worth the time, effort, and other resources involved in trying to maximize any particular good that must compete with others. Optimizing, as noted earlier, involves trade-offs to achieve the best mix of goods over time (whether subjective or objective goods). Given plural values, living the best lives we can does not involve trying to maximize wealth, brilliance and beauty in one's companions, fame or success in our careers, or other particular goods. But the irrationality of choosing less than the best overall among known available alternatives follows simply from our concepts of reasons and of better and worse. Reasons count in favor of actions: they are what make actions better than

---

[7] Compare James Griffin, *Value Judgment* (Oxford: Oxford University Press, 1996), p. 23.

[8] See Alan Goldman, *Practical Rules* (Cambridge: Cambridge University Press, 2002), pp. 79–86; also Michael Byron (ed.), *Satisficing and Maximizing* (Cambridge: Cambridge University Press, 2004) and my review of that book in *Utilitas*. For the best defense of global satisficing, see Michael Slote, *Beyond Optimizing* (Cambridge, MA: Harvard University Press, 1989).

alternatives. If satisficing is rational, there must be reasons in favor of it as strong as the reasons favoring maximization. But these reasons then make satisficing optimal from the global perspective. There therefore cannot be overriding reasons to choose what is worse overall: there must be overriding reasons to choose what is better all things considered. For global satisficing to be rational there must be reasons in favor of an option that do not make that option better, but that is not possible.

The second theory that appears to allow rational non-optimizing is one that includes "side constraints," prohibitions against certain types of actions even to prevent many more actions of the same kind. Thus, if there is a side constraint against torture, then we must not be torturers ourselves no matter how many cases of torture or other moral disasters we can prevent by torturing. Although it appears to be worse that more of such actions are performed, this theory nevertheless need not be seen as requiring the choice of worse options. It can be seen instead as giving lexical priority to certain agent relative prohibitions. This means that according to the theory, it is better that I not torture anyone myself even if this means allowing others to torture many more.

It is doubtful, however, that objective value, if it provides overriding reasons for choice, is compatible with agent relativity at the deepest level. While it may be better for parents to care for their own children, for example, all ultimately have the same aim of maximizing objective value, if more value means stronger reasons. It is also doubtful, as I will argue in the next section, that this idea of maximizing objective value can accommodate lexical priorities, giving some values absolute priority over additions of others. I have argued elsewhere at greater length that side constraints make little or no prudential or moral sense.[9] In a nutshell, aside from the difficulties of weighing side constraints themselves against one another where they might conflict, it is simply too implausible that we must allow utter disasters for the human race in order not to violate them.

Thus, if we must act on the strongest reasons we have, we must optimize. If objective values provide reasons, then the most expected objective value provides the strongest reasons, and we must act so as to

---

[9] Alan Goldman, "The Entitlement Theory of Distributive Justice," *Journal of Philosophy*, 73 (1976): 823–35. For the best defense of side constraints, see Robert Nozick, *Anarchy, State, and Utopia* (New York: Basic Books, 1974).

maximize objective value or contribute to its collective maximization. It should be noted, however, that the argument that follows does not require a premise as strong as the one just defended. I have assumed that duties could be absorbed into a calculation of better and worse states of affairs, on the ground that it is better if duties are honored. If a state of affairs is better, then it has more value and provides stronger reasons to produce or protect it. If an objection is made to this claim by critics of consequentialist theories or deontologists, then we can say that we have overriding reason to maximize objective value, should it exist, only after other irreducibly deontological duties are fulfilled. If keeping promises is not of value, then perhaps we ought to maximize value only after we keep our promises. There will remain problems for the objectivist in spelling out the connections between value and motivation, and between values and duties.

The first problem (after the problem of disagreement) is that virtually no one thinks and acts with the primary aim of maximizing a conception of objective value, or of doing so after one has performed one's duties. Our concerns, both everyday and deeper, are not generated or limited by a fundamental concern to maximize such value in the world, even assuming that we know what it would be to do so or aim to do so. We do not care about our children or provide for their welfare because we think it objectively valuable to do so, and most of us do not choose careers or leisure activities on that ground either. Our accomplishments may be of great importance to us but matter very little to the world. Very few care whether I finish writing this book, and no one (not even my wife) but I care whether I become a more accomplished tennis player. Yet I will devote many hours to both these personal goals. We set our own personal bars. Only a Mozart or Einstein makes a real difference in the amount of value in the world, and even in the case of Einstein the jury is still out on whether the difference is positive or negative.

As others have pointed out in regard to moral reasoning, the idea of maximizing objective value is not only foreign to normal agents, but often insulting as the ground of good deeds to their recipients. From the impersonal point of view from which objective value is to be accessed, my child's welfare is presumably worth no more than a stranger's, but none of us normally thinks that way. It is not that we do not think that way because we realize on a deeper level that we will better produce objective value by not aiming directly to maximize it or by attending to those people and matters closest to us that we can most effectively benefit. And it is not that we favor our own children because we think that our special relationship to them that includes favoring their interests is itself objectively valuable. We *really* just do not think about objective value in such contexts.

When we act in everyday contexts, we are normally pursuing our own goals in careers, personal relationships, leisure activities, and so on. These concerns are not developed with an eye toward objective value, and they are not hostage to any impersonal calculations. Our own good is defined largely by the satisfaction of these partial concerns. We all could produce more good than we do (conceived impartially), perhaps by working at different careers, but most of us are content not to be harming others or violating their rights in our personal pursuits. Our ordinary focus on personal matters is not irrational, as it would be if we were rationally required to maximize objective value, as would be required if our reasons derived from objective values. There are many things of value to others that I do not care about and that I see no reason to pursue. It is not that I do not think these things good: they are good for other people but not high on my list of things to do. There are even things I recognize to be of potential value to me that I do not care to pursue, such as learning to play a stringed instrument or to play soccer very well. There is only time for so much, but it is not that I think that the pursuits I do care about have more objective value than playing an instrument or even playing soccer.

As emphasized throughout, normally we do not need to deliberate about our reasons for acting, and the reason we do not is that states of affairs that present themselves as opportunities or threats already reflect our motivations. These motivations have nothing to do with maximizing anything except their own satisfaction. Only when they conflict does deliberation occur, and it is concerned to prioritize these motivations and remove the conflicts. In this process, moral constraints, which reflect a more impartial point of view, generally remain in the background, and impersonal considerations of value are absent. In regard to the way people ordinarily lead their lives, it is relevant here that even those who do devote themselves primarily to doing good for strangers most in need usually do so as a prequel or sequel to more personally oriented careers. This is not to say that most people are selfish, only that even altruistic long-term projects tend to be both personal and more narrowly directed than the goal of maximizing objective value would suggest.

It might be replied either that we all think and act wrongly in not aiming to maximize the production and protection of objective value, or that our pursuit of our personal and partial projects does unwittingly tend best to achieve that aim. I shall consider the first reply at length in the next section. It must claim that we ordinarily act not only wrongly in the moral sense, but irrationally, most of the time. Even the weaker moral claim seems false. As to the second reply, it is true that just as we need not focus on our desires in order to be satisfying them when we act on our reasons, so we need not focus on objective value in order to be maximizing it. But in the latter case as opposed to the former, it is simply implausible that we do act to maximize objective value, to the extent that we understand that concept. As noted above, it seems clear that we could all produce more good than we do if that, or anything like that, were our conscious or subconscious aim, or if our other real aims were even compatible with that goal. There is no idea here of a mechanism that would explain how we could be maximizing objective value unwittingly in the way that Adam Smith's invisible hand explains how a free market tends to maximize the satisfaction of material wants in a society.

In fact, it is questionable whether we even understand what it would be to maximize objective value in our actions. We may turn then from the question whether we do typically pursue maximum objective value—it seems so obvious that we do not—to the question whether we could do so. Of course, in one sense, if there is no objective value, then we cannot pursue it. But can we do so even as an intentional object; in other words, do we have a clear enough concept of what it would be to maximize such value? We do have the concept of an impartial and perhaps even an impersonal viewpoint from which such value is supposed to be revealed. But do we know what it would be to maximize it? The problem I want to raise here is that of an irremediable imprecision in estimating amounts of supposed objective value (beyond the usual difficulties in aggregating utilities).

It is widely acknowledged that values admit only of ordinal rankings. Incommensurability aside, an agent can judge that A is more valuable than B, but any initial assignment of units of value to A or B will be arbitrary. It might be thought that, since values come in amounts or degrees, and since real objects and their properties cannot be indeterminate, the arbitrary or initially indeterminate assignment of values to measurements in itself calls into question the objectivity of values. But in fact there is no deep problem here. The same can be said of temperature or length, for example, and these properties are not relative to subjective perspective, except in how they appear. We can correct for how temperature feels or length looks from various perspectives in order to determine objective properties once units of measurement are assigned. The real problem here for objective values is that there is no clear way to correct for subjective valuings so as to determine a precise measurement.

Consider first the values of ordinary objects: computers, cars, cool pools in summer. Ordinarily we consider such objects good to the degree that they satisfy our interests in them or our purposes in using them. My computer is good if it stores much information, processes it quickly, displays it clearly, and so on. My computer is good if it is good for me, good in terms of how I use it. An objectivist might admit that all goodness in objects is goodness for something or someone but deny that such goodness for is always relative to our purposes. Water is good for plants because it enables them to live, and this, it will be claimed, has nothing to do with us or our purposes.[10] Nothing directly to do with us, I would reply, but we conceive of goodness for plants by analogy with our own case. We have an interest in living long—we are motivated to do so—and we anthropocentrically posit an interest in plants for (long) life as well. We then see that water serves this interest and say that water is good for plants. It would make little sense to say along the same lines what is good for a rock, and therefore we do not. Furthermore, what we take to be good for plants is what serves the values we find in plants: what will help to produce a beautiful flower, for example, or improve the nutrition or taste of a vegetable.

All goodness of objects then seems to be goodness either directly or indirectly for us, goodness in serving our aims, those of other sentient beings, or those of other things thought to have aims by analogy with ours. If all goodness of objects is goodness for us or for beings like us, their value is relative to how they function for us, to our aims or interests in them. They provide reasons for us to respond to them in various ways because they serve our purposes. By responding to them or using them in various

---

[10] Kraut, *What is Good and Why*, p. 9. He builds his entire theory of value from such examples.

actions we fulfil our aims. There is no other explanation of why they should motivate us. And there is no single measurement of the value they have for all of us. Objective properties, it seems, should be determinate. But ordinary objects have a large range of values for different people. If such a property appears vague or indeterminate, this should be due to vagueness in our concepts or imprecision in the subjective states by which we apprehend it. If objective values appear imprecise or indeterminate, this should be due to some shortcoming in our ability to grasp or intuit them. Yet here there is no conceivable instrument that could give us a more precise way to measure supposed objective value.

We can make the values of various objects to a person more precise by considering what that person prefers or chooses, what he is willing to exchange for what, what gambles at what probabilities he is willing to make, assuming that these preferences meet certain conditions of rationality. The values or utilities derived will be measures of the strengths of desires for these objects, subjective values. We can also aggregate such personal preferences or subjective valuings to derive social demand at different exchange rates or prices for various goods. More contentiously, we can perhaps compare packages of goods and distributions of them over different individuals to determine which packages and distributions of goods are better from an impartial point of view. This, if successful, might give us some notion of general good, although here there is no universal agreement as to how to weigh different patterns of distribution against aggregate totals of goods, how much to value equality in distributions, for example. Even if we could achieve consensus on this central question in moral and political philosophy, this notion of general good would remain firmly anchored to our aggregates of subjective valuings.

There seems to be no sense attached to the notion of precise amounts of real or objective values of such objects, no notion of how much people should value objects, apart from how much they do value them or are willing to pay or exchange for them. If some persons ought to value some objects more or less than they do, this seems to be because those objects would satisfy or frustrate their concerns more than they currently believe. Being relative to subjective concerns, such claims about the value of ordinary objects still reflect subjective values. Furthermore, if people have different interests, and the values of objects depend on their satisfying those interests, then their values will be relative to different people for whom they are valuable. What we seem unable to do here is to move beyond impartiality in aggregation to an impersonal point of view and thereby correct for how much people informed of the nature of various objects collectively value them in terms of how much they should value them.

If the value of objects were objective or independent of subjects' interests in them, then different subjects should value the same objects to the same degree. But of course they do not. I value a tennis racquet far more than does a person who does not play tennis, and such variations hold for all such objects and the persons who use them for various purposes. Nor should it be otherwise. The objectivist must therefore move to a different level if she considers such objects at all. She must find objective value in the pleasure or satisfaction we get from using such ordinary objects. But, if we are sticking to the topic of the motivation that objective value is supposed to require of us, all the powerful arguments against psychological hedonism now become relevant. I do not go to the sports store to get pleasure, but to get a tennis racquet. As has been argued for centuries, pleasure is normally a byproduct, not a goal of successful action. We are motivated to satisfy certain needs, achieve various goals, and engage in various activities. Objects have value for us in serving those ends. Only the value of objects like chocolate ice cream can be measured in terms of the pleasure they afford. I would not know how to translate even the values of various objects for me into the pleasure that their use affords me. In any case, I will question the objective value of pleasure itself in a later section.

It might be replied that, while we do not correct for the subjective values of ordinary objects or material goods, we do in other cases. A first exception might seem to lie in the ways we speak of the appreciation or values of artworks. We say that certain individuals have bad taste, that they should value certain works more than they do. We say that certain works are better than others, even though most people enjoy or value the latter, popular forms, more than the former, fine works. We therefore imply that certain works merit greater or less appreciation than they prompt or receive. But the sense I can make of these locutions fails to imply either that the works have value independent of our responses to them or that these responses should match the independent values of the works.

In the case of individuals undervaluing works, we might mean that if those individuals understood the works, could perceive how their elements relate to each other and how the works continue or transform their historical traditions, then they would value them more. Similarly, to say that some works really are better than others might be to say that the interests that all people bring to art are more deeply satisfied by the former works.[11] There is nothing in either of these available interpretations to imply that art objects have value that is independent of the ways we respond to them and of the capacities and motivations that underlie these responses. Works merit responses only because of the ways that informed people with certain sensibilities do respond and because of the value of such appreciative responses to them. The value of such objects remains response dependent and therefore not objective in the full sense.

When it comes to the value of people's lives, as opposed to that of objects, in the first instance it seems clear that how good one's life is can be judged only from the internal personal perspective. A banker may judge her life to be very good (although again speaking of precise amounts of goodness seems out of place here), but to me, a philosophy professor, living that life might not be good at all. And there are some lives that I cannot even imagine living, cannot conceive of what it would be like to live them. The value here is the goodness of the life for the person living it, and this is clearly a subjective matter. The personal perspective cannot be eliminated from estimates of the goodness of lives in this sense. These estimates are not only person relative, but imprecise, again problematic for a concept of objective value. If we could make them precise and then aggregate the personal values of lives across people to derive a notion of the general good different from that described above, this new notion would remain that of the goodness of lives from their subjects' personal viewpoints.[12]

It is true that sometimes we are forced to weigh lives from an impartial perspective. Morality demands such when lives are at stake and decisions must be made as to who lives or dies. But in such cases we generally simply give equal weight to all lives or use some very rough measure such as age. The impartial point of view adopted in these contexts does not reveal, and is not aimed at revealing, the precise amount of objective value attached to

[11] For an account of this sort, see my *Aesthetic Value* (Boulder, CO: Westview, 1995).
[12] For more detailed discussion, see Broome, *Weighing Lives*, 122.

each life. We normally do not count the value contributed to others' lives
in such contexts, the sense in which Einstein's or Mozart's life was worth
more to society than the average person's life. Such external value is not a
measure of the objective value of a life either, in part just because it ignores
the value of the life to the person herself. Nor would combining these
perspectives, perhaps by adding the differential values added to others' lives
from their points of view to the value of the life to the person herself,
take us beyond subjective valuings to purely objective value. We are still
speaking of value in terms of satisfying the concerns that people have,
a concern to listen to beautiful music of the sort Mozart composed for
example.

In still other contexts, such as that of deciding how much to spend for
safety, we seem to weigh other goods against lives that could be saved.
There are again different ways of doing this, but I take it that no one
pretends that any of these ways gives us a precise measure of the value
of lives. We might, for example, use estimated income over a lifetime
to measure the market value produced by the person, but we would not
want to say that a person's life has just as much value as what that person
produces for the market. In rare contexts we might speak of whether it
is better or worse that a person exists or that his life is being lived. We
speak in that way when a person's life seems so bad as to be not worth
living. But this is a matter again of how good or bad the life is for the
person living it, and, even more rarely, of how that life affects the value
to other people of their lives. While loss of life almost always appears to
be negative, a diminution of value, adding more lives to the world does
not seem to increase its net value.[13] This again seems to be because the
value of a life is its value to the person living it and to others related to that
person.

The conclusion of this section is first, that appeal by philosophers to
objective value is appeal to what we ought to value and therefore to aim
at; second, that normal agents do not aim in their thought, activity, or
central concerns to maximize objective value, as they ought to if such value
exists. Third, since values come in degrees and since objective properties
are determinate, objective values ought to come in precise or determinate

---

[13] Ben Bradley, "Two Concepts of Intrinsic Value," *Ethical Theory and Moral Practice*, 9 (2006):
111–30. He suggests that we have different notions of intrinsic value referring to people's lives and
states of affairs.

degrees.[14] But fourth, there seems to be no perspective from which we have access to the precise objective values of ordinary objects or of people's lives, some of the things we might expect to have objective value if there were such. We can measure how much we value things in relation to other things we might exchange for them; but there is no measure of how much we ought to value things. In terms of reasons, the strength of internal reasons is measured by the degree to which acting on them satisfies our concerns and by how strong or deep those concerns are, while there is no measure of strength for external reasons.

It might be replied that we have no way to measure precisely other properties that we take to be both determinate and objective. We cannot, for example, assign exact degrees of baldness to persons, but baldness is an objective property. But the reason we take baldness to be objective despite not being precisely measurable is that we realize that our inability to measure results only from the inaccessibility of the evidence. People have precise numbers of hairs on their heads, but we cannot count them. In the case of value, the problem does not seem to be that we have no access to its precise degree: unlike the case of hairs, we cannot conceive of what such access would be. Once more there is no instrument or closer view that gives us an accurate measure of degrees of objective value. Thus it still seems initially doubtful that agents could aim to maximize objective value, or that determinate objective value even exists.

But suppose we could maximize objective value and in fact achieved the maximum. Then there would be nothing left to do. A world in which there was nothing to do would not be as good as one in which people continued to have important projects. Hence achieving maximum value would not be achieving maximum value. This is the paradox noticed by Yogi Berra in noting that a perfect world would not be. It can perhaps be resolved by maintaining that there is no upper bound to the amount of objective value that could be realized or produced. But then again there could be no such thing as a perfect world. No matter how much value was created, there would always be a better world waiting to be created or realized. The best of all possible worlds would not be perfect, but would be one in which we continued to produce and protect the most value we

[14] Zimmerman, *The Nature of Intrinsic Value*, 143.

could at each time, so as to continue to optimize over time. But again, none of us thinks that way when we act.

II. The Impartial and Impersonal Perspectives

"It gets late early out here."
"Little things are big."

It might be replied to the arguments of the previous section that we have been looking in the wrong places for objective value and demanding too much precision in our access to it. Perhaps it is not ordinary objects that have objective value, or even lives as such, but such states as pleasures or pains, or perhaps the satisfaction of our preferences or deepest concerns themselves. And perhaps it is not in our ordinary activities that we address ourselves to such value or aim directly to maximize it, but only in morally charged contexts in which we are required to adopt an impartial point of view and estimate as best we can all the effects of our actions on the relevant states of affairs. We may then consider first whether the moral point of view does seem proper for accessing objective value, or whether it at least approximates to a perspective from which it might be accessed.

The moral point of view might seem to take us closer to accessing objective value since morality demands that we elevate the interests or concerns of others relative to our own partial concerns and to our ordinary ways of practical reasoning. As emphasized in the previous chapter, it requires more than usual impartiality in judging what we ought to do. Furthermore, moral reasons are often taken to override partial concerns and the unfettered pursuit of personal projects, just as objective values or reasons are held to correct for our more partial perspective. But do moral codes call upon us to maximize objective value or to approximate doing so? Only if moral considerations as actually used to guide practical reasoning are so oriented does the moral point of view take us closer to accessing such value. I see two major initial problems in thinking of the moral perspective in that way: first, the agent relative prerogatives and restrictions that exist in actual moral codes, as opposed to the stark impartiality of the simpler and more abstract philosophical theories that are rarely if ever used to guide conduct in real morally charged contexts; and second, the lexical priority that we grant to rights over additions of lesser interests.

In regard to prerogatives, ordinary morality, while it elevates concern for all others over that which is natural, still allows agents to give greater weight to personal projects, their own interests, and interests of those close to them than they give to the interests of strangers. In fact, this is an understatement. As long as we are not harming others or violating their rights, we are not blamed for failing to promote the interests of others at all. Our own projects and the interests of those we care about give us reasons that are not shared by others, while, as noted earlier, the maximization of objective value would give us all exactly the same reasons, allowing only for differences in our abilities to promote or protect instances of it and the pleasure we get from doing so.

It might be replied again that having agents promote the interests of those closest to them does maximize objective value in the long run. In fact, this is typically seen as the reason moral codes allow such partiality. If morality is really impartial on the deepest level, then preference for the interests of those close to us can be morally justified only on the ground that it tends to benefit all. The problem is that this premise is very questionable: it seems that most of us could provide much more incremental welfare to those much more in need in distant places than we provide to ourselves or our friends. Furthermore, the right we grant ourselves to pursue our own projects and prefer the interests of our family and friends does not depend on our ability to show that such partiality maximizes total objective value.

While moral demands may constrain such preference beyond that which is natural, we are still understating the degree of partiality, reflecting the subjective origins, of the ordinary moral perspective. For, as noted, this perspective contains not only agent relative prerogatives, but restrictions as well.[15] Not only may we be partial, but we are required to be so by the moral perspective we adopt to guide our behavior and evaluate agents, the perspective reflected in our feelings of guilt and resentment of violations. A father who refused to feed his child in order to provide food for two other children in a distant country, or one who would not pay for his

---

[15] Contrast Samuel Scheffler, *The Rejection of Consequentialism* (Oxford: Clarendon Press, 1982). In this groundbreaking work, Scheffler justifies agent relative prerogatives but not agent relative restrictions.

child's education in order to educate two strangers, would not only be considered abnormal, but would be widely thought to have a morally defective character. It certainly seems difficult to provide a justification for such judgments from a purely impartial viewpoint, but the point here is precisely that they reflect our own values as developed from our personal perspectives. Ordinary morality retains this perspective even while elevating the interests of others in granting them rights. And again, it is not simply the objective value of the relationships themselves that justifies the partiality they include.

It was noted earlier that the requirements of duties might be held to be distinct from the values of the states of affairs that result from their fulfilment. Fulfilling these duties might be held to take priority over the reasons we have to maximize value of any sort. But not only does this claim imply the counterintuitive proposition that it is often better to realize worse states of affairs; it also seems problematic that our duties should in general so directly and sharply oppose and override a general requirement to achieve what is objectively most valuable. Is it not a better state of affairs when duties are honored than when they are ignored? If so, then the opposition between duty and value cannot be as sharp as it is posited to be by this claim. But if it is not so sharp, then there is once more a problem of how to measure the value of duties, or absent such measure, how to balance them against objective values.

An objectivist can allow that we would naturally prefer the interests and projects of those close to us, including ourselves. This would be because value, while objective, is normally viewed from a personal and partial perspective. Just as a small object appears large when viewed from close up and a warm substance feels cool to a hot hand, so an equal value will appear greater when viewed from a closer perspective.[16] And, since desire is supposed to arise in rational agents to the degree to which they experience objective value, and since they experience value from their personal perspectives, they will be naturally more motivated by closer value than by its equal but more distant counterpart. Thus the objectivist can explain why it is natural to respond differentially to the same amounts of objective value.

---

[16] See Graham Oddie, *Value, Reality, and Desire* (Oxford: Clarendon Press, 2005), pp. 60–3, 218–26, for more detailed discussion.

But while she can explain why it is natural for us to do so, she cannot explain why we are not morally or rationally required to correct for this distortion of objective perspective when deciding how to act. We do correct for perceptual perspective when judging the objective properties of objects, but we do not do so, at least not completely, when it comes to judging our reasons for acting. When the objectivist explains why we should value the interests of those close to us more than the interests of those distant, this is the wrong sense of "should". She explains why we should be expected to do so, but not why we ought to do so according to moral codes actually in use.

According to the objectivist, moral codes, if reflective of the aim of maximizing objective value, ought to correct for all partiality in perspective. They must do so if they are to serve the function of correcting our motivations in light of objective reasons. But real moral codes actually used to guide conduct do not do so. As for philosophical moral theories, which are fully impartial at their base, the utilitarian can argue once more that primarily serving our own interests maximizes utility for all in the long run, and the Kantian can perhaps allow universal willing of such preferential behavior. But again our practices and normal patterns of approvals and disapprovals are not hostage to such calculations, which are in any case suspect in this regard.[17] Is it really plausible that the degree of partiality we allow each other ultimately serves the aim of impartially satisfying the needs of all? Only if this aim is fulfilled can we achieve the objectively best state of affairs, assuming that satisfying the needs of each individual has equal value.

The second problem for thinking that morality gives us access to objective value is the lexical priority we give to rights over additions of lesser interests. Honoring rights, like doing our duties generally, can be held to have value and thus be subsumed under calculations of value produced or realized by our actions. Lexical priority seems, however, incompatible with the idea of maximizing objective value, since this idea assumes that value is simply additive across objects, states of affairs, or individuals.[18] If we

---

[17] There are "two-level" moral theories, such as Mill's and Hare's, according to which we are not to hold our common sense rules hostage to impersonal calculations, which are nevertheless the ultimate criteria of rightness. But for them this prohibition results only from our proneness to error in such calculations. Our partiality to those close to us, however, once more seems not to rest on the likelihood of such errors.

[18] This again refers to additions of value itself and does not imply that when objects have value, more of them will have more value.

do not grant such lexical priority to rights, then a person's right to life could be overridden by the interest of a sufficient number to have a mild itch relieved. But this would nullify the idea of a central right entirely. Once we do grant rights lexical priority over lesser interests, not allowing them to be violated no matter how many lesser interests are at stake, calculations aimed to maximize objective value would become hopelessly complex if not impossible.

In order to prevent all additions of relief from minor itches (which must be of some value) from overriding important rights, we would have to grant the latter infinite value. But then the problem of ordering rights themselves so as to add their values would loom hopelessly large. There are non-standard mathematics in which we can add or order infinite numbers, but it would be absurd to claim that we utilize such calculations with the aim of maximizing value in our moral reasonings. I do not know how we could do so, given that the orderings among particular rights change with contexts in which they are more or less centrally at stake. Sometimes life is more important than liberty; at other times not. Sometimes free speech is more important than the harm it might cause; at other times not. Such shifts in priorities are ubiquitous, and not all are predictable. The reasoning involved is simply not additive.

As described in the previous chapter, moral reasoning aimed at ordering rights in various controversial contexts typically proceeds from agreed cases in which those rights are uncontroversially ordered. If right A takes priority over right B in context C, then it must take priority in context D where the rights again conflict, unless there is some morally relevant difference between C and D. Intuitions in the agreed cases are properly considered reliable because they reflect our own moral values. A full description of this process of reasoning is again beyond our scope here,[19] but it is equally clear that this reasoning is not a matter of adding and subtracting aimed at maximizing. It is instead a matter of working out shared priorities in contexts that may alter those priorities, a matter of what we are willing to do and suffer in different situations. The contextualized values that are thereby prioritized derive from different sources or concerns, without a single objective measure that would allow for simple addition and subtraction.

---

[19] For my description, see *Practical Rules*, ch. 4, and *Moral Knowledge* (London: Routledge, 1988), ch. 5.

As also noted earlier, the central constraint of consistency that governs moral argument—that we are not to judge cases differently without specifying morally relevant differences between them—aims at avoiding moral incoherence, the defeat of some moral values by others we judge to be less important in the relevant contexts. This aim is formally similar to that involved in prioritizing prudential concerns, except that moral argument can succeed only where values are shared. We must begin moral arguments from cases or orderings of rights on which we agree and then assimilate controversial cases to these agreed ones if we cannot find morally relevant differences. Using the example of abortion again, if we allow contraception or abortion at an early stage of pregnancy, then we must allow it at a later stage if we cannot find a morally relevant difference between the stages, a difference that is relevant in other moral contexts as well.

This method of settling moral disputes, and its limitation of beginning only from agreed cases would not be paramount if values were objective and recognized to be so. The actual development of moral codes through the working out of priorities among rights in new cases is like the development of legal codes: gradually to be filled in by arrivals at consensus under the constraint of consistency and compatibly with the social function of moral restraints. We must maintain that degree of impartiality in the form of respect for rights that is necessary for social living with cooperation. The aim of maximizing objective value, by contrast, would give us an already completed and waiting to be discovered moral code.

For the subjectivist, our emphasis on individual rights reflects our roles as autonomous valuers or creators of value. Rights protect autonomy by creating a personal space not to be invaded by collective interests. Nagel, by contrast, claims that the priority we grant to certain interests over others actually reflects the greater attention paid by moral demands to objective values. He points to the fact that we feel obligated to feed a person who is starving, but not to aid that person in a personal project, even if she would be willing to starve in order to complete the project. The reason for this priority, he believes, is that the latter represents only a subjective value, while the person's health or life are more objectively valuable.[20] But it is not clear to me why all such projects must be counted as only subjectively valuable by the believer in objective value, and I argued earlier that we are

---

[20] Nagel, *The View from Nowhere*, ch. 9.

not rationally required to be concerned about our health (although being concerned, it makes sense to grant a right to health care). The priority in Nagel's example can instead be explained in terms of which obligations individuals would be willing to assume in return for catastrophic insurance from others. A contractarian framework of this sort will reflect shared and central, but not necessarily objective, values.

Our actual moral codes, with their emphasis on individual rights, reflect not the aim of additively maximizing objective value, but restraints that we are willing to accept in order to provide such insurance, reduce conflict, and promote cooperation so that we may all pursue our deepest concerns. These restraints require a certain degree of impartiality not in order to reveal objective value, but because, in order to serve their real functions, they must be acceptable to all. Where they conflict with the pursuit of personal projects, this need not be seen as a conflict between subjective and objective values, but instead between the interests of one person and those of others. We have seen that the degree of impartiality required, while greater than we naturally grant, falls short of what we would expect from an objectivist viewpoint.

There are yet other features of common morality that indicate its subjective basis, as opposed to an orientation toward objective value. Why, for a first example, is harming people considered worse than not helping them, and not helping those in your vicinity worse than not helping those more distant? From an objective point of view, there are no answers to these questions. Harm is harm whether caused or not prevented, and distance is a matter of subjective perspective, not objective weight. But people care more about not being harmed than about being helped; not all need help, but all need protection against harm. People care more about those with whom they are in direct contact, and they want limits to the demands that morality can make on them. Then too, there are evolutionary origins of morality in concern for kin and pressures favoring the development of self-reliance.

Second, the vagueness and imprecision emphasized in the previous section regarding values generally infects moral values as well. Do I kill one person in order to save two, five, one-hundred? Do I save my child in danger or two strangers, five strangers, one-hundred? Objectively, there should be right answers. They should depend only on the values of the lives and relationships. But in fact there is not enough precision in our subjective values to give us clear answers. The reason there is such lack of precision might be that we fortunately do not often have to reflect on or make such tragic choices. Lacking clear precedents, the only justification for any such choice we might have to make would be simply that we had to make it. Once more the lack of precise answers does not seem to derive from any remediable difficulty in epistemic access to the facts or from the unique strangeness of objective values. There simply is no subject independent way to weigh all moral reasons against each other, let alone weigh moral against prudential and other sorts of reasons.

Third, as I will argue in the next section regarding pleasures and pains, the relativity in the moral valences of various actions to contexts makes objective measurement obscure if not impossible. Killing and lying are sometimes right and loving someone sometimes bad, and we cannot exhaustively state the conditions in which the usual valences reverse. As the examples of killing some to save others also indicate, it does not seem to be just a matter of maximizing value or minimizing its loss.

The final problem for thinking that the moral or impartial point of view takes us closer to accessing objective value is, as described in the previous chapter, the broader issue of moral relativism. Whose moral perspective is to provide such access—the egalitarian's or libertarian's, the individualist's or collectivist's, the utilitarian's or Kantian's? Again we need not try to answer this question. It now seems that if we are to access objective value, we need to move beyond impartiality to impersonality, beyond merely human projects altogether.

Before leaving morality behind altogether, however, we should note that there is one moral methodology that might yet take us closer to objective value. One might attempt to move closer by imposing ever thicker Rawlsian-type veils of ignorance. Thus, we might imagine being ignorant not only of all partial and personal concerns, but of our culture and place in history, of our natural endowments and vulnerabilities, and then imagine what reasons might remain for us to act. Or, to complete the move as Nagel suggests, we might even more radically imagine the viewpoint of the universe as a whole, with its virtually infinite time and space, and conceive of how our reasons and values appear from that perspective. The problem here is that, instead of objective values and reasons revealing themselves from such perspectives, all value and meaningful purpose seems to disappear entirely. From our perspective little things are big and it might get late early for us, as Yogi Berra reminds us, but from the point of view beyond all personal concerns what is big or important to us becomes vanishingly small, and there is no appreciable difference between having more or less time for our projects or lives.

If the Rawlsian method leaves us ignorant of all our actual concerns, it removes all reason to choose anything. It is a standard criticism of Rawls' ascription of purportedly universal values or "primary goods" that they turn out to be not only culturally, but personally, relative. Rawls sees goods such as wealth as useful for acquiring all other goods, and more of these primary goods as always better. But for ascetics, for example, wealth is corrupting, not liberating. More of it is more corrupting. If such values appear to us to be universal or objective, as coming to us from without, it is because they are largely given to us by our culture, and it is difficult to see beyond the culture in which we are so deeply embedded to imagine concretely very different choices of what to care about. But even for those within our culture, Rawls' primary goods vary in value: some care more about wealth or liberty than others. Primary goods are of variable worth even to different individuals who care about them. And not only could a human from a very different culture see our pursuit of wealth and power, for example, as completely pointless; a non-human alien could describe the most thorough genocide as we might describe the workings of an antibiotic or insecticide, or the replacement of one type of grass with another.[21]

As Nagel himself sometimes emphasizes, the cosmic perspective induces an absurdist or nihilistic vertigo in which all our most passionate undertakings, soon to be annihilated from all memory, appear pointless. In the long run, as they say, we are all dead, and there is not much else to say from that perspective. The trick, according to Nagel, is to find a mid-range perspective between the personal and the cosmic, in which objective values appear before they disappear.[22] But wherever we stop short of complete impersonality, the tension remains between the claim that an objective perspective reveals a different kind of value and the claim that it reveals the

---

[21] This point is made by Joseph Mendola, "Objective Value and Subjective States," *Philosophy and Phenomenological Research*, 50 (1990): 695–713, p. 700. Having made it, however, he surprisingly goes on to identify what he takes to be objective values (to be considered in my final section).

[22] Nagel, *The View from Nowhere*, p. 209. I have been representing Nagel as a proponent of objective value, and indeed he is. But it would certainly not be fair or accurate to portray him as a pure objectivist: for him it is a major and partly unsolvable problem how to integrate the subjective and objective perspectives.

absurdity of all valuings. What is revealed from the mid-range perspective is once again shared values, those shared more or less widely. This is the perspective of impartiality. Objective properties would persist from the more distant view of impersonality or pure objectivity, where it appears instead that values disappear.

Thus it seems that the personal perspective cannot be eliminated entirely from judgments of value. Every evaluative judgment is made from the perspective of a person with a history of cultural inputs, a set of tastes, and a set of concerns more or less widely shared. This motivational set remains in the background as states of affairs present themselves as reasons, as opportunities or threats, culminations, rewards, and pleasures, or dead-ends, frustrations, or pains. That we do not typically focus on our own motivations is one reason why values may appear to be objective. But to attempt to transcend this personal perspective entirely and give everyone the same objective reasons and concerns is to nullify personal identity as well. The view from nowhere is the view of no one.

A person's identity is determined and defined in large part by the values she pursues, by her deepest concerns that generate many other concerns as specifications of them or means to satisfy them. As argued earlier, these deepest concerns—for our families and personal relationships, careers, and so on, including second-order desires to be a certain kind of person with certain kinds of concerns—require no reasons themselves beyond being satisfiable in current social settings, but they provide reasons for many other desires and actions. Certainly they are not all universally shared: the pursuit of philosophical wisdom, for example, is not of value to all people, and not simply because not all are capable of achieving it. Yet it may be among the deepest concerns of some. The self is created by the integration of these concerns of the individual into a coherent structure, the basic task of practical reason.[23]

These two points—that we cannot eliminate the personal perspective and that this perspective is defined largely by the person's set of prioritized concerns—implies that we cannot question all of our concerns or motivations at once and retain any sense of who we are. And that is not only true, but it is once again why the attempt to transcend the personal and achieve

[23] Compare Harry Frankfurt, *The Importance of What We Care About* (Cambridge: Cambridge University Press, 1988), p. 170.

a purely objective perspective results in a kind of value vertigo. If values were objective, independent of all our actual motivations but demanding nevertheless that we be motivated by them, then it would be possible that our informed and coherent set of motivations could be nonetheless mistaken or misguided, just as our best evidence as to the nature of objective properties could be misleading. What it means to be an objective property is to be independent of the evidence we have for it or the way it appears. An objective property is not reducible to the way it appears to subjects: it can appear one way and be another way. Similarly, what it means to be an objective value is to be independent of subjective concerns. If objective values are what we ought to pursue, if their function is to correct subjective values, and if they therefore can be different from all our actual concerns, then all these concerns could be mistaken.

But in the case of values, there seems to be no such possibility. If we are maximally satisfying our deepest concerns, and if our second-order desires mesh with our first so that we are self-satisfied, then there seems to be no way that the world (apart from other beings with other interests) could demand that we have different motivations. These deepest concerns, we noted, require no support from reasons. We do not need a reason to care for or prefer our own children. Reasons come from, not to such concerns. They derive from the needs of the type of beings we are, although culture and personal differences shape and translate these needs in very different ways and orders. As I asked in the Introduction, could we be mistaken in being concerned for the welfare of our children? Could their welfare lack objective value, making our concern misguided? Of what concern to us could it be if it were so?

If there were objective value, it might be totally out of tune with our concerns and with how our lives are going, which is a function of the satisfaction of those concerns. But such a conflict would only render the objective values irrelevant to us and our reasons for action. How could we judge these values except from the perspective of what we find valuable? Things that are objectively good might not be good for us, but then we would have no reason to pursue them. Certainly we could see no such reasons. The tie between value, reasons, and motivations would be lost. The objectivist needs to have it both ways—again, that values be independent of actual motivations but rationally require motivation. But this dual demand is incoherent. If our whole informed and prioritized set of concerns were out of tune with objective value, we could find no reason to pursue it instead. If we could find no reason, we would have no reason, since reasons are what should guide our conduct, and they could not guide our conduct if we could not become aware of them.

There is one sense in which our collective concerns might have gone wrong: if they were completely unsatisfiable. Of course then we would not have survived as a species. That we have survived indicates that the world had to play some role in shaping these concerns, as it did through natural selection. Given the required cooperation of the world in providing value for us, we may think of values as relations between objective properties and our concerns. External objects and their properties are valuable, but only because of the ways we respond to them. Values are response dependent properties, as are secondary qualities such as colors. But while normal people see roughly the same colors in the same conditions, normal people do not value the same objects in the same ways. Thus values are not only relational properties, but more strongly relative to different subjects than are secondary qualities.

Nagel claims that once we get some distance from our desires by adopting an impersonal perspective, we recognize that, whatever the facts may be about our psychology, we can always ask what we have most reason to do.[24] This is again an "open question" argument for the irreducibility of value to any subjective origins. I have been arguing the opposite: that there is no perspective from which we can coherently question our informed and prioritized entire set of motivations at once. The question is not open to us whether we ought to try to fulfil our coherent deepest concerns. To be concerned is to be concerned to fulfil those concerns, and they can be called into question only by other concerns with which they might conflict.

One might reply that the case is no different with belief in an objective physical world. We cannot look beyond our entire set of beliefs to compare them with the world as it is in itself. We can question particular sets of beliefs or theories if they come into conflict with immediately acquired perceptual beliefs. But we cannot strip away all our beliefs at once and apprehend an objective reality that retains epistemic import. But this does not show that there is no objective physical world to which the beliefs

---

[24] Thomas Nagel, *The Last Word* (Oxford: Oxford University Press, 1997), pp. 105–6.

214 THE CASE AGAINST OBJECTIVE VALUE

should correspond. Likewise, it might be argued that the fact that we have no subjectively value-free perspective from which we might question all our values at once does not show that there is no world of objective value to which our subjective values should correspond.

There are two crucial differences that destroy the analogy, however. First, even though we cannot check our entire belief set against the physical world as it is in itself, and even though our criterion for rational belief must therefore be coherentist, as is our criterion for rational values, in the case of belief the thought that our beliefs might contain wholesale error is intelligible (although we probably would not have survived if beliefs about the locations of physical objects were all false). We have no difficulty imagining that physical reality might be very different from how it appears to us. Contemporary science suggests as much. By contrast, the idea that all values might be entirely other than we conceive them to be seems unintelligible on reflection. Once we have become informed of the (non-normative) nature of the objects of our concerns, including what it is like to experience them, and once we have determined what we care about most, there is no remaining question of what we rationally ought to care about or do.

Second, while the criterion for rational belief, like that for value, is coherentist, belief in an objective physical world adds to the coherence of the belief system. This is because genuine satisfactory explanations provide coherence, and only appeal to physical objects as the causes of our perceptual beliefs satisfactorily explains those beliefs.[25] What explains my belief that there is a black object on my desk before me is that my computer is causing me to have that belief as I look at it. There is no other explanation for that belief. In the case of value, by contrast, appeal to objective values as the causes of our subjective valuings adds only mystery since, in contrast to the detailed specifications of the physical causal chains involved in perception, the supposed causal process in the case of values remains unspecified. The explanation is genuine in the one case, hence coherence enhancing, but not in the other.

As noted earlier, the objectivist can reply that the causal efficacy of value lies in the fact that values are realized or instantiated in ordinary physical

---

[25] For the full argument, see Alan Goldman, *Empirical Knowledge* (Berkeley: University of California, 1988), ch. 9.

objects. The causal chains that link us to objects also connect us to their values. Causal explanations can appeal to values and not only to the objects or other properties in which they are realized because we respond to the same values in the same ways no matter where they are instantiated, and because the objects in which the same values are realized may have little else in common. I respond to beauty in both the *Pietà* and *Taj Mahal* without focusing on any other properties they might have in common. It is their aesthetic value to which I respond in both cases, which causes me to react pleasurably as I do, although their beauty is realized in their other properties.

But there are three problems with this reply. First, we have now seen in the previous section that ordinary physical objects do not admit of determinate degrees of objective value and that this makes it doubtful that they have objective value at all. We will see the same problem in regard to other candidates for objects of value in the next section. Second, on the objectivist account it remains mysterious why values attach to all the otherwise diverse objects or properties in which they seem to be realized. The subjectivist reverses the order of explanation and says that the *Pietà* and *Taj Mahal* are both similarly valuable to us because we respond to them in very similar ways, and we desire to have such pleasurable responses. To insist instead that we ought to respond in these ways because these objects are similarly aesthetically valuable is to beg the questions why and how they are similarly aesthetically valuable. No objectivist aesthetician has ever been able to answer these questions satisfactorily.[26]

Third, there is an epistemic question that mirrors the metaphysical questions just raised. If we are to recognize similar objective values across their diverse instantiations, the question arises how we do this. How do we know that objects different in all their other intrinsic properties are nevertheless objectively valuable in the same way, for example aesthetically? The answer typically given is intuition. If this is a special faculty akin to the senses but not physically located, it is entirely mysterious. The objectivist must offer a different explanation of our ability to intuit objective value.

---

[26] The best attempt historically to reduce beauty to objective properties is probably Hutcheson's account in terms of unity amidst variety. But while the account fits some paradigm cases, it is easily counterexemplified both by objects that have this property but are not beautiful and by those that lack it but are. See Francis Hutcheson, *An Inquiry into the Original of Our Ideas of Beauty and Virtue* (New York: Garland, 1971).

One type of explanation involves a version of a transcendental argument. Such arguments appeal to the necessary conditions for possessing certain concepts, in this case normative or value concepts. Proponents argue that certain epistemological and metaphysical conclusions follow from a proper characterization of these necessary conditions.

To possess any concept, one must be able to use it correctly. One has the concept "red," for example, only if one can correctly pick out red things. It follows that if people have this concept, there must really be red things to pick out. For more complex concepts, there must at least be the simpler elements from which these concepts are constructed. More to the point, one has various value concepts, for example the concepts of what is beautiful or admirable, only if one can use them correctly to pick out otherwise diverse beautiful or admirable objects or people. One must be disposed to do so correctly—to apply these concepts, absent certain sources of error, only to objects that really are beautiful or admirable, that is, valuable in these ways. But then one's intuition that an object is beautiful or admirable can be simply a recognition of one's own disposition to apply these concepts to the object. And one can recognize the disposition in the very application.

This looks like an ingenious explanation[27] of what otherwise seems to be a magical ability. But it fails to establish that the value properties to which these concepts refer are objective or response independent. That remains an open question. And if values are objective, then we still lack an explanation of how we are able to acquire these concepts, how we come to recognize objective values across their diverse instantiations. The recognitional capacity cannot consist only in the disposition to apply the concepts in question: it must underlie the ability to acquire the concepts or the dispositions to apply them. In the case of perceivable qualities, we have senses that register the presence of the properties and that thereby explain how we can acquire such concepts as "red". But we cannot perceive value by means of our senses. The answer here must be that we tend to react to values with such responses as pleasure or desire. This may appear to still leave it open whether we desire an object because it is valuable or whether it is valuable because we desire it. But another

---

[27] An explanation like this is offered by Ralph Wedgwood, *The Nature of Normativity* (Oxford: Oxford University Press, 2007), pp. 239–242.

difference from secondary qualities tips the scale again to the subjectivist account.

In the case of colors, for example, we can correlate our responses to certain objective ways of reflecting or emitting light. In the case of values, by contrast, I do not know of any objective correlates that valuable objects share. It might be replied that we can find such correlates at least in the case of "thick" value concepts, courage, for example, as opposed to goodness or beauty. Courage is a valuable trait and manifests non-normative properties in virtue of which a person is courageous. Courageous people do not flee from dangerous threats. Perhaps also in the case of a valuable property like beauty we can specify for each beautiful object those physical properties in virtue of which it is beautiful. I doubt it, but in any case those other properties, for example curved lines and bright or subtle colors, will have nothing in common except their beauty. Once more the only explanation we have for why they are beautiful lies in our pleasurable responses to them (the status of pleasure itself will be addressed in the next section). And even in the case of courage, the ultimate explanation for why it is a valuable trait seems to be that we desire to have it or its effects. In general, the only clue we have as to what we ought to care about is what we do care about once all the relevant factual information is in. This is our only epistemic access to value, for which we can find no objective correlates. Objective value would again remain practically irrelevant if it did not already match our subjective valuings. And if it does match them, it is practically superfluous. Nor can we find clear defects in those with whom we disagree about value, as we can in the case of sensory conditions such as color blindness.

Despite these differences, the analogy, such as it is, between values and secondary qualities like colors has encouraged some contemporary philosophers, most notably David Wiggins and John McDowell, to seek to develop intermediate positions between subjectivism and objectivism in regard to values. McDowell and Wiggins hold values to be relational or response dependent properties, as I do, but they interpret the relation differently. I take as the mark of the real or objective the distinction between appearance and reality, between the way a real object appears to a subject and the way it may be independently of subjective appearance. The distinction implies, as I have emphasized following Michael Dummett, the ubiquitous possibility of error on the part of subjects about objective properties. For Dummett, the truth value of a statement about a real property is independent of any evidence we have or any means we have for knowing its truth or falsity.[28] If values are real or objective in this sense, then they may differ entirely from the ways that we value or desire things. But Wiggins and McDowell reject this characterization and classify as real many response dependent properties about which we could not all be mistaken. Here the real contrasts with what are figments of our imaginations, as McDowell writes of a property's "being there to be experienced, as opposed to being a mere figment of the subjective state that purports to be an experience of it."[29] In this sense colors are real—out there on the surfaces of objects—even though they appear as such only to creatures with visual systems like ours. In the same way McDowell and Wiggins see values as out there among the properties of objects even though they appear as such only to creatures with our sorts of desires and values. As colors are supposed to consist in objects being such as to cause certain visual experiences in us in certain conditions, so values consist in their objects being such as to merit certain positive responses.

Their way of characterizing values allows them to be objective to some degree in my sense in the same way that colors are supposed to be. As noted, we could not all be mistaken about such properties, but any individual could be mistaken on a given occasion if not grasping the object in the right way or in the right conditions. But is this characterization really sufficient for ascribing objectivity? For any way that we respond to any object, there must be some property in the object that consists in its being such as to cause that response. How then should we describe the difference between a subjectivist and an objectivist account of such properties? McDowell and Wiggins claim that holding values to be objective in this way even though response dependent allows us to give justifying explanations of the ways we respond to them, for example with desire. If an object is such as to merit such a response, then we are justified in responding in that way. But we have seen that objects cannot require responses totally other than the ways we do respond, so that the merited responses must be our responses

---

[28] Dummett writes: "Realism I characterize as the view that statements of the disputed class possess an objective truth value independently of our means of knowing it." Michael Dummett, "Realism," in *Truth and Other Enigmas* (Cambridge, MA: Harvard University Press, 1978), p. 146.

[29] John McDowell, "Values and Secondary Qualities," in T. Honderich (ed.), *Morality and Objectivity* (London: Routledge, 1985) p. 114.

in favorable conditions that actually obtain. If our responses cannot in general go wrong, but my or your responses can, then the justification or normative demand must be the demand to conform our responses to those of others in favorable circumstances, assuming that those conditions can be spelled out non-circularly. Real or objective values must then be those that prompt desires in normal or competent subjects in such conditions.

As Wiggins recognizes, this account first of all assumes large-scale agreement or convergence among competent evaluators as to what objects are valuable and a realist explanation for that agreement. Properties that lack objective status are not only those that are figments of our imaginations, but those that are radically relative to different subjective tastes in the same external conditions. Wiggins then stipulates two criteria for objectivity, or what he calls "plain truth," of even this weaker, response dependent sort: "If x is true, then x will under favorable circumstances command convergence, and the best explanation of the existence of this convergence will either require the actual truth of x of be inconsistent with the denial of x."[30] Thus, in simpler terms, if a property is objective (although response dependent and therefore also partly subjective), people in favorable conditions should agree on its presence, and their agreement should be explained by this presence of the property in the object. In my view these conditions are met by neither colors nor values, and so the analogy between them in fact weakens the case for objectivity in any sense.

I will comment briefly for purposes of clarification on Wiggins' first condition in relation to colors. Given the vast number of discriminable shades and the many variables, including those internal to perceivers, which affect apparent shades, it is overwhelmingly likely that normal perceivers will see slightly different shades on the same surfaces in the same external conditions. The relevant internal conditions include the adaptive states of their neurons deriving from previous perceptions and their prior perceptual expectations. Thus, even if we could stipulate certain external conditions as uniquely favorable for identifying real or objective colors (and these would have to isolate particular colored patches from others), the relativity of perceived shades to variable subjective conditions in visually normal subjects would leave us ascribing incompatible shades to the same surfaces

[30] David Wiggins, "Truth, and Truth as Predicated of Moral Judgments," in *Needs, Values, Truth* (Oxford: Blackwell, 1991), p. 147.

if we took objects to have the colors they appear to have to normal subjects in these conditions. Our everyday agreements in ascribing colors such as red to objects derive from the breadth of such color concepts, from the fact that they cover a very large number of discriminable shades. But if every instance of red is an instance of some specific shade, then Wiggins' first conditions fails and colors are subjective ways of appearing.

This is not the place to defend this account of colors or even to cite empirical evidence. Disagreements about values are far more obvious and less controversial. Here, in contrast to colors, we do not find agreement in ascribing broad value properties such as goodness or rightness. Where there is agreement, it usually involves subsuming one heavily evaluative term under another, as in "Wanton cruelty is wrong." But, as Hume pointed out in regard to aesthetic evaluations, such apparent agreement may often mask disagreement about which descriptions of actions count as satisfying the evaluative concepts. We may agree that wanton cruelty is wrong but disagree over what counts as wanton cruelty. This is not to deny that we can find genuine and virtually universal agreement on some cases, for example that inflicting severe pain on infants in order to hear them scream is wrong. But such examples do not get us very far in resolving issues regarding what is of positive or negative value generally. What we find is a spectrum from broad agreement on some cases to very little on many others, so that objectivists and subjectivists can both cite evidence to their liking. We could think of this as a spectrum of more and less objective values, or we could favor the positive evaluations and explain disagreement as due to value blindness. In regard to the latter option, in practice we are unwilling to grant the falsity of our negative responses to what some others find valuable, and again, there is no independent criterion or physical evidence for value blindness, as there is for color blindness. As to more or less objectivity, there is still Wiggins' second necessary condition to consider: that the explanation for agreement should appeal to a real property in the object itself as the cause of the responses.

So let us counterfactually grant convergence and think about its explanation. The key point here is one that I emphasized earlier: that there appears to be nothing that objects which we value have in common except our positive responses to them. This indicates that the subjective side of the relation is the determining factor in the relational properties that constitute values. Any purely objective property we could ascertain across the diverse objects that we find valuable would be hopelessly disjunctive, and the disjunction would be open-ended. As such it would not provide any comprehensible explanation for our responses. The idea of an object's "meriting" a positive response in virtue of such a property would be empty. Thus the attempt to forge a position between subjectivism and objectivism in regard to values in effect collapses back into a subjectivist position, despite the fact that values are relational or response dependent properties and that it is therefore properties in objects that we find valuable.

Thus, to summarize, objects or properties that are valuable appear so from subjective viewpoints and not from the impersonal perspective that abstracts from all subjective concerns or desires. I have maintained that we cannot make sense of the world requiring all our concerns to be other than they are. We can question coherent value systems only from the perspective of other values or concerns with which they conflict. Of course, we can also criticize particular concerns, pursuits, or values. The key critical question is whether the pursuit of any particular value is likely to lead to self-defeat, either because its object is unattainable, or because the agent is uninformed about the nature of the experience of the object, perhaps infatuated by certain of its properties while ignoring others, or because its pursuit or attainment will block the satisfaction of more central first- or second-order concerns. It is clear that these sorts of practical error do not imply objectivity in value, although the possibility of subjective error is often a premise in the argument for objectivity. Practical error of these sorts is mainly a matter of incoherence within motivational sets, and such incoherence explains why achieving particular things that one wants can disappoint. Values can be questioned in terms of other first- or second-order values, but only in such terms.

Any concern can be criticized, but only from the perspective of some set of values, either the agent's or that of some other evaluator. The attempt to adopt a completely impersonal perspective results not in the appearance of a new set of values or reasons, but in the disappearance of value entirely. We have seen also that subjective values or concerns, especially deepest concerns, can provide all the reasons we need for having other concerns or desires. What makes desires for or pursuit of certain objects rational is not the independent value of the objects, but the reasons for the desires deriving from these deeper concerns. An object can merit desire in light of these reasons. And it will merit desire only in light of them, given our earlier conclusion that there is no purely objective property in light of which it merits a positive response, no such property independent of our concerns that we can ascertain.

Perhaps the most difficult case for the subjectivist is when we care intensely about what we nevertheless admit or judge to be of little real value, for example whether our clothes are in fashion, or which team wins the World Cup or Super Bowl. Here we once more want to criticize each other for caring about what has little real importance or objective value. I will take up such cases in the final section. Before that we need to consider yet other candidates for objects of objective value. If we cannot locate such objects (and so far we have not), belief in objective value is empty.

III. Pleasures and Pains

"Nobody did nothin' to nobody."

Having argued that normal agents fail to be motivated by objective value without being irrational, and that ordinary objects lack determinate degrees of objective value that we can discern, we have yet to consider the most widely endorsed candidates for objects having such value. Somewhat ironically, they turn out to be subjective states. The irony appears to be mild, since there seems to be no contradiction in a subjective state's having objective value. But to have such value states or objects must have it independently of people's attitudes toward them, whether they want them to continue or cease, for example. The states themselves must provide reasons for all to want them to continue or cease, whether or not they do so desire. On reflection this might again seem problematic for such states as pleasure and pain, since, as we shall see, the kind of pleasure endorsed by most contemporary hedonists as the sole objective good includes in its analysis a positive attitude, an attitude held to be in itself good. One way to characterize this attitude is as a desire that its intentional object, itself a state of affairs that may be a mental state, persist. Robert Nozick, for example, defines pleasure as a feeling desired because of its felt qualities.[31] If taking pleasure in something involves a desire, and states having objective value

---

[31] Robert Nozick, *The Examined Life* (New York: Touchstone, 1989), p. 103.

must have it independent of subjects' desires, how can pleasure in this sense be objectively good?

The answer is that, while the second-order state of being pleased may include a desire that the first-order state about which one is pleased persist, we might not desire to be pleased or take pleasure in anything. While being pleased at something or taking pleasure in it involves a "pro-attitude" toward that thing, we might irrationally not want to have such attitudes toward anything. While objectivists hold that taking pleasure in things is always good, that such states are intrinsically good or good in themselves and therefore provide reasons for all to want to be in them, some people in irrational frames of mind such as depression might fail to respond to such reasons. Thus pleasure or taking pleasure in some state of affairs might be good independently of whether we desire or seek such pleasure. Almost all the objectivist authors cited earlier hold that pleasures and pains are objectively good and bad in this way. According to them, we should be motivated to pursue pleasures or things to take pleasure in and avoid or prevent pains whether or not we are so motivated.

Many philosophers who hold that pleasure is intrinsically or objectively good hold further that it is the only thing that is intrinsically good. Since we desire many things for their own sakes besides pleasure, since the objectivist maintains that such desires are rational only if those things have some value, and since it does not appear that we are all irrational for desiring these other things, it looks like objectivists ought to be pluralists about value. But there is also a reason why monism, the view that only pleasure, for example, is intrinsically valuable, is attractive to objectivists. Pluralism in regard to objective values is mysterious, as I suggested earlier. While value supervenes on other properties, these other properties of valuable things appear to have nothing else in common except their value. We might say that what they have in common is that they provide reasons to desire them, but then we could ask why they provide these reasons. The only obvious answer closes a small and unenlightening circle by saying that we should desire them because they are valuable. There seems to be no helpful answer to the question why objective value attaches to just these otherwise diverse properties.

The subjectivist holds that what these objects and their properties have in common is that we rationally desire them. If these objects have no intrinsic non-normative properties in common, we should look to what they share in our responses to them. Rationally desiring them gives them subjective value. The objectivist's counterpart explanation is that what they have in common are the responses they cause—pleasurable responses. Other properties of objects would then be instrumentally valuable in producing pleasure, which would remain independent of desire in the way described above. The objectivist would then have an answer to this central puzzle about value. The problem with this answer is that we would then be rational to desire other things only as means, only for their instrumental value in producing pleasure. But it seems clear that we desire such things as knowledge and accomplishment independently of whatever pleasure they produce. And it is not the case that we come to desire them in themselves only after desiring them as means to pleasure.

Let us set this advantage of subjectivism aside for now in order to assess just the claim that pleasures and pains are objectively valuable and disvaluable, whether or not they are the only things intrinsically so. In order to assess this claim to objective value, we must first disambiguate the terms 'pleasure' and 'pain,' since, as hinted above and widely noted in the literature, they refer ambiguously to two different kinds of states. Some pleasures and pains are phenomenal sensory states, having physical causes but lacking objects, for example the pleasure of a massage or the pain of a headache. These are sensations we literally feel, whether or not we know their causes. Sensations are typically physically located. They are distinguished by their locations and causes, although they are not intentional states: they do not refer to the objects that cause them. Although they are all good or bad feelings, they are quite diverse in the ways they feel. The pleasure of a warm shower is quite different from that of a cold drink or the touch of velvet. The question then arises why all these diverse feelings are classified as pleasures. Do not answer that they all feel good; the question is what we mean by that.

One more enlightening answer appeals to the other kind of pleasure and pain: intentional, attitudinal states that do take objects, for example the pleasure taken in one's accomplishments or the pain of one's defeats or embarrassments. We take pleasure in various states of affairs, including phenomenal or sensory states we might be in. While this positive attitude might then be accompanied by pleasurable sensations, it need not be and is in any case distinct from them. Taking pleasure in something is enjoying it, and we may enjoy many things other than our sensations. Enjoying an activity need not involve feeling any particular sensations while engaging in it.

Although these two senses of pleasure and pain seem to be distinct, attempts to reduce one kind to the other persist. Traditionally, the tendency was to conceive of the intentional state as a sensation, without recognizing it as intentional. Such pleasure was thought to be a non-local, mental sensation, as opposed to the usual physical sensations localized in particular areas of the body. This was supposed to be a "higher" pleasure, as opposed to the lower pleasures of the body.[32] The actual experience that proponents of this account had in mind was probably the global feeling we might describe as a "warm glow" that we get at just completing a major accomplishment, or less dramatically, at the end of a particularly good day, or the kind of intense enjoyment of something that we call a feeling of joy, which might be a hybrid between sensational and attitudinal pleasure. But while a global sensation of this kind accompanies some situations we intensely enjoy, it does not accompany, let alone reduce, every pleasure we take in the various activities we enjoy. On the negative side the hybrid state might be the feeling we get when we are about to cry. But again not every state of affairs that causes displeasure involves sensations of this sort, so that the reduction in this direction does not work.

More common these days, although far more recent, is the attempt to reduce sensory pleasure to attitudinal. This attempt is motivated, as indicated earlier, by the need to specify what all the otherwise diverse pleasant sensations have in common. According to this account, what they have in common is only that the subject takes pleasure in them. A sensation is a sensory pleasure if its subject takes pleasure in it or enjoys it, if it is a sensation that the person finds pleasing in itself.[33] The alternative account of sensory pleasure, of what all pleasant sensations have in common for the objectivist, is to say that there is a separate and distinct sensation of pleasure that accompanies such otherwise diverse sensations as that of a warm bath or velvet surface. But first, these sensations seem uniform and not divisible into two distinct feelings; and second, I at least do not know what this purported second sensation feels like. So the attitudinal reduction of sensory pleasure seems preferable.

[32] See e.g. Rem Edwards, *Pleasures and Pains* (Ithaca, NY: Cornell University Press, 1979), pp. 36, 113.
[33] Fred Feldman, *Pleasure and the Good Life* (Oxford: Oxford University Press, 2004), pp. 57, 79–80.

Nevertheless, in the end it seems to fare no better. For one thing, we think more naturally of pleasure as attitudinal than we think of pain that way. We naturally think more readily of pains as sensations. This is not decisive, however, since just as we take pleasure in things we enjoy, so we take displeasure or are pained by things we suffer. Nevertheless, that we have attitudinal pain as well as pleasure does not mean that the sensation itself is amenable to attitudinal analysis. The first more serious problem for this account is that it makes a mere sensation depend on a more sophisticated intentional attitude. Lower animals can feel pain, while it is at least doubtful that they have such intentional attitudes.

Second, the attitudes seem neither necessary nor sufficient for feeling the sensations. On the one hand, we can take pleasure in sensations that are not sensory pleasures, for example the sensation of falling for those who like roller coasters; and we can feel averse to sensations that are not pains, for example itches or the sensation of falling for those who do not like roller coasters. On the other hand, we can fail to take pleasure, be pleased by, or enjoy pleasant sensations or have a negative attitude toward sensory pains. We can be indifferent to a pleasant sensation or feel guilty for having it if we think it is sinful (you, not me). Those under certain sorts of anesthesia can still feel pain but not mind it; a weightlifter can be pleased at being in mild pain, which indicates the effectiveness of the exercise; and masochists apparently generally take pleasure in sensory pains. If one can take pleasure at being in pain, it seems that we cannot reduce the one to the other, since the same sensation cannot be both a pain and a pleasure.

Fred Feldman, who defends this attitudinal account of sensory pleasure and pain, bites the bullet in the case of feeling pain and not minding it by saying that the sensations felt by the anesthetized patient are not really pains. By contrast, he does not deny that masochists take pleasure in their pains, but he analyzes their situation as their having a second-order positive attitude toward their having a first-order negative attitude toward their sensations.[34] But this is again too complex or sophisticated. A masochist does not take pleasure in an intentional attitude, in having such an attitude, but instead takes pleasure in the painful sensation itself. Thus again it seems that we require both attitudinal pleasure and sensory pain as irreducible in

---

[34] Fred Feldman, 89.

order to understand this situation properly. Our question is whether either kind of state has objective value or disvalue.

In regard first to the phenomenal states, there is first once more the problem of measuring the amount of supposed objective value in these states. The amount of value in a sensory pleasure or disvalue in a pain is supposed to equal the product of the intensity of the sensation and its duration. This is most plausible for comparisons of sensations of the same kind, for example feelings of warmth, but does not apply as well to comparing warm baths to touches of velvet. How are we to compare the intensities of these different pleasures? Even in the case of like sensations the measure is already problematic. It seems, as noted, that a pleasurable sensation of warmth is a single uniform sensation, not distinct sensations of warmth and pleasure. Yet increasing the intensity of warmth does not uniformly increase the intensity of pleasure. In fact, the pleasure may increase at first before reversing and turning to pain, and there will be subjective variance here, depending on how much warmth one likes to feel. I, for one, do not like warm baths at all, but others do. In the case of different kinds of sensations, such as those of warm baths and velvet, one will count as the more intense pleasure that which one desires more to have. But this is a measure of subjective, not objective value, and it seems once more to confuse attitudes and sensations.

A related and more obvious problem in measuring the supposed objective value of these states involves the assumption that sensory pleasure is always objectively good and pain bad. Certainly most instances of pain are considered bad, but, as indicated above, the broader context can affect the degree of badness and even give net positive value to some pains. As noted, some pain in the context of strenuous athletic endeavors adds to the sense of accomplishment; under some anesthetics one can still feel pain but does not mind it or want it to cease; and even intense pains considered very bad at the time of their occurrence can in retrospect be seen as not so bad, or even as being good in having made one a better person. In this third case, one could say that the pain in itself is bad but its effects good. One might offer the same reply to the first case, but here it is less clear that the pain, bad in itself, can be distinguished from its good effect of providing a sense of accomplishment. For one thing, the two are simultaneous. For another, a pain that heightens one's pride or sense of accomplishment can seem good in itself. If one is glad it is there, it will not seem bad.

Even if we can separate the intrinsic value of the pain from the value of its effects, the problem of specifying the proper temporal perspective from which to judge its intrinsic value remains. The natural temporal perspective here would seem to be the time of its occurrence, but this runs counter to our general tendency to think that gaining some distance from an object improves one's ability to judge its value. Past pain may again seem to lack disvalue when one does not regret its having occurred. And the seeming value of past pleasure will depend on how nostalgic one is. The disvalue of present pain seems to be exaggerated when its victim judges half sincerely that he would rather die than suffer one more minute of it. A minute after its having ceased, it once more seems far less bad and certainly not worth dying for.

Given the difficulty of separating the value of a state from the value of its effects and the difficulty of specifying the correct perspectives for judging that value, it becomes tricky how to measure the overall objective badness of pains. Pain in general serves the function of warning us of injury or disease, and since any other sort of warning might not be heeded with the same urgency, pain begins to look not so bad.[35] Again an objectivist would reply that pain is intrinsically bad although sometimes instrumentally good. But is all pain intrinsically bad? What of a slight pain in my toe that I do not mind at all? Perhaps the reply is that only intense pain is always intrinsically bad. Here it is hard to imagine not minding it when it occurs, but the example of the slight pain indicates that it is the minding it that determines it to be bad and not the phenomenal feel itself.

If the case of phenomenal pain that is not minded is problematic, the problem becomes worse in the case of pains that are desired, by masochists or by those who see it as deserved punishment for guilt. When we turn attention from phenomenal pains to phenomenal pleasures, it is clearer that people seek them with more or less priority and urgency, that their value for particular persons varies greatly, and that there seems to be little force to the claim that all ought to seek them to the same degree. Given similar

---

[35] I might have considered disease, then, instead of pain as a candidate for a state with objective disvalue, although it is not mentioned as often. Candidates could be multiplied, but similar arguments will apply.

if less obvious variation in reactions to and attitudes toward pain, the same point applies. There is not only temporal perspective that affects evaluation, but personal perspective as well.

We saw earlier that if a state has objective value or disvalue, it provides the same reason to pursue or to avoid and relieve it to all agents. Given its objective disvalue, I would have the same reason to prevent or relieve your pain as mine. But once more no one thinks or acts in that way. I may be concerned about your pains, but I am more concerned about mine and those of my family members, and this does not strike me as irrational. Furthermore not only do we find different sensations pleasurable or painful—I do not like the feel of warm baths but like the touch of velvet; you may be the opposite—but the sensory pleasures I care about pursuing may be different from the pleasures you pursue. They do not have the same value for us, and again there seems to be no way to correct for these differences so as to arrive at a measure of objective value. We might say that amounts of objective value exist for these sensations even though we cannot calculate them, but then again they remain superfluous from the point of view of practical reason.

If the attitude toward phenomenal pleasure and pain counts more than the phenomenal feel itself in determining its degree of goodness or badness, this takes us back to the second sense, in which we are referring to intentional, attitudinal states. While sensational pleasure and pain cannot be reduced to attitudinal, perhaps it is only the latter that has objective value and disvalue. Here any state or activity is pleasurable in which one takes pleasure, a common occurrence for normally fortunate people. It is surprisingly difficult, however, to say in what taking pleasure in something consists. Most writers equate taking pleasure in something with being pleased at it, but the two are not the same. I can be pleased that the dentist will see me right away without taking any pleasure in that fact. Given this distinction, one might be tempted to say that taking pleasure requires pleasant sensations beyond merely being pleased, which does not, but that analysis would lead us back to our previous set of comments.

As noted earlier, a worry for the objectivist is that taking pleasure in something may be just having a certain kind of desire for it satisfied. This might sound more plausible as an analysis of being pleased, where being pleased at something is simply having one's desire for it satisfied and not counterbalanced by a resultant frustration of some other desire. This will not quite do either, however, as one can be pleased by the occurrence of some state of affairs that one had not desired in advance.

In a recent article, Chris Heathwood defines being pleased at something, which he seems to equate with taking pleasure in it, as desiring it while believing that one's desire for it is being satisfied. This analysis does not compute with my earlier claim that one can strictly desire only what one does not yet have. Desires proper, whose function is to prompt action, are not directed at the past or at that with which one is presently satisfied, as no actions can or need be directed at those states of affairs. In regard to the past, I can hope that my team won if I do not know whether they did, or I can desire to learn of their winning, or I can wish that they had won if they did not, or I can be pleased at their having won, but I cannot want them to have won if I know they did. Hopes and wishes are not central types of desires, but offshoots lacking the typical function that lies at the center of our cluster concept. In regard to the present, I would not say that I want my team to be winning if they are (unless I am awkwardly saying that I am pleased that they are winning), but I can want them to continue to win or continue to play as well as they have been.

Perhaps, then, as others have suggested, to take pleasure in something is to desire that it continue. But again there are problems with this account. I can take pleasure in a good meal or good dessert without desiring that it continue (certainly not indefinitely). And if I think I deserve some punishment, I (fictional I) can desire that it continue for at least some time without taking any pleasure in it. There still seems nevertheless to be some conceptual connection between taking pleasure in something and having some desire that relates to it. Let us assume that is so without struggling further with the exact specification of the relevant desire. The worry again to be noted here for the objectivist is that taking pleasure in something might then become merely a measurement of its subjective value, its value for the particular subject who has this desire.

That might be so, but it does not defeat the claim that being in this state, including having this desire, is objectively good; at least it does not empty this claim of all content. But if the claim is simply that having certain desires satisfied is objectively good, then it will once more remain superfluous from a practical point of view and indeed burden us with excess metaphysical baggage. If rational desires create subjective value and in themselves determine how we rationally ought to act, there is no point in holding that their satisfaction is objectively valuable. Thus, if there is to be some point in saying that taking pleasure in things is objectively valuable, there must be something more to taking pleasure than having certain desires and having them satisfied (and, given our prior discussion, that something more must not consist only in pleasant sensations).

I do not have a full analysis of attitudinal pleasure at hand, although in this context the burden seems to be on the objectivist to provide one so that we can assess her claim that such pleasure has objective value. I want to turn to a different but by now familiar problem that she faces here, whatever her full analysis. It is the problem of broader context, again looming as insuperable for determining degrees of objective value. Consider first the case of taking pleasure in another's plight. Is this pleasure good? Noah Lemos argues that what is bad about this whole situation is that the person has a good—pleasure—that he ought not to have.[36] But since all pleasure of this sort is intentional, there are not two components here, pleasure and pleasure in another's plight. All pleasure of this sort is pleasure in something; none is separable as just pleasure (unlike phenomenal pleasures), just as there are no beliefs that are not beliefs in something. Beliefs simpliciter are not components of beliefs in . . . , and similarly pleasure simpliciter is not a component of pleasure in . . . And if some intentional pleasures are good and some bad, we might wonder why we should privilege the good instances by saying that pleasure in itself is good. The answer as to why we are inclined to do so is that we tend to think here from the first person perspective, in which we want or seek such pleasures, which may be just to say trivially that we seek states that we desire or like.

The alternative strategy for the objectivist here is to narrow the descriptions of the states that are said to have objective value.[37] Here the amount of pleasure taken in some object is adjusted at least by the worthiness of the object as a source and the desert of the subject to have the pleasure.[38] Its value depends, to paraphrase Yogi Berra, on who did what to whom. In regard to worthiness of the object, if pleasure in another's pain is bad, is pain in another's pain good? Good in itself or only in its effects? How good? There seem to be no fixed general answers to whether pleasure taken

---

[36] Lemos, *Intrinsic Value*, p. 44.
[37] This is the strategy, for example, of Zimmerman, *The Nature of Intrinsic Value*.
[38] Fred Feldman makes just these adjustments in *Pleasure and the Good Life*.

in unworthy objects and pain taken in worthy objects are good or bad, let alone to what degree. Is harmless pleasure taken in bad art objectively good, when it instantiates terrible taste? Those who take aesthetic value seriously will likely disagree here with those who do not.

In regard to the desert of the subject, once more just adding this factor alone raises unanswerable questions about the amount of objective value. Does under- and over-deserving have equal effects in opposite directions; that is, is it worse to get less rather than more pleasure than deserved? Does reducing the disparity by n units count for more when the disparity is greater, or for less at higher levels of pleasure? When one gets much less pleasure than deserved, but still gets pleasure, is this good or bad? These questions are independent of how we calculate desert itself, which will have to figure fulfilment of partial obligations among many other factors over a lifetime. When we add worthiness of the object as the source of pleasure to the desert of the subject in augmenting or discounting the values of amounts of pleasure, the calculations become hopelessly complex. We would have to calculate, for example, under-deserved pleasure taken in another's over-deserved pain, and thirty-six permutations thereof.[39]

Any degree of discounting for pleasure based on false belief about its object also seems arbitrary, as is evidenced by the wide variety of responses to Nozick's pleasure machine, in which one takes pleasure in an illusory world that one thinks is real.[40] How about the pleasure of one who generally deserves it in another's pain in an illusory world? Is there really a precise amount of objective value in this situation? There must be if pleasures and pains have such value.

Thus, adjustments in purported objective values for false pleasures, base pleasures, undeserved pleasures, deserved pains, and pains taken in others' pains, especially when these adjustments must be combined, become not only hopelessly complex, but seemingly arbitrary. Once more we are either magically tuned in to the values of such complex states, allowing us somehow to intuit that value, or, if they have objective value, it is beyond our grasp. Once more we might continue to insist that such states of affairs have objective value even though we cannot calculate it, but then again it

---

[39] See Owen McLeod, "Adjusting Utility for Justice," in K. McDaniel et al. (eds.), *The Good, the Right, Life and Death* (Burlington, VT: Ashgate, 2006).

[40] Robert Nozick, *Anarchy, State, and Utopia* (New York: Basic Books, 1974), pp. 42–5.

would lack practical import. The need to make such calculations, if we had the goal of promoting objective value and we thought these states were among its main bearers, would not be rare, since most attitudinal pleasure and pain is more or less deserved and directed at more or less worthy objects. It is not always the case that "nobody did nothin' to nobody."

Remember that attitudinal pleasures and pains are held to comprise a large, if not unique, class of states with objective value. Once we adjust for worthiness of objects to give pleasure, however, we acknowledge that the objective goodness or badness of pleasures and pains presupposes that of other things, and that the former, although it is most widely endorsed, cannot be primary. Objects worthy of giving pleasure might have value only in doing so, but we would still need to assign determinate levels of worthiness to such objects. And when it comes to things that are pleasurable, as opposed to pleasures themselves, it is not only obvious that people take pleasure in things others find painful (when spending a semester in Colorado, I was shocked to see people voluntarily dangling off sheer cliffs, a torture than which I can imagine few worse), but also that when one initially takes great pleasure in a new acquisition, the pleasure in that object rather quickly fades to a more normal hedonic level. I questioned in the previous section whether we can assign amounts of objective value to such everyday objects.

Yet when we think of other states that might be held to be objectively good or bad, for example companionship or loneliness, or excitement or boredom, we seem to be driven back to the pleasure or pain taken in them as the source of their goodness or badness. What is loneliness to one person is independence to another; what is companionship to one is lack of "personal space" to another; what is excitement to one is stress to another; what is boredom to one is comforting routine to another. It all depends on the subjective attitude of finding these objective states of affairs pleasurable or painful. That is another reason why the latter are the most widely endorsed candidates for states having objective value or disvalue in themselves.

I have not yet mentioned here the problem of incomparable values; those that seem neither better nor worse nor equally good. Such values have a ready explanation if their source is subjective. We may prefer neither A over B nor B over A, and yet admit that small additions to A improve it without making it preferable to us over B (negating initial equality). The notion of objective incomparable values may be puzzling enough in itself, if such values come in degrees, but the problem I have been emphasizing

234   THE CASE AGAINST OBJECTIVE VALUE

is the rational obligation we would have to maximize such value. Erik Carlson has shown that we can order and add incomparable values, but that this process involves vectors in n-dimensional space.[41] It almost goes without saying that no one makes such calculations or ought to do so. And even objectivists can take the appeal to intuition only so far.

This discussion of attitudinal pleasure as a basic bearer of objective value reinforces earlier points in the main argument of this chapter. If objective value exists, then we ought to maximize it: we ought to choose what is objectively better overall over what is worse, and our calculations of what is objectively better all things considered should correct for our initial subjective valuings. But, I have argued, we cannot calculate objective value for even this one supposed primary bearer of it, and so there is no practical relevance to the concept. Yet practical guidance and explanation of the rationality of our choices is the principal reason for positing objective value in the first place. If it exists, then we all have the same reasons to promote it in proportion to its degree. Thus, if attitudinal pleasure is what has objective value, then if I care more about pursuing some goal than about enjoying it, I must nevertheless pursue enjoyment instead if I am rational. But this seems wrong.

While we have no way to calculate objective value, we can discover, if we do not already know, what our preferences or values are, cheerfully admitting (as it is problematic to admit for objective values) that they may be indeterminate in many places. They may remain indeterminate until the necessity for choice arises, to be made determinate in the acts of choosing. Such choices will be rational if informed and coherent in the ways described in earlier chapters. We do not need to appeal to the maximization of objective value in order to explain their rationality.

IV. Good and Meaningful Lives

"I'd rather be the Yankee catcher than President."

If, as concluded in the previous section, we do not need the concept of objective value in order to explain the rationality of our everyday choices,

---

[41] Eric Carlson, "Incomparability and Measurement of Value," in McDaniel et al. (eds.), *The Good, the Right, Life and Death.*

the objectivist will argue finally that we do need it to explain when people are leading good and meaningful lives. Thus we arrive at our last topic, one which philosophers generally approach only when they are older (as I am) and wiser, only when younger philosophers think they are going soft in the head in part for addressing this topic. We may distinguish at least initially, as some philosophers want to do, between a life's being good, high in personal welfare or well-being, from its being meaningful, although the two are related in that meaning in life, if indeed that is a legitimate notion, would seem to contribute to that life's being good.

In regard to personal welfare, the measure of how well one's life is going, as internalists (which by now I hope we all are) we will equate this notion first with what I earlier described as broad self-interest. Recall that broad self-interest was defined as the satisfaction of the subject's rational—informed and coherent—desires or concerns. Recall also that practical reasons motivate rational agents by indicating ways to satisfy their prior and deeper motivations. If we add to the truism that it is rational to act on one's reasons the claim that it is rational to act to promote one's well-being, and add also that reasons indicate ways to satisfy central concerns, we get that one's well-being consists in the satisfaction of these central concerns. These concerns that ultimately determine which states of affairs count as reasons are also those whose satisfaction contributes to a good life. One's life is going well during a time when one's central concerns are being satisfied. They will be satisfied when various specifications of them are being satisfied at different times. A life that is going well is a good life, at least for the person who is living it.

Just as we argued earlier that not all desires create reasons, but only those sets of desires anchored by broader and deeper concerns, so now we can conclude that not all satisfactions of desires contribute to personal welfare, but only the satisfaction of those desires that enter into the creation of reasons, those that are reflective of or specifications of these deeper concerns. It must be understood also that one must know of the satisfaction of these concerns in order for it to make one's life go better, and that the satisfaction of desires for means contributes to personal welfare only in so far as it facilitates the fulfilment of desires for ends or for things desired in themselves. That the depth of desires being satisfied determines how much their satisfaction contributes to well-being explains why achievements later in life tend to count more. They count more if they culminate the fulfilment of many subsidiary desires organized over long periods of time by the deeper or more central motivating states.

This account of personal welfare or the goodness of a life to the person living it handles many of the objections raised to earlier desire satisfaction accounts. These objections point to various kinds of desires whose satisfaction does not seem to contribute to personal well-being. These include self-destructive desires, reduced or shallow desires, those whose satisfaction disappoints, those felt as alien by the subject, those satisfied after death or not known to be satisfied, desires for the welfare of others or for such things as cures for diseases other than one's own or for peace in distant parts of the world, desires no longer had when satisfied, and programmed desires, those acquired as a result of brainwashing or hypnotism for example. The account suggested above nullifies the purported counterexamples.

I explicitly added to the earlier account of broad self-interest the exclusion of desires not known to be satisfied. Other counter-examples to desire satisfaction accounts of personal welfare are excluded by the requirement that the desires in question be rational—informed and coherent, and reflective of broader, deeper and therefore more stable concerns. Self-destructive desires are those whose satisfaction would frustrate that of more central concerns, that is, desires that are incoherent with one's broader motivational set. Desires felt as alien will also be those that fail to reflect these concerns that enter into one's self-identification, and they will fail to cohere also with second-order desires to be (or continue to be) the kind of person one is. The satisfaction of shallow and reduced desires will contribute little to personal welfare for a similar reason. My desire to eat some ice cream might reflect a broader concern to have pleasant sensations, but its satisfaction makes only a fleeting and minor contribution to the fulfilment of that concern, which itself ranks fairly low among my central cares. Desires whose satisfaction disappoints are those whose subjects are ignorant of what it is like to act on them, subjects who are not relevantly informed. In all these cases there is no significant satisfaction of deep concerns that anchor other desires in coherent sets.

The last three purported counterexamples on the list are somewhat more problematic. The satisfaction of a desire that has faded completely by the time it is satisfied does not add to a subject's well-being at that time. But first, since our account counts only the satisfaction of deeper concerns as contributory to personal welfare, and since these concerns are far more stable than specific desires that derive from them, the desires whose satisfaction might cause a problem for the account in this regard will rarely if ever exist. Second, if there are such desires, we can simply add to the account the stipulation that desires must exist at the time of their satisfaction (or just before) for their fulfilment to make a life go better. This addition is not *ad hoc*: it may be already implied. It is doubtful that a subject would know of the satisfaction of a desire he no longer has, and more to the point, it is questionable whether a desire can really be satisfied if it no longer exists (just before its satisfaction). A state of affairs can come about that was formerly wished for, and this is what was referred to above, but this does not really appear to be the satisfaction of a desire if no such desire exists.

In regard to programmed desires, all desires are in some way programmed, by nature if not by society or specific other people. I want to be a good philosopher and tennis player because these are roles available in my society and encouraged by my role models. But some ways of instilling desires disqualifies their fulfilment from contributing to a good life, while other ways do not. In earlier characterizing the relevant information requirement for rational desires, I allowed that knowledge of the origins of the desires could count as relevant. The question here is whether a subject fully capable of processing such information would endorse the desires on such reflection. Presumably a victim of hypnotism, for example, would not. If not, an incoherence is introduced with a second-order desire, and the programmed desire is disqualified as irrational.

Persons seen by others to be leading subservient lives might nevertheless continue to endorse their desires in knowledge of their socially programmed origins. There are two responses to such persons by the proponent of the rational desire satisfaction account of personal welfare. First, it can be claimed that the satisfaction of their coherent and informed desires still makes their lives go better than they would if their desires remained unsatisfied. Satisfied privates in the army have better lives than unsatisfied privates in the army. Second, it can also be claimed that their lives would be improved if they had satisfiable more ambitious desires as alternative specifications of their basic natural concerns (such as a concern to control their own lives), desires they would have in full knowledge of what it would be like to act on and satisfy them. The basic natural concerns are themselves less subject to manipulation than more specific desires. In regard to the latter, if more ambitious desires could not be satisfied under the existing social scheme, it would not make their lives go better to have them.

Finally, there are desires exclusively for the welfare of others or for states of affairs such as world peace. I desire complete peace in the world, and this desire seems rational on my part. It is neither incoherent with my other desires nor based on lack of relevant information. But does it really make my life go better if a war in remote Africa ends? One reply is that it depends on my degree of involvement with this goal. If I contribute to or better work for peace groups and organize some of my time and energy doing my small part to contribute to this goal, then its achievement or partial achievement could make my life go better. But if it is simply an idle desire on my part that does not dispose me to do anything about it, then it remains pretty much irrelevant to how my life is going (that is, unless the war interferes in some way with my activities). Similarly, if it is my children's welfare that I pursue, and if their concerns are very much bound up with my own, then it is not implausible that their doing well contributes to my doing well. All this is not only in keeping with the account offered, but follows from it. It all depends on how deep and central is the concern in question.

It nevertheless also makes sense to say that I can sacrifice my own welfare for that of my children, just as one could sacrifice one's life for others. Here the distinction drawn earlier between broad and narrow self-interest becomes relevant. Recall that narrow self-interest is defined by desires that make essential reference to oneself. The personal welfare equated with how well one's narrow self-interest is being served is needed for the same reason. A person can sacrifice that part of his welfare that makes essential reference to himself while acting rationally or in his broad self-interest. Thus we need concepts of both broad and narrow welfare following from like concepts of self-interest.

The concept of narrow welfare is needed also to avoid the conclusion that all rational agents are egoists. If reasons indicate ways to serve one's broad self-interest, defined by the satisfaction of one's coherent and informed concerns, if rational agents always act on their reasons, if personal welfare equates with self-interest or with how well it is being served, if egoists always act in their self-interest, and if broad self-interest is the only kind of self-interest there is, then all rational agents are egoists. But they are not. Hence we sometimes think of personal welfare, like self-interest, in narrower terms to exclude the satisfaction of desires for the welfare of others. When an agent acts to satisfy those altruistic desires, she acts in her broad self-interest but not in her narrow self-interest or egoistically. Egoists, by contrast, always act for their narrow personal welfare.

The crucial point for our purposes here is that we do not appear to need to appeal to objective value, its pursuit or achievement, in order to account for personal welfare or a good life in either the broad or narrower senses. Externalists, however, will continue to worry that the requirements of coherence and relevant information could still fail to aim desires at what is truly valuable or even good for the agent. For externalists, in order to explain what is truly good for people, what contributes to their lives going well, we need a notion of goodness independent of what they happen to desire. For them desires are too socially and individually contingent and variable to have genuine normative force in themselves.[42] Adding information and coherence does not guarantee goodness in their objects: we still must be lucky or wise to have our values aligned with true value. As no parent can deny, the disconnect between desire and value or welfare is most clear in the case of young children. Whether or not they have rational desires at all, certain things are clearly good and bad for them. In order to know as parents that vegetables are good for them and soft drinks bad, we do not need to consider what they desire or would desire in different conditions. We do not think about their desires at all in educating them, including educating them as to what is good for them and what is not, and as to which values are worth pursuing.

Thus it is claimed that coherent and informed desires are not necessary as indicators of what is good for us. Another example that purports to show this is when we are benefitted or made happier by very pleasant surprises that we had not sought or desired in advance, for example unexpected honors or gifts bestowed upon us. These can make our lives go better, contribute to our welfare, without being satisfactions of pre-existing desires. Just as informed and coherent desires are not necessary indicators of values, so externalists maintain that they are not sufficient either. According

[42] This is argued, for example, by William Fitzpatrick, "Robust Ethical Realism, Non-Naturalism and Normativity," in Russ Shafer-Landau (ed.), *Oxford Studies in Metaethics* (Oxford: Oxford University Press, 2008).

to them, people can coherently desire what is bad for them even with information as to what it is like to act on or satisfy those desires. I might desire my next cigarette with no concern for my health with which that desire is incoherent, but that cigarette is still bad for me. Given this distance seen between desires and what is good for people, externalists will posit instead a list of things that are good for people, that make their lives go well or contribute to their welfare. These things might include health, material comfort, freedom or autonomy, love, companionship or close personal relations, achievement, the development of our natural capacities, and happiness.

Of course these lists will once more differ in their entries, making us suspicious again that they reflect mainly the socially programmed and individual values of their proponents (just the source and variability that made them suspicious of the normative status of desires). Among philosophers, the development of intellectual capacities and achievements are likely to be high on the list, but being in tune with nature will not make their lists at all, while the farmer's list is likely to be the reverse. Once again each must accuse the other of value blindness or of ignorance as to what really makes a life go well. Or the temptation will be to let a thousand flowers bloom, to be tolerant and optimistic and say that all those things are of value and can enter as ingredients in a good life. But then we find among the billions of us those who think that counting blades of grass, turning on radios, or watching sports events or TV soaps makes for a good life—just those people whose lives the appeal to the pursuit of objective value was intended to criticize or demean. Once we let them into the club of those enjoying good lives, we have not only lost the distinction between objective value and objects of desire, but we have multiplied beyond reason the types of desires that correlate with value. No proponent of objective lists of things good for people wants that big a list, but they so far lack a principle for limiting their lists.

One way to limit them is to emphasize one entry as the key to which the others are means, specifications, or signs. Making the development of our natural capacities central, freedom might be seen to facilitate that development; companionship or personal relationships might be a manifestation of the development of our social capacities or skills; intellectual achievements might be the result of the development of our minds; and happiness a sign of overall flourishing from the successful development of all these capacities. This particular notion of a good life of course dates back to Aristotle, who equated happiness with this idea of flourishing as the full realization of our natural kind and its unique excellences. Its latest proponent is Richard Kraut.[43] One concrete implication of the view is that those contemporaries who have led the best lives must be Bill Bradley and Jack Kemp! They developed social skills to the high degree required for election to the U.S. Senate. Bradley at least is of superior intellect, having been named a Rhodes Scholar from Princeton, and both men authored books. Both also developed physical skills to the degree that they were prominent professional athletes. Of course for all we know both might have been miserable for failing to be elected President, a position to which both, unlike Yogi Berra, aspired. They might have been miserable for failing to get what they most wanted and spent their lives pursuing, even if they took pleasure in developing all their natural capacities.[44]

If that were so, would their outstanding development of all these capacities have given them the best lives? A negative answer points to the obvious problem with this idea of flourishing as the key to an objectively good life, indeed a problem for any objective list or principle for ordering its entries. If we simply posit a list of goods for people, what are we to say when some people do not care about having those goods or care much more about some other goals such as becoming President? A person may have developed capacities but her life may be going badly if she is not getting what she wants. Similarly for freedom, material comfort, and other items on such lists. If one has but does not care much for these items and lacks other things of more concern, one's life will not be going well.

Some goods, as Rawls realized, may be relatively uncontroversial because they are necessary for acquiring many others and/or because they reflect basic instincts. Such are food, shelter, health. But whether these are necessary for good lives (some people have had good lives without much of them), they certainly are not sufficient. And other entries on objective lists are not necessary. Many intellectuals who do not care about further developing their physical skills would not be better off for trying to do so, and for many athletes and manual workers the reverse is true. (This

---

[43] Kraut, *What is Good and Why*.

[44] Kraut adds taking pleasure in such development as also necessary to having a good life, but this move itself seems *ad hoc* in the context of his Aristotelian theory. *What is Good and Why*, p. 164.

allows that developing mental or physical skills *can* be useful for satisfying many other concerns.) The development of our unique capacities is neither necessary nor sufficient for a good life, yet it has been most prominent on lists of what is good for us.

Of course things can be good for one even if one does not care about them: vegetables might be good for me even if I do not care about eating them. But for the internalist this is because I care about my health and they promote my health, or because I care about doing things for which my health is necessary. (Despite the externalist's earlier example, the same will be true of children, as we tell them when trying to get them to eat their vegetables.) Even things that I care about that are good for me seem to be means to my welfare and not constitutive of my welfare as such. It is at least possible, in the ballpark or right category, that one's life going well consists in having one's central concerns satisfied. But developing one's capacities or being in love or loved is not personal welfare, but at most means to it,[45] and that only for those who desire such things. The development or full realization of social, intellectual, and physical capacities is one life project, albeit a rather egocentric one, that can organize many activities and more specific desires, but there are many other central concerns that can play the same role without being so focused on oneself.

Happiness (divorced from the notion of developed capacities) remains to be considered from our original list. Equating happiness with personal welfare is not refuted by the objections raised to other entries since happiness is not typically considered a means to anything else, and since it can plausibly be claimed to be something that all rational people desire. Furthermore, in objecting to the Aristotelian notion of welfare by pointing out that one could satisfy it and yet still be miserable, I may seem to have suggested that happiness is our real criterion of personal welfare. One problem with this suggestion, however, is that equating happiness with personal welfare is no more plausible than equating it with the satisfaction of our central concerns. That, of course, would reduce to the internalist's account of personal welfare. A desperate objectivist could still claim that happiness or the satisfaction of central concerns is itself of objective value

---

[45] This point is made by L. W. Sumner, *Welfare, Happiness, and Ethics* (Oxford: Clarendon Press, 1996).

and its pursuit what makes a life go well, but this superfluous move simply adds excess metaphysical baggage once more to the internalist account that already would be sufficient if correct.

But in addition, these analyses of happiness are not quite correct. We aim automatically to have our concerns satisfied, but as many have pointed out, we do not ordinarily aim at happiness. (Nietzsche said that only Englishmen do.) Happiness is in part a byproduct of having our concerns satisfied. While pleasure is a short-term byproduct of satisfying desires, happiness reflects a longer term view of the status of our more central and stable concerns. It is not the same as personal welfare, but instead consists in a positive appraisal of how one's life on the whole is going, of one's level of personal welfare. As Nozick's virtual reality machine again illustrates, we want not just happiness or a positive appraisal of our situation, but also want the appraisal to be warranted, to reflect the actual satisfaction of our central concerns, among which may be desire for real achievement or love, for example. Furthermore, we may desire achievement or love whether or not they will make us happy. Being too happy or satisfied can even stifle sustained effort for achievement or make one unprepared for obstacles or setbacks.[46]

Happiness is then distinct from personal welfare in being an appraisal of it, and an appraisal that is not infallibly correct. It seems that we tend to overestimate how much satisfaction of desire in the future will contribute to our happiness. Our self-appraisals are also overly influenced by recent emotions, and when temporary feelings of pleasure from achievements or satisfactions of desire fade, we tend to return to earlier baseline levels of overall contentment. These levels vary more with persisting personality types than with changes in situations.[47] Such data do not refute the analysis of personal welfare in terms of the satisfaction of central concerns as long as we do not identify happiness with welfare, but we have seen ample reason in the previous paragraphs not to do so.

Having exhausted the usual items on objective list accounts of personal welfare, we may conclude that the internalist account in terms of get-ting and keeping what we most care about is superior. The objections

---

[46] These last points are emphasized by Joel Kupperman, *Six Myths About the Good Life* (Indianapolis: Hackett, 2006), ch. 2.

[47] Studies demonstrating these facts are summarized in Daniel Nettle, *Happiness* (Oxford: Oxford University Press, 2005), pp. 39–43, 110, 141.

raised earlier to this account are easily handled. Children, we noted, do
have basic concerns such that these concerns and further specifications
and developments of them render various things good and bad for the
children. As for things that pleasantly surprise us and make our lives go
better even though we had not desired them in advance, as noted much
earlier, we find pleasant what we are disposed to find pleasant, including
various unexpected specifications of what we generally care about. So the
satisfactions we feel still have an internal explanation. Finally, the cigarette
that is bad for me is bad for my health, and therefore bad for me if
but only if I care about my health or care about anything for which
my health is necessary. We say that the cigarette is bad for me without
mentioning these qualifications because almost all people satisfy this last
condition or because our statement is shorthand for its being bad for
my health.

Aside from the advantage in handling examples, the internalist account of
personal welfare is once more simpler and more intelligible, again eschewing
appeal to the mysterious non-natural property of being objectively valuable.
But the externalist has one card left. She can still maintain that, while our
lives may go well when we get what we most deeply want, they will
lack meaning if we are not pursuing objects or objectives of real value.
Susan Wolf, who has made this topic respectable among contemporary
analytic philosophers, argues that meaningfulness is an element of a good
life distinct from happiness. Meaningful lives according to her involve
engagement with projects of real worth.[48] Worthy projects are objectively
valuable. One can be engaged in activities and values that are shallow,
and these do not lend meaning to life.[49] Furthermore, not all valuable
or pleasurable activities contribute to a meaningful life: her examples of
those that do not are riding roller coasters and writing checks to charities.
The latter activity, while valuable, does not produce a sense of fulfilment
reflective of activities that do make a life meaningful. Finally, we may be
committed to activities that we find pleasurable and meaningful, but we
may be mistaken about their being meaningful. Even if Sisyphus found
his endlessly repetitive action of rolling a stone up a hill pleasurable and

[48] Susan Wolf, "Happiness and Meaning: Two Aspects of the Good Life," in E. F. Paul,
F. D. Miller, and J. Paul (eds.), *Self-Interest* (Cambridge: Cambridge University Press, 1997): 207–25,
p. 209.
[49] Ibid. 210.

meaningful, a life of such endless repetition would still be a wasted, not a meaningful, life.[50]

The possibility of mistake is why Wolf believes that she needs to appeal to objective value in explaining meaningful lives. Subjective impressions of meaning are insufficient. Even though she admits more frankly than other philosophers that she has no theory of what objective value is, or of what has it and why, and even though she has no way to compare lives in terms of it—she says that there is no fact of the matter whether the life of a lonely philosopher or that of a beloved housewife is more meaningful or valuable—she believes that she needs this concept in her account.[51] Commitment in itself does not create meaning in life, if what one is committed to is objectively worthless. A life of watching television soaps or sports events is not meaningful, no matter how committed to such activities a person is. What is needed beyond commitment according to her is the objective value of the pursuits to which one is committed.

Again the suspicion recurs that Wolf's appeal to pursuits of objective worth independent of people's concerns reflects simply her own subjective values. This suspicion is reinforced by her examples of lives with and without meaning. According to her, the lives of corporate lawyers and pig farmers are highly suspect on this account, while presumably those of labor lawyers and epistemologists (whom others might accuse of playing glass beads games) are not. Does this amount simply to disparaging the lives of others who find satisfaction in pursuits that seem worthless to her?[52] Farmers and business executives would judge very differently even if they accepted her notions of objective value and meaningfulness. Nevertheless, there does seem to be something genuine in the intuition that a life of mindless repetition lacks something significant that is present in a life of deep personal relationships and self-fulfilment.

Our questions are these. Is this significant thing properly termed meaning? If so, can we give a respectable account of meaning in life without equating it with the pursuit of objective value? Combining the two questions for the moment, there seems to be no obvious connection between

---

[50] The example is from Richard Taylor, following Albert Camus. Taylor claims that the agent's attitude toward his activity is all that counts. Richard Taylor, "The Meaning of Life," in *Good and Evil* (Amherst, NY: Prometheus, 2000), pp. 319–34.

[51] Wolf, "Happiness and Meaning," p. 209.

[52] Steven Cahn dismisses the concept of meaningful lives as pernicious on this ground. "Meaningless Lives?" in *Puzzles and Perplexities* (Lanham, MD: Lexington, 2007), pp. 89–91.

engagement in objectively valuable projects and having meaning in any ordinary sense of that concept. That something is meaningful does not imply that it has objective value. The word "something" in the previous sentence has meaning but not much value. Wolf is not helpful here, since she does not worry over her use of the term "meaning". And she is not alone in invoking the notion of objective value to distinguish meaningful from meaningless lives. Stephen Darwall and John Cottingham, to name two, agree with her that meaning in life cannot derive from purely subjective values, but instead derives from engagement in objectively valuable pursuits.[53] In rejecting this notion I admit at the same time that Wolf is right that being actively engaged and content in some mindlessly repetitive activity does not make one's life meaningful. We face the task then of accepting this intuition without appealing to differences in objective values of different lives or activities in explaining it.

What is the connection between meaning and objective value supposed to be? We may focus first on the concept of meaning. Meaning is always a three term relation: something means something else to an interpreter. The paradigm, although probably not the origin of our concept of meaning, is linguistic meaning, based on conventional associations between terms and their referents. That this is the paradigm may be why the question of the meaning of lives seems inappropriate or even senseless to some philosophers. Lives do not literally refer to or symbolize anything, except perhaps for the lives of historical figures who are known for one action or effect. Patrick Henry symbolizes liberty to many, but you and I are not like that.

We can also say somewhat non-literally that certain people symbolize certain things to other people because of the way they affect their lives: decent parents mean security to their children. This comes a bit closer to what some see as the source of meaning in lives: their effects on others. It takes us, however, to a natural, as opposed to conventional, use of "meaning": causes mean their effects and effects mean their causes. Clouds mean rain and smoke means fire. Similarly, we can say that person A means something to person B because of the effect that A has on B's life. But again this is not the primary sense we seek when we ask whether lives

[53] Stephen Darwall, *Impartial Reason* (Ithaca, NY: Cornell University Press, 1983), p. 164: *Welfare and Rational Care* (Princeton: Princeton University Press, 2002), pp. 89–90. John Cottingham, *The Meaning of Life* (London: Routledge, 2003), p. 66.

are meaningful, because usually we are interested in whether people's lives are meaningful to themselves, not to others. This allows, however, that an important source of meaningfulness in the life of a person can be its meaningfulness to others, the way it contributes to the meaning in their lives. Yet another related sense of meaning equates it with importance. "You mean a lot to me" means that you are very important to me. But when we ask whether a life is meaningful, we are not simply asking whether it is important, either to others or to oneself. Sisyphus might have thought it important that he stay alive even though he was leading a meaningless life.

There is a final yet more relevant sense of meaning that we invoke when we ask what people mean by various actions or remarks. "What did he mean by interrupting her speech, by running out on the field in the middle of the game, by saying that he would not run for office?" We raise such questions when we do not understand the point or purpose of the action or remark, the broader plan into which it fits. We want to know what broader concern of the agent makes her action intelligible to us or rational for her. When we ask for the meaning of a remark in this sense, it is not that we do not understand the language, but that we do not see the point or significance of the remark in the broader scheme of things, how it relates to an ongoing conversation or figures in the speaker's broader purposes. "He interrupted her speech because he means to undermine her candidacy." That was his point or purpose. "The artist means this work to be a political protest." That was his intention or purpose.

Traditionally, the solution to the problem of the meaning of life appealed to just this notion of a broader plan or purpose into which each person's life fit. A life was considered meaningful by fitting into God's plan for it in his broader plan for all humanity or the universe as a whole. A person's life means something because God means it to play a certain role in his grand plan or purpose according to this account. But while this answer involved a proper sense of meaning, it did not reveal the meaning of lives to those living them, since no one knows what such all encompassing plans are. And the idea that one's life is merely a miniscule tool in some super being's infinitely larger plan or purpose does not seem to afford that life an uplifting kind of meaning. All such grand narratives, whether supernatural or historical and political, simply swallow up the lives of the individuals who are unwitting pawns in them.

If God's plan for us has little or nothing to do with our concerns in this world, then it cannot give our lives a meaning we can grasp. But if his plan for us is revealed in the projects and goals we have, then it does not add to the meanings we can derive from those projects. I suggested earlier that objective value plays the role of God in contemporary philosophy by providing a ready-made goal for us to pursue and a validation of the subjective values we seek to enforce. I also suggested a similar objection in the form of a dilemma regarding its practical import: if objective value validates the subjective values we already have, then it is practically superfluous; if it is different from what we value, then it is beyond our grasp and irrelevant. The same objection applies when we narrow the focus of practical import to the role of adding meaning to life.

Nevertheless, although the notion of an external plan for our lives, like that of external value, might not provide a fully satisfactory account of the meaning life has for us who live it, the question of meaningful lives may not appear pressing until belief in such a plan is challenged or given up. At that point, just when the question becomes pressing, it may at the same time seem senseless, since there is no longer any super narrative scheme into which each person's life can fit and in terms of which it can have a purpose. In the modern and post-modern ages we have lost faith in these religious and secular grand narratives that provide external purposes or plans for our lives. At least there is no such plan for the lives of ordinary people, but perhaps only for those fanatics who devote their entire time to a single cause. The causes to which we do commit ourselves are self-chosen, diverse, and not all-consuming. So we have lost faith also in the idea that life itself, or all lives, have a single essence that could give to each the same sort of meaning. There is no single meaning of life. Thus, some philosophers will dismiss the issue entirely if they cannot accept the older responses to it. But here again others will see the notion of objective value residing in diverse objects and projects as providing a unifying goal for us to pursue in very different ways.

Some such overarching single goal or plan seems necessary if we are to speak of *the* meaning of life, some purpose our lives can share such as maximizing objective value or fulfiling God's intentions. Can the internalist speak of life's meaning without invoking such an external purpose to pursue or realize? Must there be a meaning of life to contrast with meaningless repetitions of totally trivial pursuits? As Kurt Baier points out, there can be meaning *in* lives even if there is no meaning *of* lives.[54] Changing the subject just this much allows us to rescue what does make sense in the notion of a meaningful life far better than does equating the concepts of meaning and value. So, despite that misstep, Susan Wolf was correct to ask about meaningful lives and not the more traditional question of the meaning of life. Meaningful lives have meaning within them as they unfold. This meaning is internal to the lives as they are lived. But if internal to a life, the meaning must attach to aspects or episodes in it, since, as noted, meaning is a relation of an element to something outside it. "Meaning in life" therefore refers to episodes or events in one's life that are meaningful and that thereby lend meaning to life as it is lived.

Events in a life acquire meaning by relating to each other as episodes in the pursuit of long-term projects and personal relationships. Others have noted that such projects and relationships give life meaning, while merely repeating particular actions or flitting randomly from one activity or brief pleasure to another do not. Indeed, life does seem to acquire new meaning when one embarks on a new project or relationship or deepens an old one, refocusing one's concerns and activities. But if left at that description of meaning generating projects, we are left wondering why meaning is what such projects but not particular actions in themselves provide, and the explanation may seem elusive. The answer emerges when we focus on events that point to other events as developments or precursors of them, giving them meaning in the most relevant sense, especially initiating and culminating events and those that change the course of an ongoing project or relationship.

This sense of meaning is quite ordinary in applying both to linguistic terms and to other sorts of non-linguistic entities. Especially linguistic terms without concrete referents are said to derive their meanings from their places within sentences and inferential patterns. Like the life events we are discussing, they acquire meaning by relating to other terms in larger intelligible structures. The meanings of logical connectives, for example, are exhausted by the terms they relate and the inference patterns they allow.

An equal or perhaps better analogy is to elements within artworks. In musical pieces, for example, the musical phrases acquire meaning for

---

[54] Kurt Baier, "The Meaning of Life," in E. D. Klemke (ed.), *The Meaning of Life* (Oxford: Oxford University Press, 2000), pp. 101–32.

competent listeners through their places in developing themes and harmonic progressions, pointing the listeners behind to what prepared for them and ahead in anticipation of developments and resolutions of dramatic tensions. A phrase or theme heard in a recapitulation has a meaning different from its first appearance in an exposition and from its transformation in a development section. A listener who hears and understands these differences grasps the unfolding meaning of the piece. This meaning derives from internal relations among the musical elements unfolding in an orderly way toward the ultimate goal or finale. Similarly, events in a fictional narrative are understood to foreshadow future developments or to fulfil earlier promises or resolve earlier tensions. When the reader grasps these relations, she interprets and understands the meanings of the fictional events in terms of their roles in the narrative structure. And it is the same in the messier domain of real life.

Just as artworks and works of literature admit of different interpretations according to which the elements or episodes within them will have different meanings, so, as interpreters of our own lives, we can relate its events, and relate to them, in different ways. Trivially, events will take on different meanings for the optimist than for the pessimist, as they interpret them in different ways, as fulfilments or precursors of worse things to come. And different and incompatible ways of interpreting may be equally supported by the events themselves, which will have multiple and branching effects and causes. But not just any way of interpreting is justified. We may to an extent give meaning to the events we experience, but we are constrained by their actual sequences, just as interpreters of literary or musical works are constrained by the texts or scores as written.

We get a better sense of the concept of meaning here by comparing it to its negation, grasping the contrast drawn. From the negative point of view, to say that a life lacks meaning is to say that it lacks direction or intelligible progression. As usual, no one says it better than Shakespeare. When Macbeth complains that life is a tale told by an idiot, he is lamenting its lack of narrative intelligibility, the fact that its events fail to relate to each other in a progressive, intelligible pattern. But this very powerful lament suggests what meaning in life could or should be, and according to Macbeth, pompously purports or pretends to be (pretense in the person of a poor player strutting on the stage). A meaningful life, even according to Macbeth, who could find no such meaning, would be an intelligible succession of events giving meaning to each by relating it to others in an unfolding narrative that makes sense of each as a precursor of the next and culmination of the prior. Of course, Macbeth was wrong about his own narrative: more than in the life of any real person, the logic of events in his life simply led inexorably in the direction of a tragic end.

As the case of Macbeth makes clear, this account of meaningful lives does not reduce or equate the concept of meaning to that of value, but it does maintain a possible link between the two. The episodes in Macbeth's life were pregnant with meaning, but most had negative value for him. For those of us more fortunate or less evil, meaning can derive from engagement in worthwhile or valuable projects or relationships, more easily sustainable than heinous projects and exploitative relationships. Agents pursue projects that reflect their own values, and meaning derives from the way that pursuit of these concerns connects various activities and events into intelligible narratives. It is not the value of the goals that generates meaning, but the complex relations among the activities involved in their pursuit. That is why challenging goals that require sustained pursuit through a variety of means provide more meaning in the long run, and why satisfactions that come too easily seem shallow and relatively meaningless.

Of course success matters in several ways. Pursuits that fail may seem pointless in retrospect, especially if there was little or no chance of succeeding to begin with. My trying to be a great professional basketball player will not lead to a meaningful life for me no matter how long I persist in pursuing that impossible goal. In contrast, success brings a sense of fulfilment that heightens the meaning of the struggle to achieve it. And it relates the entire project to its external effects, giving it a meaning that failure lacks. If I am able to contribute significantly to the philosophical literature, then my philosophical pursuits have a meaning they would otherwise lack. They point beyond themselves to their results. But success is not a necessary condition for activities to contribute to meaning in life, since it is the ongoing pursuit of goals and relationships that ties these activities together in intelligible structures.

Just as meaning does not derive from the objective value of the goals pursued, so it does not derive from the nature of the activities in themselves. As noted earlier, in itself shooting a ball through a hoop makes no more sense than throwing it as high as one can into the air; hitting a ball over a net is no different as an isolated action from hitting it into a net. These activities become meaningful when nested in a connected set of concerns validated by a social structure that orients them toward various goals. Throwing a ball through a hoop, as opposed to high in the air, can be at the center of such concerns as developing physical skills, competing, winning, earning respect of peers, creating school spirit, and having a lucrative career. That is why it can be a part not only of such long-range goals, but even of a life plan for those with some chance of success at it. And these various goals into which the activity can fit relate it to many others and thereby render it a meaningful activity, while throwing the ball in the air is a strange waste of time.

Meaning here is distinct from but also related to not only value, but happiness. The continuous achievement of our central concerns that lends meaning to the activities involved connects, albeit very imperfectly, with happiness as the global approval of the course of our lives over time. Just as success and the feeling of fulfilment that accompanies it reflects meaning in the activities that led up to it, so it leads itself to happiness, other things equal and for those personalities prone to being reasonably content. But contentment with one's projects and relationships is again neither necessary nor sufficient for meaning. Wolf is right to reject Richard Taylor's claim that Sisyphus' accepting his lot and remaining content with his mindlessly repetitive task makes that activity meaningful. If Sisyphus thinks that the activity is meaningful, he is simply mistaken. It might symbolize something to him, such as the injustice of the world or the need to keep up the struggle, but it lacks relations to other activities and goals that would give it meaning in the full-blown sense we invoke when we speak of meaningful lives. Conversely, many people with challenging and complex long-term projects that lend meaning to the different stages in them are not thereby made happier. Such projects typically involve delayed gratification, and it may be lack of contentment at each stage that keeps one's nose to the grind.[55]

As in the mythical world of Sisyphus rolling his stone, in the real world a life devoted to making sure one's clothes are in fashion by making trip after trip to the shopping mall, or one devoted to watching sports on television, seem meaningless even if the people leading those lives are perfectly content

---

[55] Suggested by Nettle, *Happiness*, pp. 26–7.

to do so. Such examples lead Wolf to conclude that a meaningful life must instead be devoted to objectively worthwhile projects. But we have seen that the contrast can be drawn without appealing to the notion of objective value. It is revealing in the examples just cited to compare the life of a professional fashion designer or baseball player to that of the consumer or fan. Winning the World Series can meaningfully be at the center of the player's concerns because it relates to and indeed organizes many other activities and concerns—desires for accomplishment, a successful career, and wealth, for example—and it culminates years of endeavor. For the fan there are no such organizing relations; the new season of passive watching simply begins shortly after the previous one ends. The actions and events in his life are simply repetitive instead of cumulative. This contrast between the meaningful and meaningless life can be drawn in terms of the internal relations among the activities that make it up, and not in terms of the objective value of the activities themselves. The challenge we posed to ourselves to account for commitment to or contentment with meaningless projects without appealing to objective value that merely disguises our own values has been met.

From the viewpoint of our subjective values we can also distinguish meaning from value. Imagine that the baseball fan organizes a whole set of concerns and activities around watching baseball games. (We can also imagine that he does not neglect his family, that he has sufficient income to indulge his passion, and so on, so that moral questions do not interfere with our judgment.) He scrupulously plans trips to various stadiums in different cities, collects souvenirs from these trips, collects and trades baseball memorabilia, gradually building a collection that reveals the history of the sport, memorizes statistics from all the games he watches and from the sport's history, follows trades, potential trades, salaries, and so on. Furthermore, his expertise and involvement in the sport increases over time.

This life certainly does not fit my taste. I would not value it highly, although I am a sports fan. But the events in it do have meaning. As elements in a complex ongoing project, they refer back to earlier events whose promise they fulfil or forward to future ones for which they prepare. Of course, this type of meaningfulness is a matter of degree, and it remains true in our modified example that each new baseball season simply begins a new cycle much like the previous one. But there is repetition in any life, perhaps necessary for stability and security, and in this one there is also progression as the memorabilia and experiences in different locales add to the earlier ones.

We can imagine lives we would value still less while granting them meaning. People have organized their lives around the pursuit of fame; others have sought only revenge. Wolf would dismiss their pursuits as meaningless. Others offering advice on how to live have done so also,[56] although it is strange for those publishing books to criticize the quest for fame, as if they seek only to enlighten their readers (my goal of course). As we learn from the Count of Monte Cristo, seeking revenge, while perhaps not morally admirable, can be not only rational if coherent with one's deepest concerns, but also can make for an intensely meaningful narrative. Other yet more blamable pursuits, such as seeking constant supplies of heroin, in addition to being typically irrational in opposing deeper evaluative judgments, may fail to impart meaning to their merely repetitive actions and events. Meaning in life is distinct from moral goodness as well as from value more generally, although it is more often connected to the latter.

It is clear from the distinctions between meaning, welfare, and happiness that the meaningfulness of a life is only one aspect relevant to its evaluation, and a goal for the person leading the life that may have to be balanced against others. Meaning in life is not only distinct from happiness, as Wolf rightly claims, but might come into conflict with it. Unlike fictional characters, no real person's life is fully coherent, let alone coherent with those of all others. Seeking a perfectly coherent narrative for one's life would again be fanatic and narcissistic, not to mention that meaningless activities and events can be fun. As with all other values, meaning in life itself matters only to those who care about it. If all value for us derives ultimately from our concerns or from what we care about, this will be true also of the value for us of meaning in our lives. And this value will differ depending on how much we care about it.

Some people prefer challenge, complexity, diversity, and long-range projects in their lives that lend to them cumulative progression and narrative intelligibility. Others might prefer the more relaxed and comfortable routine of repetition. Still others prefer the excitement of living in the moment

---

[56] For example, Kraut, *What is God and Why*, p. 185.

to seeking narrative continuity. The fashion in psychology these days is to downplay the strength and influence of character that might be seen to underlie, but more accurately reflects, such continuity. We seem to have returned to Hume's claim that the self is a mere bundle of separate experiences, or in more contemporary jargon, of distinct reactions to different circumstances. But even bundles can be more or less intelligibly or coherently organized.

As opposed to Aristotle and other philosophers who advise us on how to live the good life, Hume's indirect advice to philosophers themselves was on the mark:

We come to a philosopher to be instructed, how we shall chuse our ends . . .We want to know what desire we shall gratify, what passion we shall comply with, what appetite we shall indulge . . . I am sorry then, I have pretended to be a philosopher.[57]

If I were to ignore this admonition, I would advise developing diverse deep concerns and relationships, imparting different strands of meaning while protecting against failure in any one. But that is just personal taste. Eventually we all reach a point where the quest for new meanings itself seems pointless, and there is nothing wrong with looking forward to retirement on the golf course. And I have no reply to those at earlier stages who prefer the slogan "If it feels good, do it!" If asked what is objectively the best life, I would reply as Yogi Berra did when a reporter challenged his managerial skills with the question "Don't you know anything?" "Lady, I don't even suspect anything."

[57] David Hume, "The Sceptic," in *Essays* (Indianapolis: Liberty Fund, 1985), p. 161.

6

Conclusion

"We have deep depth."

We have raised a number of seemingly unanswerable questions about purported external reasons and the objective values they are supposed to reflect. Given that we act most often without deliberation but with reason, how is it that we are automatically tuned into these reasons and values, and how could we know that we are? What causal mechanism could allow us to recognize and be motivated by these values if they are independent of our subjective concerns, as external reasons would be? If the reply is that the values are realized in ordinary physical properties that have usual causal effects on us, the question becomes why values attach to just these properties that are otherwise completely diverse or only randomly related. If pursuit of these randomly collected objects fulfils none of our concerns, is therefore of no benefit to us, why should we pursue them? If instead these objects are united by satisfying concerns we have, then what practical effect could appeal to their objective value have? In short, how could appeal to such values call into question our deepest concerns to the effect that we should abandon the latter and pursue the former instead? How would this be possible, let alone desirable, if such concerns are not a matter a choice for us? How could we attempt to maximize objective value in the world if we have no precise measurements of it in any objects in which it is supposed to inhere? Finally, if we are automatically tuned into external reasons such that we act rationally almost all the time without deliberating, how are we to explain the degree of disagreement we find among people as to what is valuable and what is not? Who is value blind and how are we to identify these unfortunates except by their disagreement with our own subjective values?

The externalist has some questions for us too. He wants to know how we can derive normativity, or what we ought to do, from our desires, since we can always desire what we ought not to, and what we ought to desire depends on reasons that reflect how worthwhile or desirable the objects we desire really are. For externalists, basic and irreducible normative principles determine that we ought to believe what our evidence supports and do what will produce states of affairs that we find desirable. But the questions whether we should believe what strikes us as true, what our evidence supports, or pursue what we care about most do not seem as genuine as those we posed above to the externalist.

For one thing, we have little or no choice in these matters. While our evidence can always mislead us, we must believe what strikes us as true on the evidence of which we are aware. We have nothing else to go on except coherence with evidence or other beliefs. We can irrationally engage in wishful thinking, but then we will be ignoring, failing to seek, or hiding evidence from ourselves. Likewise, if we fail to pursue what we most care about, this will be due to irrational weakness of will in the face of temptation, lack of will from depression, or being in the grip of emotion. Normally, and when we are rational and yet fail to pursue some object, it is because we care more about doing something else.

More strongly, believing is believing true, and acting is attempting to fulfil the motivations behind the actions. These are constitutive aims. And they are natural constitutive aims in that we have evolved as creatures who believe and act. Reasons indicate and reflect ways of satisfying these aims of truth and desire fulfilment. Although evidence can mislead us and we can desire what we ought not to, we can no more ask whether we should act to fulfil our deepest concerns than we can ask whether we should believe what seems true on all the available evidence. Beliefs, including perceptual beliefs, provide all the evidence for truth we have, and so coherence among beliefs is our only indication of what to believe. Similarly, desires for known objects, including basic concerns, provide our only clues as to what is desirable, and so coherence among desires or subjective values is our only indication of what to do. The coherence criterion of practical rationality is the stronger of the two, since in the case of doxastic or theoretical rationality we could be victims of systematic error despite being coherent and aware of all available evidence, while there seems to be no such possibility in the practical sphere. The pursuit of what we care about most could completely fail or disappoint, but then it would be incoherent with our desire to succeed or survive, or lacking in prior information about what it would be like to so act.

Other questions posed to internalists have been answered too. First, how can we explain how reasons for desires themselves seem to derive from the values of their objects? The answer is that objects are valuable when they fulfil our deeper concerns and that these concerns provide the reasons for having the desires. Thus the object does not directly or in itself provide the reason for desiring it, but its value indicates that the desire for it either has a reason or is itself basic. Second, if some desires create reasons, why do not all desires do so? The answer again is that only desires that cohere in sets anchored by deeper concerns, reflected in evaluative judgments as opposed to bare urges, create reasons.

If the internalist theory can handle the questions and purported counterexamples posed to it, then it is clearly the preferable theory even aside from the mysteries attached to externalism. This is because, as emphasized, internalism is the simpler theory, both metaphysically and epistemologically. We have seen that absent measurements of supposed objective value for other candidate objects, the most plausible candidate for what has objective value is the satisfaction of our rational desires or concerns. But this proposal clearly adds nothing to the internalist account except excess baggage. According to it, what has objective value is the fulfilment of our subjective values, which adds words but not understanding to the claim that the only values are subjective. The account I have offered is not only the simplest explanation of the data, but fully unified as well. All reasons, doxastic and practical, are states of affairs that motivate rational agents in accord with the natural aims of belief and action. All rationality is a matter of paying attention to relevant information and being coherent or avoiding self-defeat.

If internalism is clearly superior on these accepted theoretical grounds of simplicity and unity, we might finally speculate on why so many philosophers favor the objectivist account. First, of course, they do not believe that the internalist can explain or dismiss the purported counterexamples, including prominently wrong desires, desires with reasons, and concerns we are required to have, specifically prudential and moral concerns. You will have to judge whether my accounts of relevant information and coherence as the avoidance of self-defeat explain wrong desires and reasons for desires, and whether my dismissal of substantive requirements for prudential and moral concerns in terms of the distinction between reasons there are and reasons agents have, are adequate.

Second, phenomenology, which on the face of it favors the externalist, plays a prominent role. When we act and especially when we deliberate, we are focused on the values of the objects we pursue and the reasons these objects or states of affairs provide. This exclusive focus suggests to us the objectivity of values. If there is a reason to save a building, for example, it would be its noteworthy architecture or historical significance, not simply the fact that some people desire to save it. Other people will desire to replace it, and a head count is not always the most rational way to decide the issue. I have admitted that reasons are states of affairs and not desires and that we focus on the values and disvalues of these states of affairs in deciding how to act, but I have argued that these facts are not metaphysically decisive. In perceptually distinguishing objects, we focus on their colors and not on our visual systems, but colors reduce to the ways they appear to our normal visual systems. Likewise, values can reduce to our rational valuings, despite appearing to be features of objects. Would the building be worth saving if no one attached any historical significance to it and all saw its architecture as a scar on the city's landscape?

There are other phenomenologies to consider in addition to the experience of apparent objective value and external reasons. On the externalist's side, there is the experience of resisting urges, of seeming to rise above one's base desires, exercise will power, and act on the basis of reason instead. There is of course a philosophical tradition from Plato through Kant of opposing reason to desire, and Hume's response of arguing that passions can be countered only by other passions. I have argued that desire itself is a complex state, that resisting urges is indeed a matter of acting on one's better evaluative judgment, but that such evaluative judgments, often implicit and automatically activated, are themselves motivational elements of desires reflective of deeper and more stable concerns. The exercise of will power consists of focusing on these elements, enabling their motivational force to operate. Then there is the phenomenology of everyday activity, of the very different and sometimes opposed personal projects that people ordinarily pursue. And this, I argued, tells strongly against the notion of objective value as what rational agents ought to pursue and protect.

Externalists will emphasize not only the experience of value, but the fact that they can offer a deeper explanation and justification of our subjective values and desires than the subjectivists can. In the face of the ever present possibility of misguided desires, they can show why others will be mistaken in their values and why they, whose values have objective grounding, can be justified in seeking to impose them on those less enlightened. It simply cannot be the case that their deepest concerns, including their acceptance, support, and enforcement of moral requirements, rest on no objective foundation at all, that some entirely different coherent motivational set could be equally justified. Concerns that are bedrock for the subjectivist receive an explanation and justification by appeal to objective values and external reasons deriving from them. But in reply, we may consider it a fundamental rule of inquiry to take explanations only to the depth before which further explanans add more mysteries than they resolve. That is why we do not appeal to divine explanations of natural laws in science.

Objective value is the god of the contemporary philosopher in taking the explanation of our subjective values to this deeper depth and in so doing introducing mysterious non-natural properties. Both objective values and divine commands provide presumed external standards for our concerns and pursuits to meet, but not ones that we can understand. Having posited them, we are immediately faced with questions about their natures that we cannot answer. Perhaps both myths are mutually supporting, for if reasons and values do not derive from the concerns of natural sentient beings, what could their ultimate origin be except God? And both myths are closely linked to a third: the myth of contra-causal free will that can oppose action from natural desires. If external reasons are to be independent of all our desires and yet have practical effect, this could be only because we are able to act in opposition to all our natural motivations, that is, with Kantian contra-causal free will. Kant himself refused to locate such agency in the natural world, but later libertarians have not been as clear-headed or forthright. And indeed, the notion flies in the face of science to no less a degree than divine intervention.[1]

Of course we can resist any particular urge just as we can question the rationality of any particular desire. But in both cases we can do so

---

[1] For a summary of the experimental data, see Daniel M. Wegner, *The Illusion of Conscious Will* (Cambridge, MA: MIT Press, 2002).

only from within our own broader subjective perspective. We need no miraculous powers or mysterious external standards in order to raise these reflective questions and act in light of them. We rise above other animals not by ascending into some non-natural realm inaccessible to them, but by being able to reflect on our motivations as a whole, including second-order motivations to be and act in certain ways.

When we say that values are subjective, we mean that they are relational in somewhat the way that secondary qualities like colors are. The difference is not that objects merit our concerns while they only cause us to perceive their colors.[2] This idea of objective meriting reintroduces all the unsolvable mysteries of non-natural, irreducible normative properties. What we mean instead is that the world, both natural and cultural, must cooperate if our motivations are to be satisfied. And it is no mystery why it does cooperate to the imperfect degree that it does: our motivations have been shaped by our natures and cultures, and we have reshaped the natural world to reflect our motivations.

"Too many works finish before they end."[3]
"It ain't over 'til it's over."

---

[2] John McDowell suggests this distinction. "Values and Secondary Qualities," in *Mind, Value, and Reality* (Cambridge, MA: Harvard University Press, 1998).

[3] This one sounds like it comes from Yogi Berra, but it's from another genius of the twentieth century, Igor Stravinsky.

Index

Notes are indexed in bold.

relevant 45–6, 47, 48, 49, 51, 53–4, 55,
57, 180, 186, 237, 258
insincerity 157
instrumental rationality 27, 61
    practical norms 59–60
instrumental reasons 42, 58, 59
intellectual capacity 240
intelligibility 186
intentions 58, 178
    actions 70, 170
    demand to 59, 60, 61
    pleasures 231
    risk 76
internalism 9–16, 30, 34, 38, 71–2, 94,
    113, 114, 121, 122, 125, 129, 140, 178,
    179, 242
    advantages 20–8
    arguments against 93
    desires 31, 46
    Hume on 28
    internalism 186
    irrationality 45
    lives 235
    personal welfare 244
    rationality 60
    reasons 23, 60, 72, 75, 98, 99, 177, 183,
        201
        for desires 258
    theory 186
    values 17
    versus externalism 9–16
intransitivite preferences 76, 176
introspection 43–4
intuition 22, 52, 53, 109, 110, 117, 118,
    120, 121, 133–4, 175–6, 206, 215,
    216, 234
irrationality 2, 9, 10, 14, 27, 37, 38, 41, 43,
    45, 46, 53, 54, 59, 68, 72, 73–4, 75,
    80, 88, 98, 99, 100, 109, 132, 133, 136,
    137, 138, 139, 141, 145, 151, 153, 158,
    160, 191, 223
    actions 8, 32, 158
    charge of 167
    depression 107
    incoherence 108, 142, 164–5
    information requirement 47, 52, 55
    morality 175
    motives 147
    paradigm cases 145, 158, 159
    rational agents 177

self-neglect 134
see also weakness of will

jealousy 85, 86, 87, 88, 89
Johnson-Laird, P. N. 85n, 87n
judgment internalism 143–4
judgments 27, 76, 86, 88, 170
justification 19, 29, 30, 31

Kant, I. 81, 97, 164, 205, 259, 260
Kemp, J. 241
knowledge 68, 224
Kolodny, N. 131, 131n
Korsgaard, C. 165n
Kraut, R. 187n, 196n, 241, 241n, 254n
Kupperman, J. 189, 189n, 243n

legal obligations 154, 155
Lemos, N. 188, 188n, 231, 231n
lexical priorities 192, 203, 205–6
liars 173
libertarians 260
light 217
Lindsey, S. 103n
linguistics 249
literature 250, 251
lives 202, 235, 237, 249–50
    bad 241
    choices 51, 55
    events 87, 91, 105, 105, 249, 250–1
    good 235
    loss of 200
    meaningful 234, 244, 245
    mindless repetition 245
    plans 150, 252
    rationality 56
    repetition 253–4
    value of 200
    see also meaningful lives
local satisficing 191
logical truths 22
love 129–30, 130–1
loyalty, to institutions 5–6

McConnell, A. R. 103n
McDowell, J. 217, 218, 218n, 261n
Mackie, J. L. 21n, 186, 186n, 188
McLeod, O. 232n
Mandelbaum, E. 172n
Martin, L. 103n, 105n